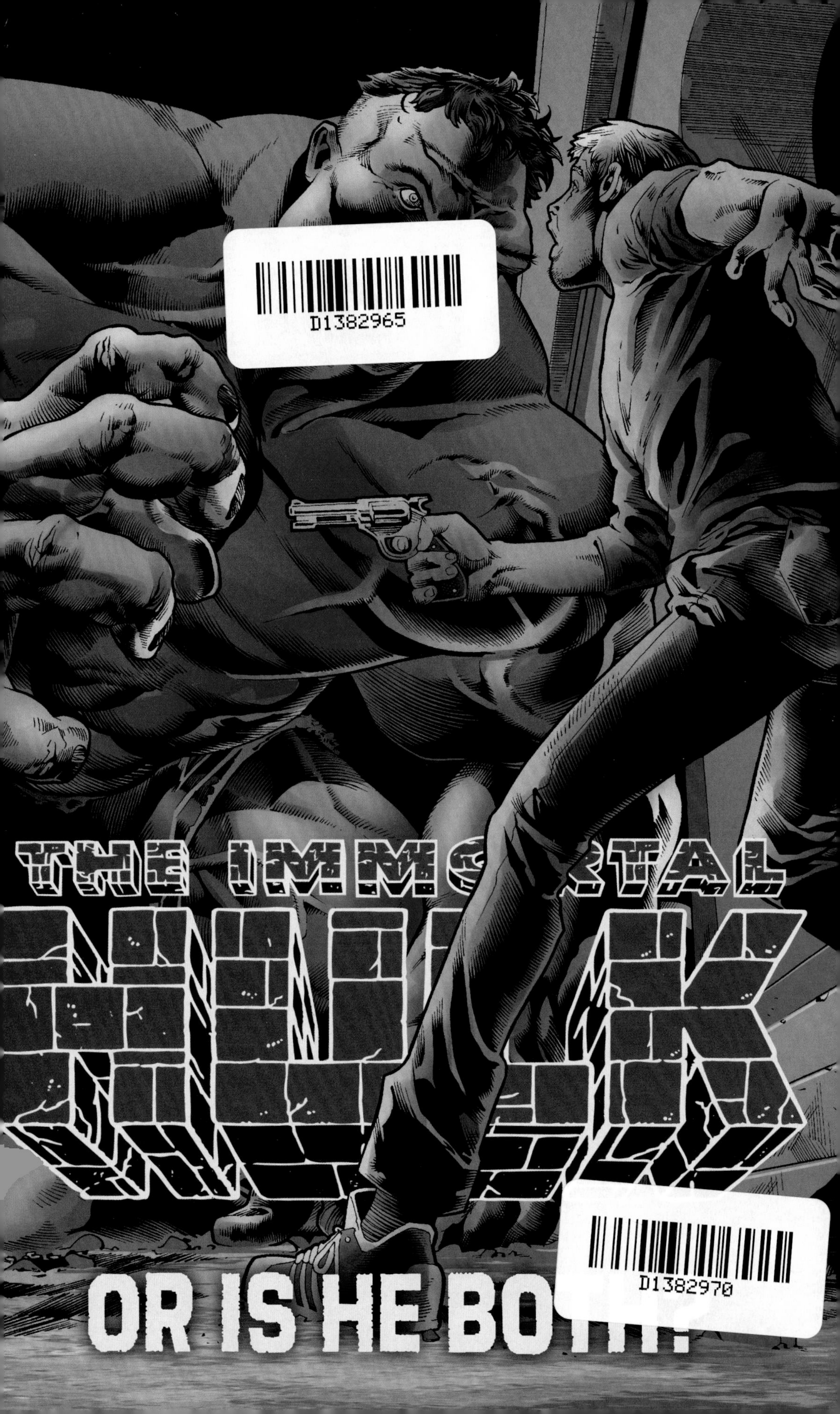
THE IMMORTAL
HULK
OR IS HE BO

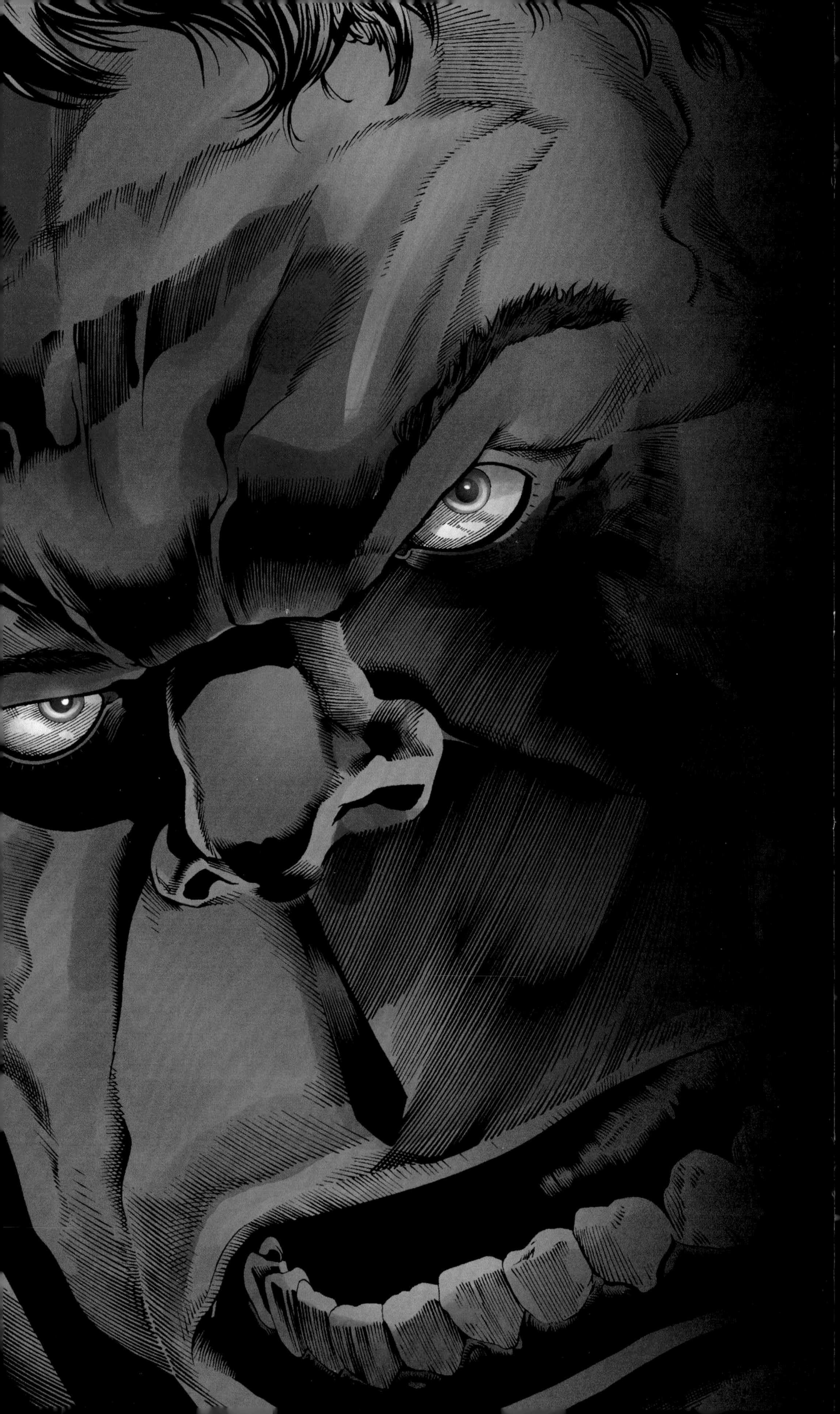

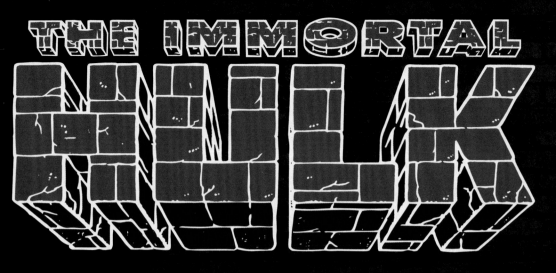

# THE IMMORTAL HULK

## OR IS HE BOTH?

**AL EWING**
WRITER

**JOE BENNETT**
PENCILER

**RUY JOSÉ**
INKER

**PAUL MOUNTS**
COLOR ARTIST

**VC's CORY PETIT** [#1-5] WITH **TRAVIS LANHAM** [#2]
LETTERERS

**PAUL HORNSCHEMEIER**
#3 THE BARTENDER'S STORY
ARTIST, COLORIST & LETTERER

**MARGUERITE SAUVAGE**
#3 THE OLD LADY'S STORY
ARTIST & COLORIST

**GARRY BROWN**
#3 THE PRIEST'S STORY
ARTIST & COLORIST

**ALEX ROSS**
COVER ARTIST

**ALANNA SMITH & SARAH BRUNSTAD**
ASSOCIATE EDITORS

**TOM BREVOORT & WIL MOSS**
EDITORS

AVENGERS #684

**JIM ZUB, MARK WAID & AL EWING**
WRITERS

**JOE BENNETT**
PENCILER

**RUY JOSÉ**
INKER

**MORRY HOLLOWELL**
COLOR ARTIST

**VC's CORY PETIT**
LETTERER

**MARK BROOKS**
COVER ARTIST

**ALANNA SMITH**
ASSOCIATE EDITOR

**TOM BREVOORT**
EDITOR

COLLECTION EDITOR: **MARK D. BEAZLEY**
ASSISTANT EDITOR: **CAITLIN O'CONNELL**
ASSOCIATE MANAGING EDITOR: **KATERI WOODY**
SENIOR EDITOR, SPECIAL PROJECTS: **JENNIFER GRÜNWALD**
VP PRODUCTION & SPECIAL PROJECTS: **JEFF YOUNGQUIST**
BOOK DESIGNER: **ADAM DEL RE**

SVP PRINT, SALES & MARKETING: **DAVID GABRIEL**
DIRECTOR, LICENSED PUBLISHING: **SVEN LARSEN**

EDITOR IN CHIEF: **C.B. CEBULSKI**
CHIEF CREATIVE OFFICER: **JOE QUESADA**
PRESIDENT: **DAN BUCKLEY**
EXECUTIVE PRODUCER: **ALAN FINE**

**HULK**
CREATED BY
**STAN LEE & JACK KIRBY**

**IMMORTAL HULK VOL. 1: OR IS HE BOTH?** Contains material originally published in magazine form as IMMORTAL HULK #1-5 and AVENGERS #684. Fourth printing 2019. ISBN 978-1-302-91255-0. Published by MARVEL WORLDWIDE, INC., a subsidiary of MARVEL ENTERTAINMENT, LLC. OFFICE OF PUBLICATION: 135 West 50th Street, New York, NY 10020. © 2018 MARVEL No similarity between any of the names, characters, persons, and/or institutions in this magazine with those of any living or dead person or institution is intended, and any such similarity which may exist is purely coincidental. **Printed in Canada.** DAN BUCKLEY, President, Marvel Entertainment; JOHN NEE, Publisher; JOE QUESADA, Chief Creative Officer; TOM BREVOORT, SVP of Publishing; DAVID BOGART, Associate Publisher & SVP of Talent Affairs; Publishing & Partnership; DAVID GABRIEL, SVP of Sales & Marketing, Publishing; JEFF YOUNGQUIST, VP of Production & Special Projects; DAN CARR, Executive Director of Publishing Technology; ALEX MORALES, Director of Publishing Operations; DAN EDINGTON, Managing Editor; SUSAN CRESPI, Production Manager; STAN LEE, Chairman Emeritus. For information regarding advertising in Marvel Comics or on Marvel.com, please contact Vit DeBellis, Custom Solutions & Integrated Advertising Manager, at vdebellis@marvel.com. For Marvel subscription inquiries, please call 888-511-5480. **Manufactured between 6/5/2019 and 7/1/2019 by SOLISCO PRINTERS, SCOTT, QC, CANADA.**

10 9 8 7 6 5 4

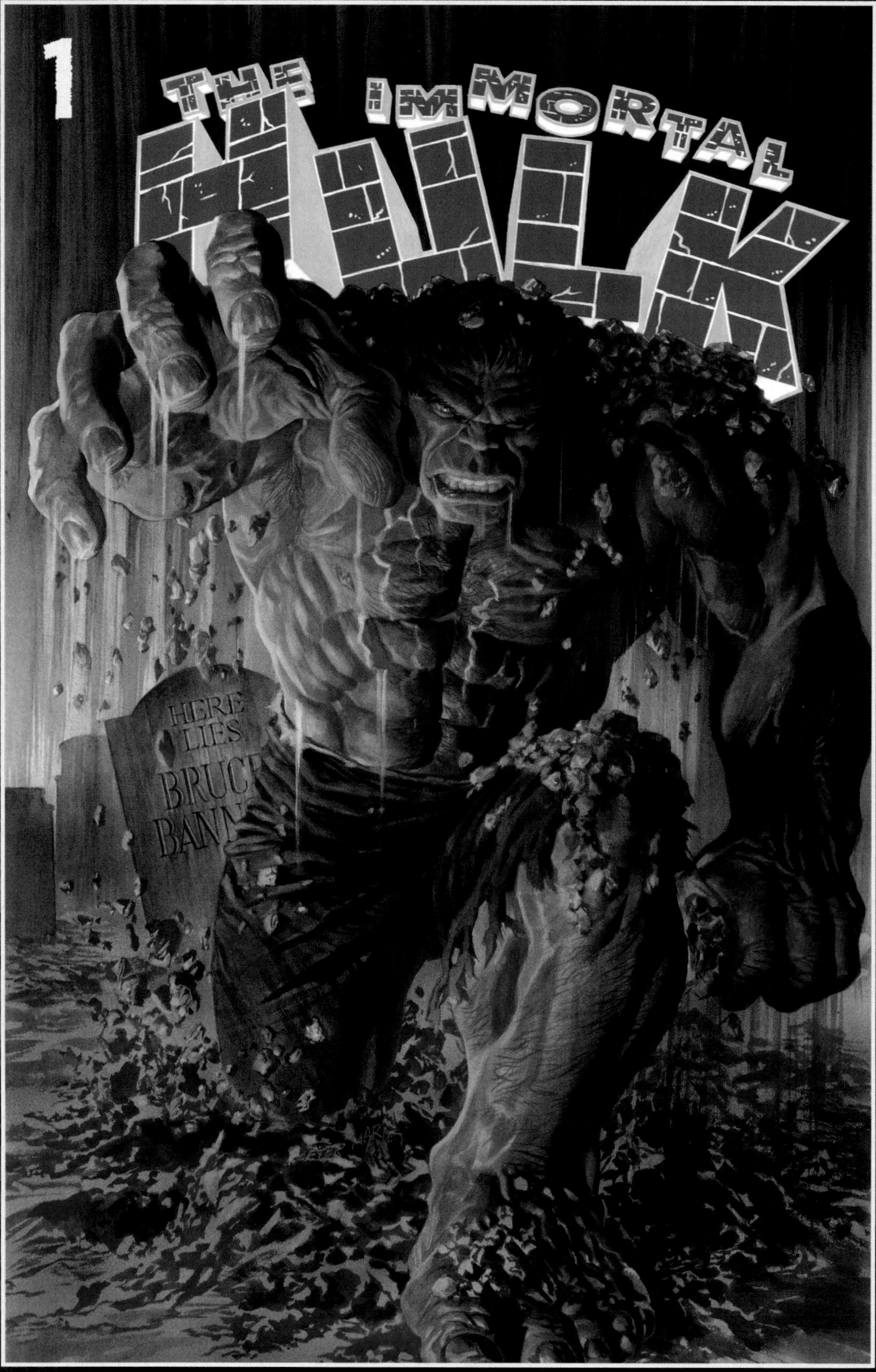
1
THE IMMORTAL
HULK
HERE LIES
BRUC
BANN

**"MAN IS, ON THE WHOLE, LESS GOOD THAN HE IMAGINES HIMSELF OR WANTS TO BE."**

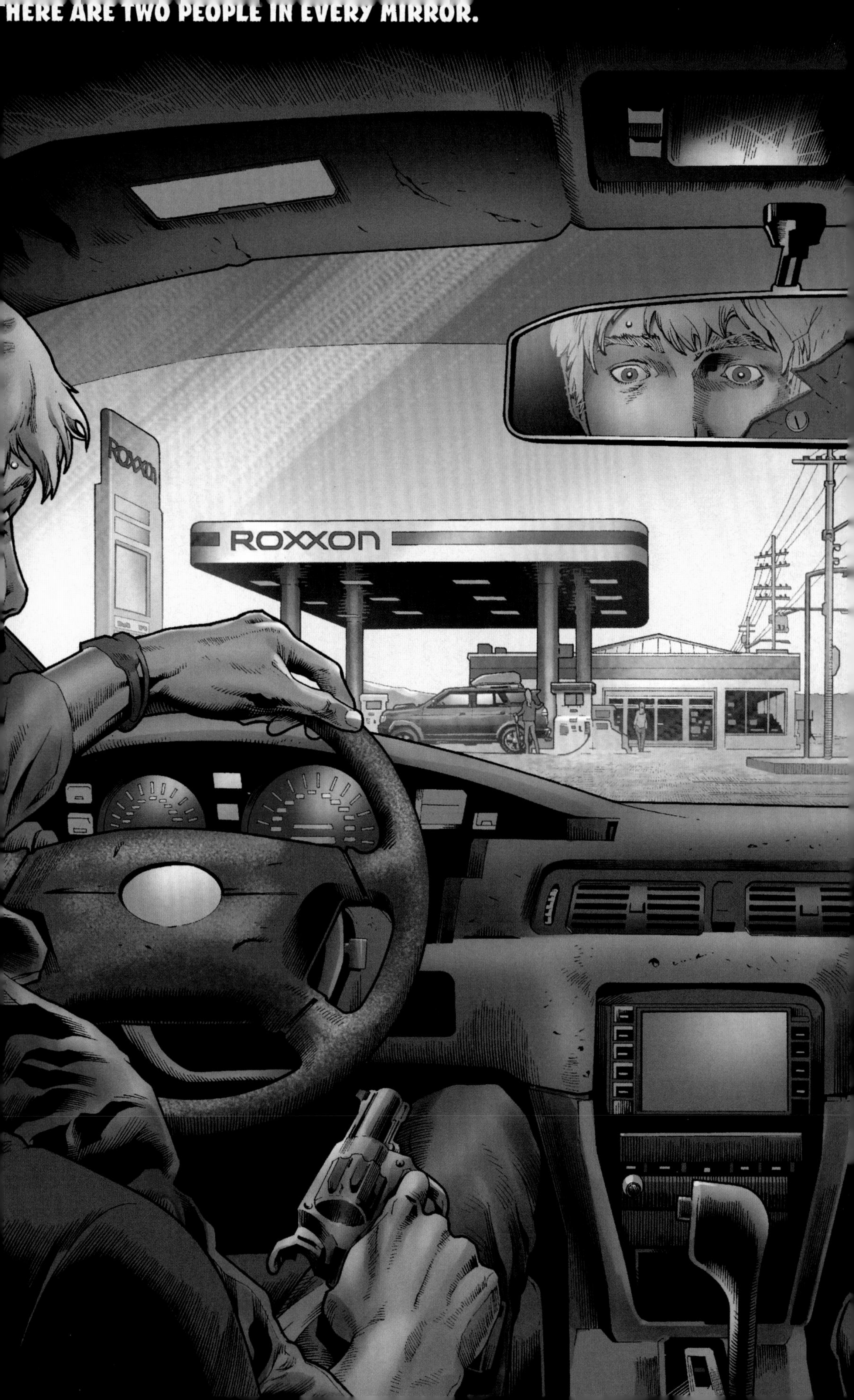
HERE ARE TWO PEOPLE IN EVERY MIRROR.
ROXXON
ROXXON

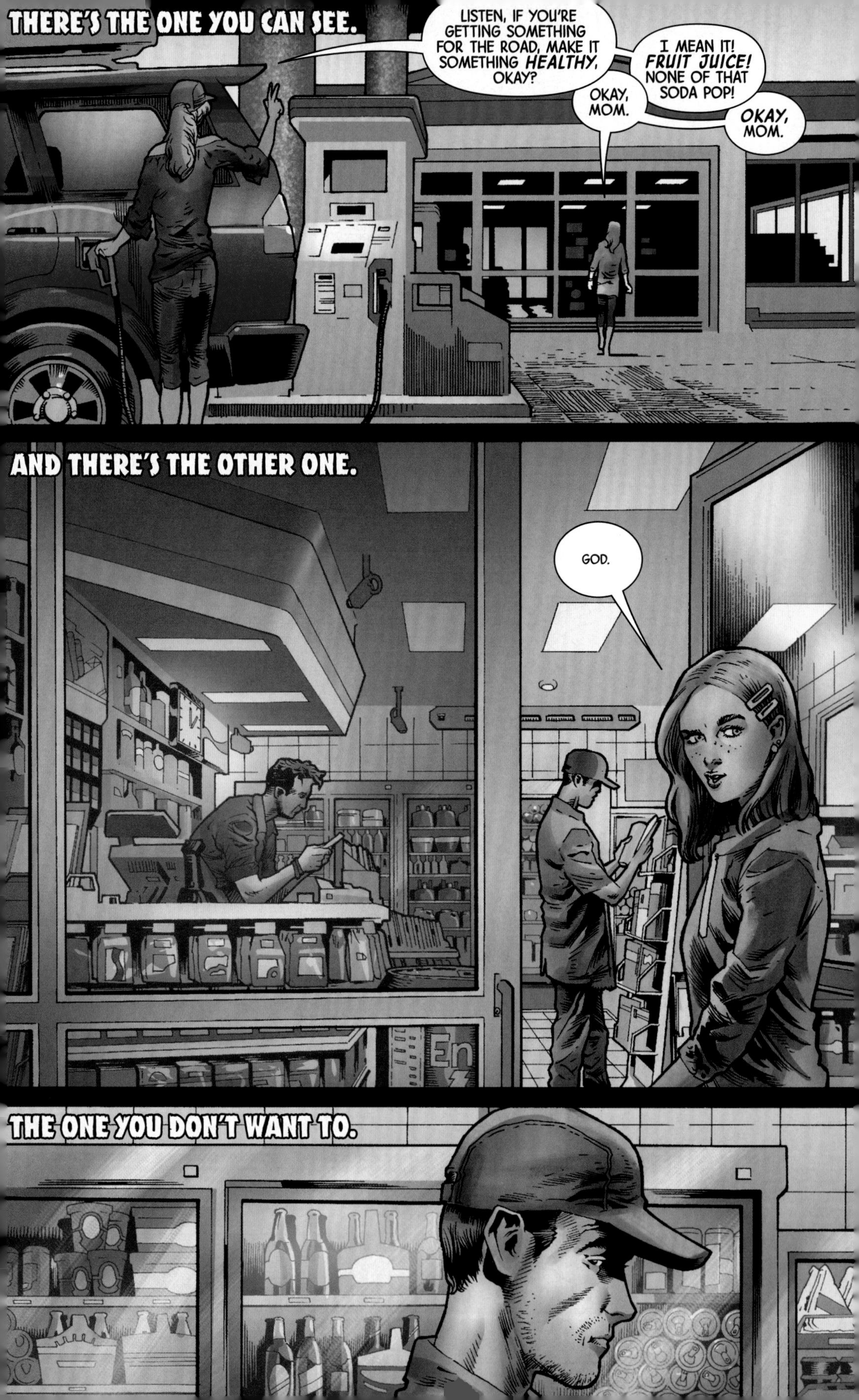
THERE'S THE ONE YOU CAN SEE.
LISTEN, IF YOU'RE GETTING SOMETHING FOR THE ROAD, MAKE IT SOMETHING HEALTHY, OKAY?
OKAY, MOM.
I MEAN IT! FRUIT JUICE! NONE OF THAT SODA POP!
OKAY, MOM.
AND THERE'S THE OTHER ONE.
GOD.
THE ONE YOU DON'T WANT TO.

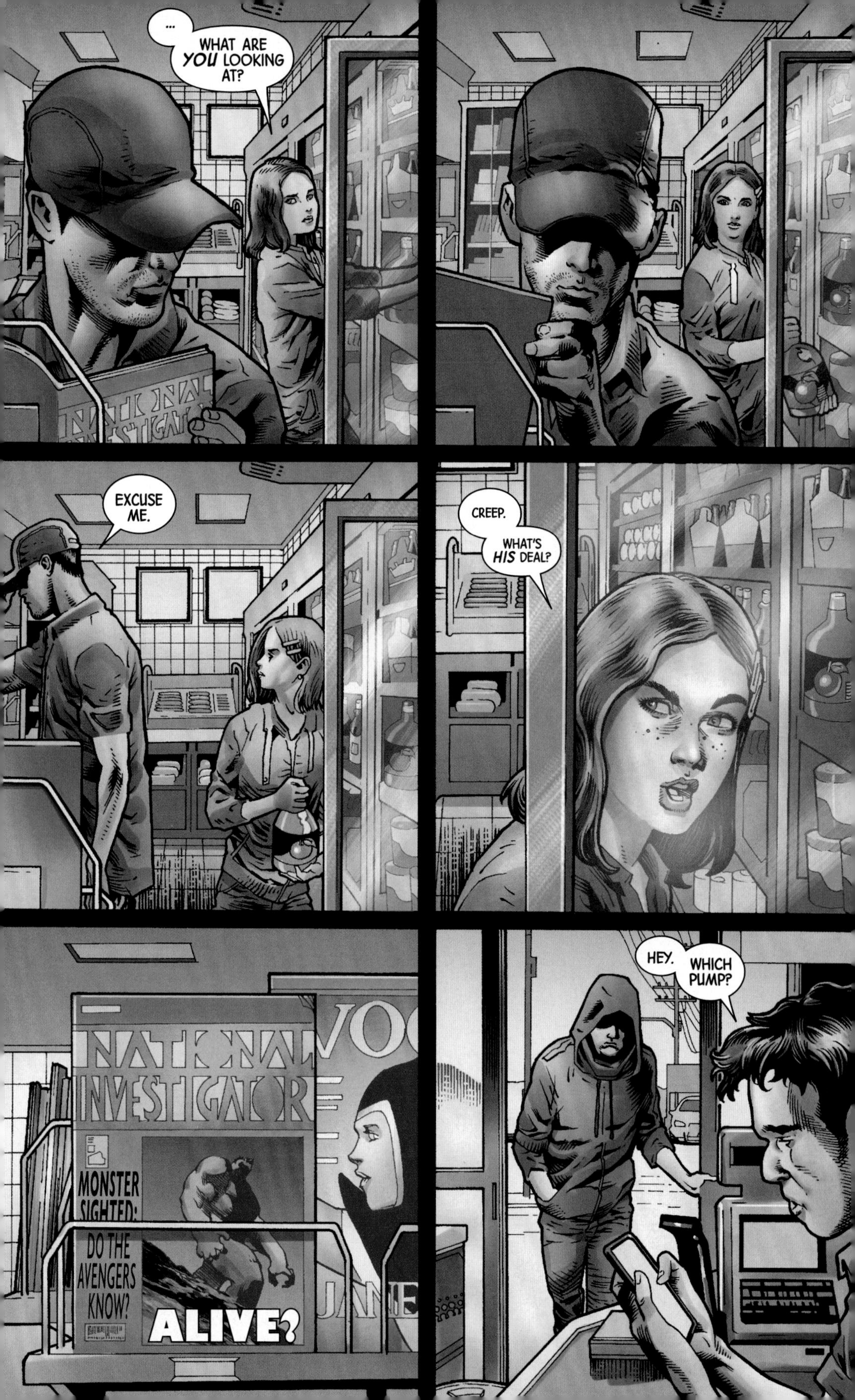
...
WHAT ARE YOU LOOKING AT?
EXCUSE ME.
CREEP.
WHAT'S HIS DEAL?
NATIONAL INVESTIGATOR
MONSTER SIGHTED:
DO THE AVENGERS KNOW?
ALIVE?
HEY.
WHICH PUMP?

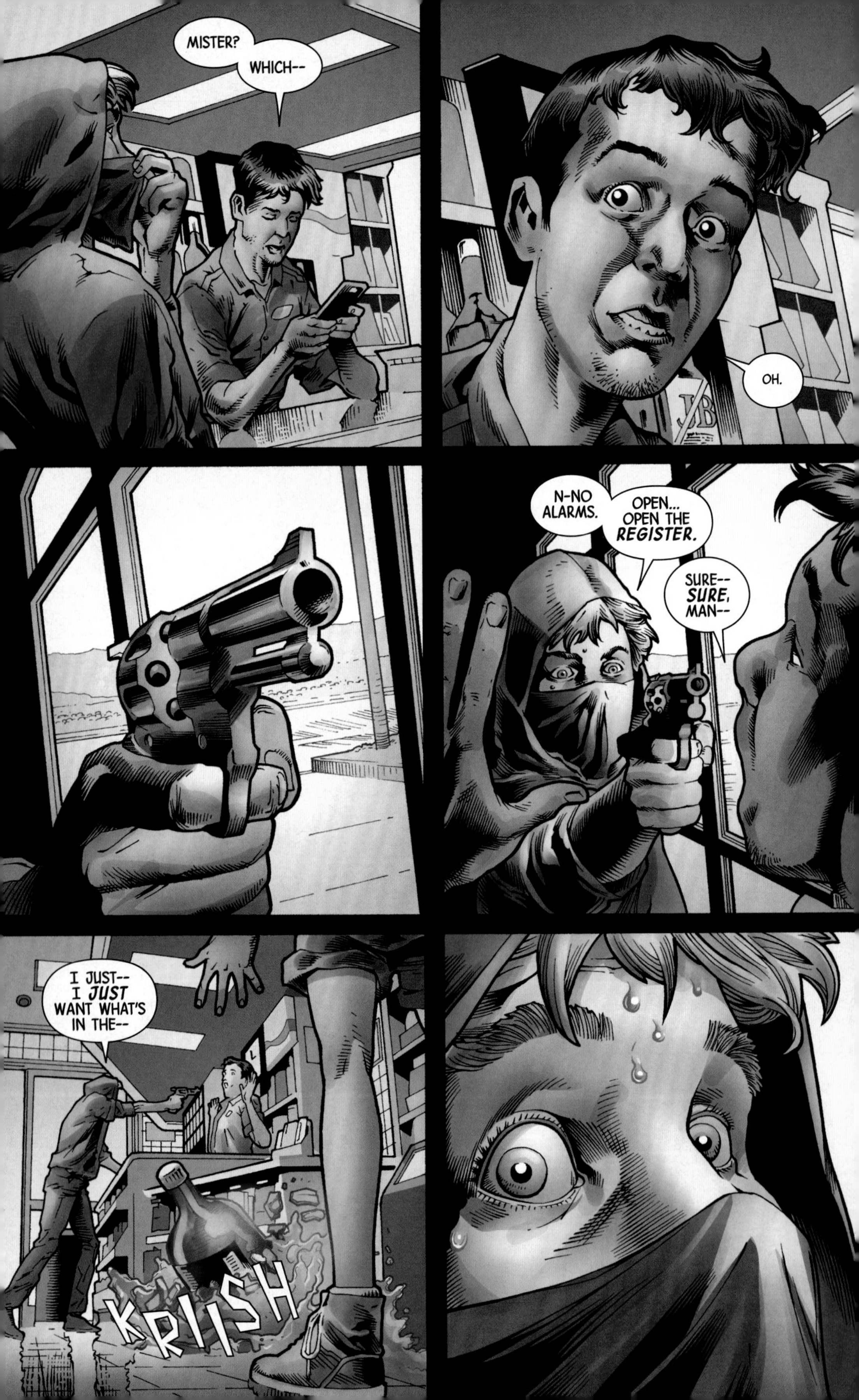
MISTER?
WHICH--
OH.
N-NO ALARMS.
OPEN... OPEN THE REGISTER.
SURE-- SURE, MAN--
I JUST-- I JUST WANT WHAT'S IN THE--
KRIISH

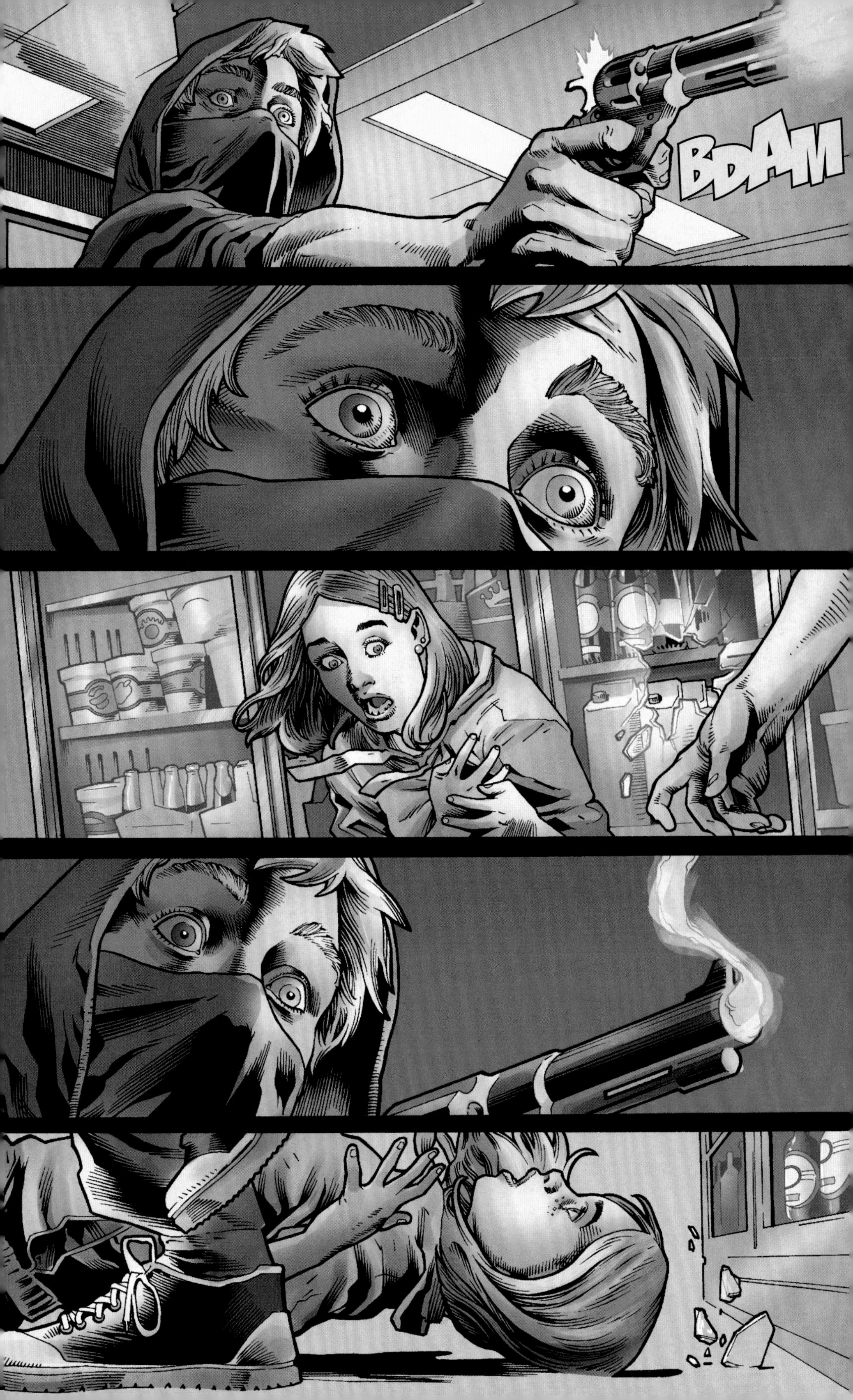
BDAM

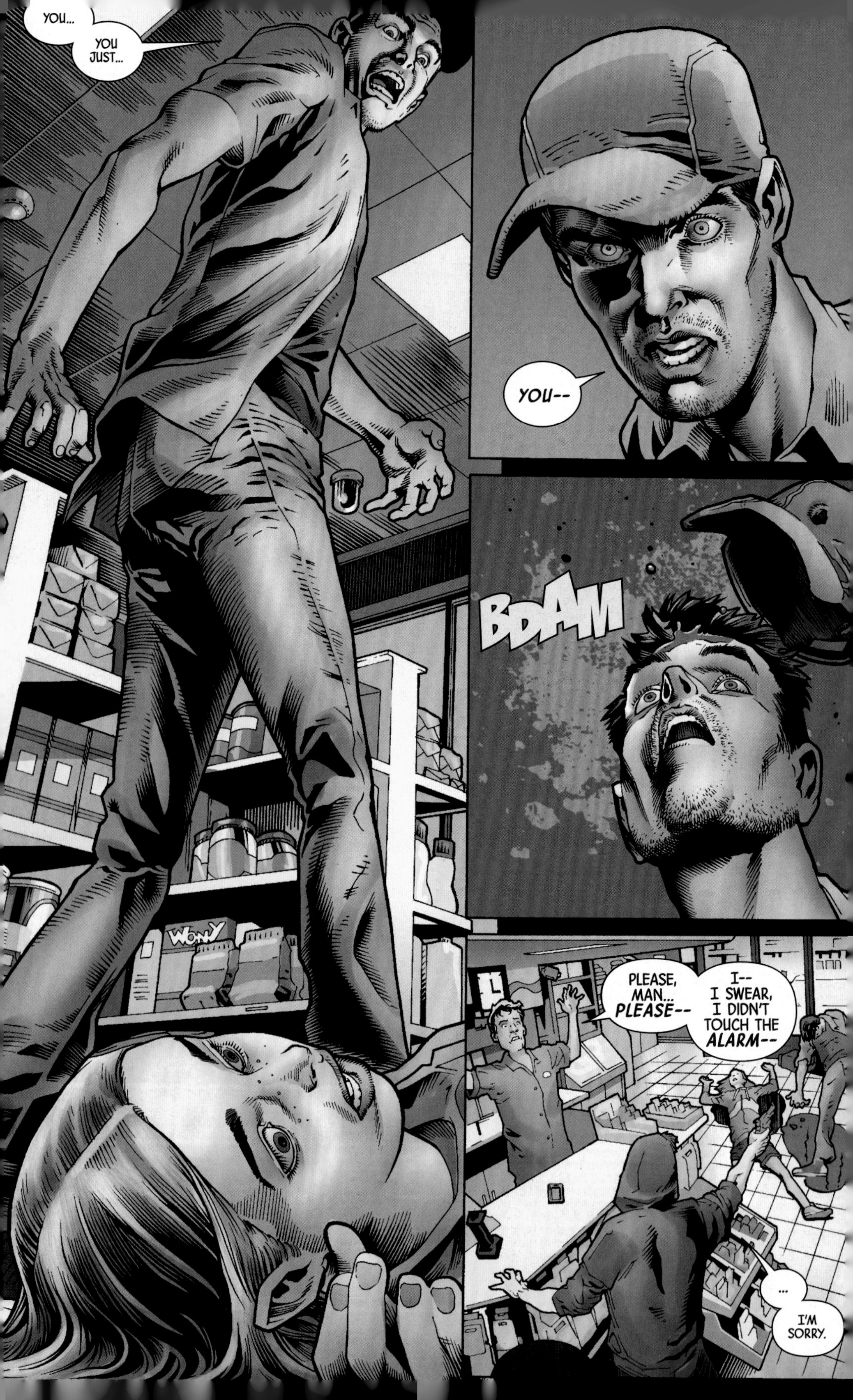
YOU...
YOU JUST...
YOU--
BDAM
PLEASE, MAN... PLEASE--
I-- I SWEAR, I DIDN'T TOUCH THE ALARM--
...
I'M SORRY.

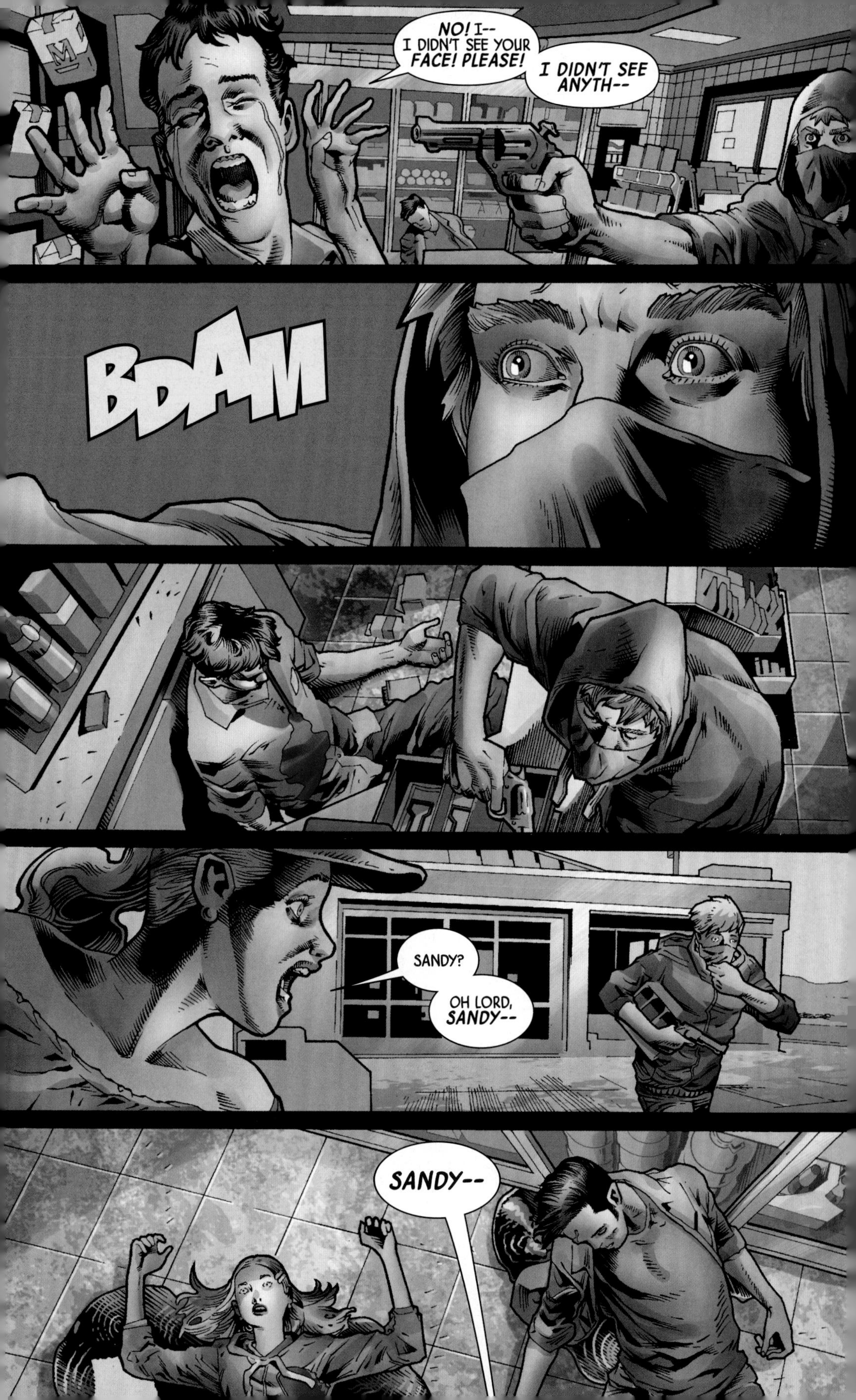
NO! I--
I DIDN'T SEE YOUR
FACE! PLEASE!
I DIDN'T SEE
ANYTH--
BDAM
SANDY?
OH LORD,
SANDY--
SANDY--

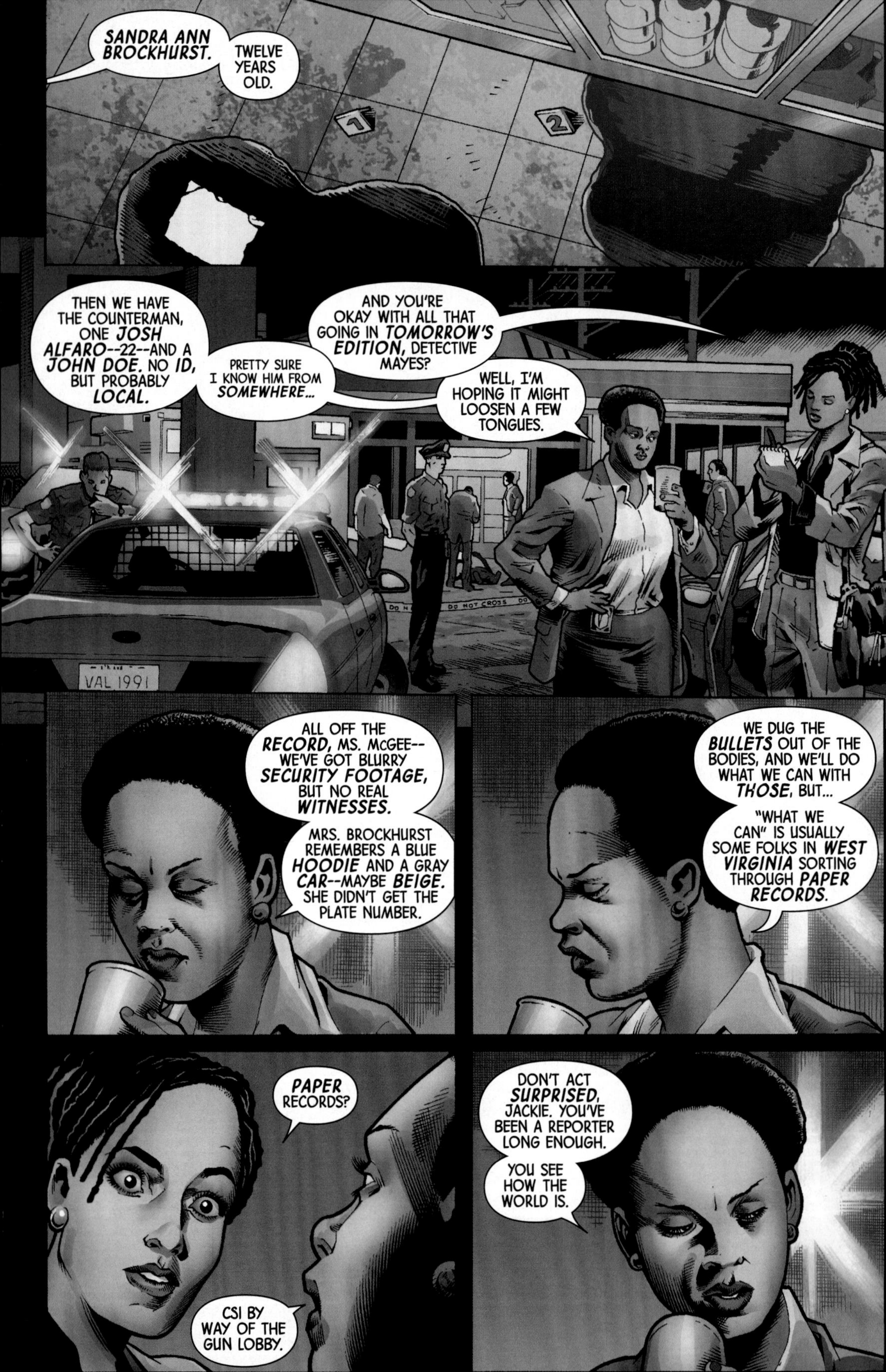
SANDRA ANN BROCKHURST.
TWELVE YEARS OLD.
THEN WE HAVE THE COUNTERMAN, ONE JOSH ALFARO--22--AND A JOHN DOE. NO ID, BUT PROBABLY LOCAL.
PRETTY SURE I KNOW HIM FROM SOMEWHERE...
AND YOU'RE OKAY WITH ALL THAT GOING IN TOMORROW'S EDITION, DETECTIVE MAYES?
WELL, I'M HOPING IT MIGHT LOOSEN A FEW TONGUES.
DO NOT CROSS
VAL 1991
ALL OFF THE RECORD, MS. McGEE-- WE'VE GOT BLURRY SECURITY FOOTAGE, BUT NO REAL WITNESSES.
MRS. BROCKHURST REMEMBERS A BLUE HOODIE AND A GRAY CAR--MAYBE BEIGE. SHE DIDN'T GET THE PLATE NUMBER.
WE DUG THE BULLETS OUT OF THE BODIES, AND WE'LL DO WHAT WE CAN WITH THOSE, BUT...
"WHAT WE CAN" IS USUALLY SOME FOLKS IN WEST VIRGINIA SORTING THROUGH PAPER RECORDS.
PAPER RECORDS?
CSI BY WAY OF THE GUN LOBBY.
DON'T ACT SURPRISED, JACKIE. YOU'VE BEEN A REPORTER LONG ENOUGH.
YOU SEE HOW THE WORLD IS.

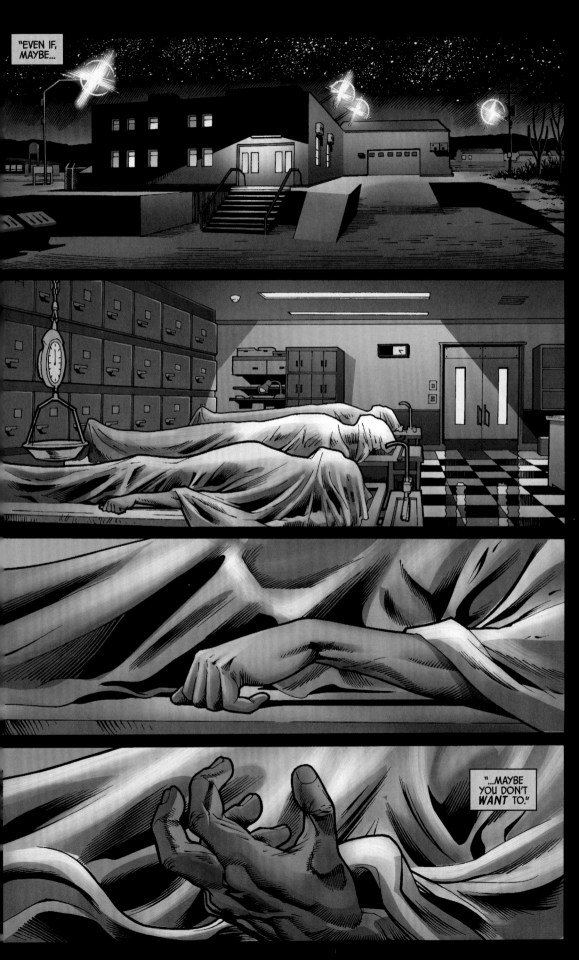

"EVEN IF, MAYBE...

"...MAYBE YOU DON'T WANT TO."

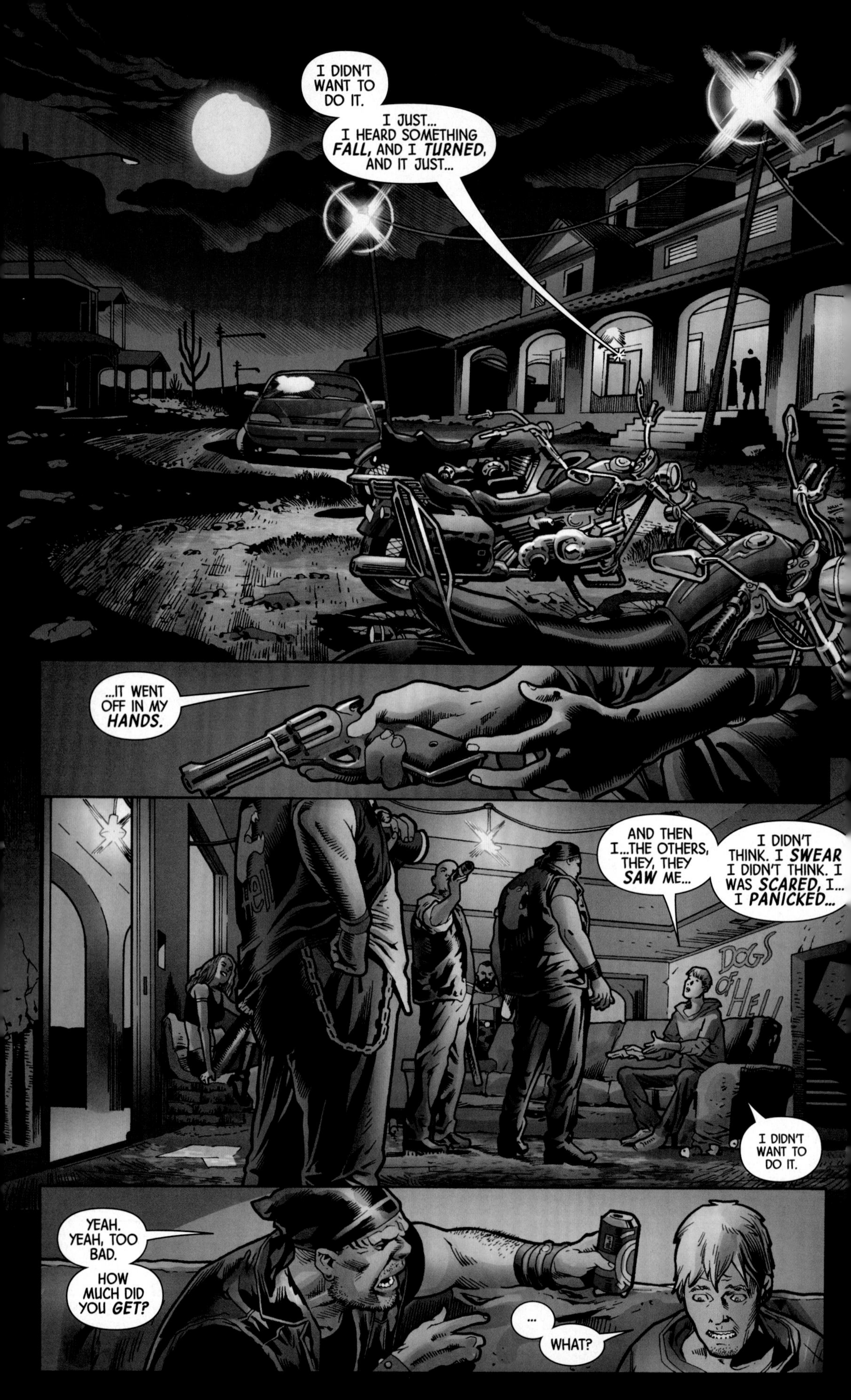
I DIDN'T WANT TO DO IT.
I JUST... I HEARD SOMETHING FALL, AND I TURNED, AND IT JUST...
...IT WENT OFF IN MY HANDS.
AND THEN I...THE OTHERS, THEY, THEY SAW ME...
I DIDN'T THINK. I SWEAR I DIDN'T THINK. I WAS SCARED, I... I PANICKED...
DOGS OF HELL
I DIDN'T WANT TO DO IT.
YEAH. YEAH, TOO BAD.
HOW MUCH DID YOU GET?
...
WHAT?

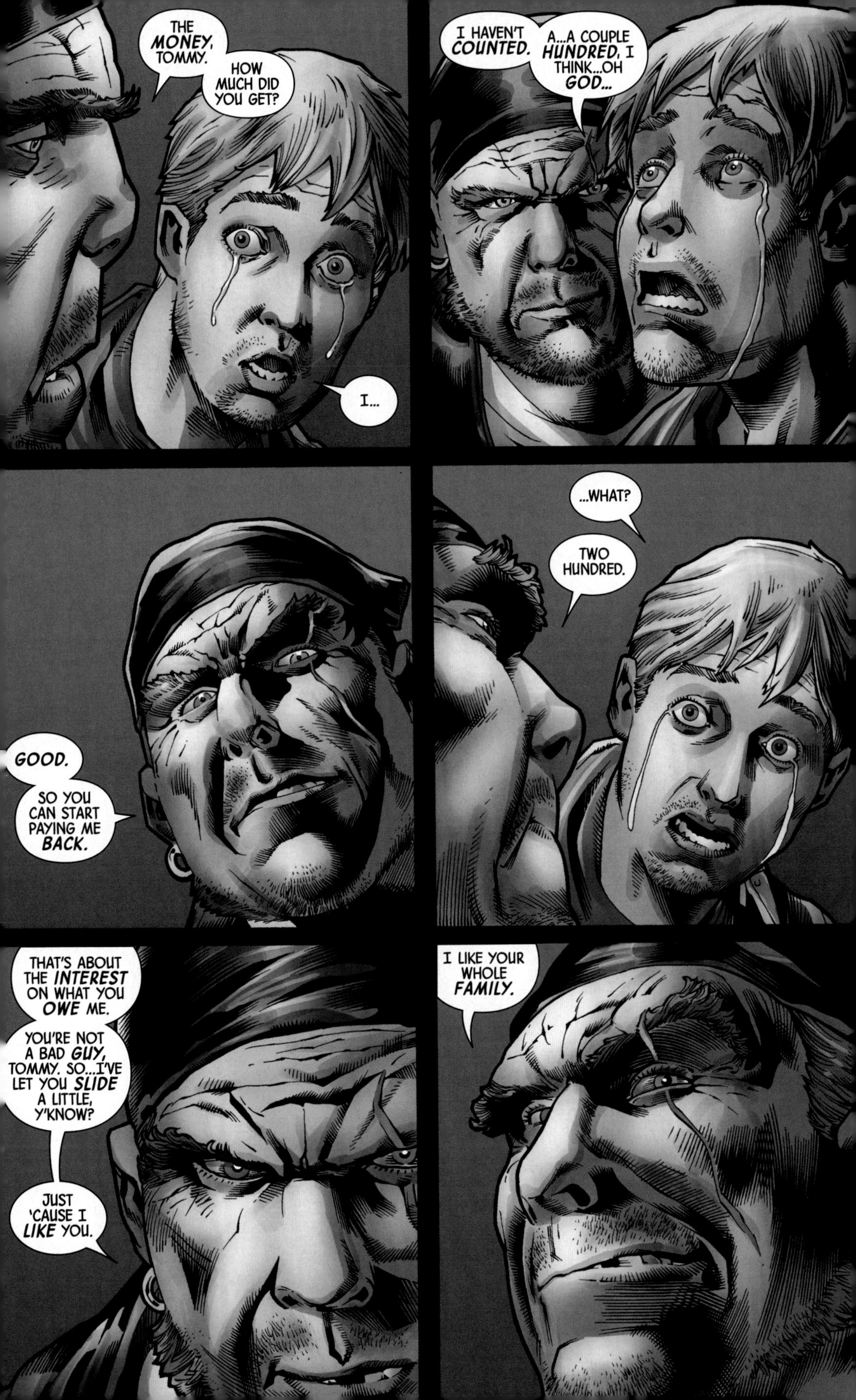
THE MONEY, TOMMY.
HOW MUCH DID YOU GET?
I...
I HAVEN'T COUNTED.
A...A COUPLE HUNDRED, I THINK...OH GOD...
GOOD.
SO YOU CAN START PAYING ME BACK.
...WHAT?
TWO HUNDRED.
THAT'S ABOUT THE INTEREST ON WHAT YOU OWE ME.
YOU'RE NOT A BAD GUY, TOMMY. SO...I'VE LET YOU SLIDE A LITTLE, Y'KNOW?
JUST 'CAUSE I LIKE YOU.
I LIKE YOUR WHOLE FAMILY.

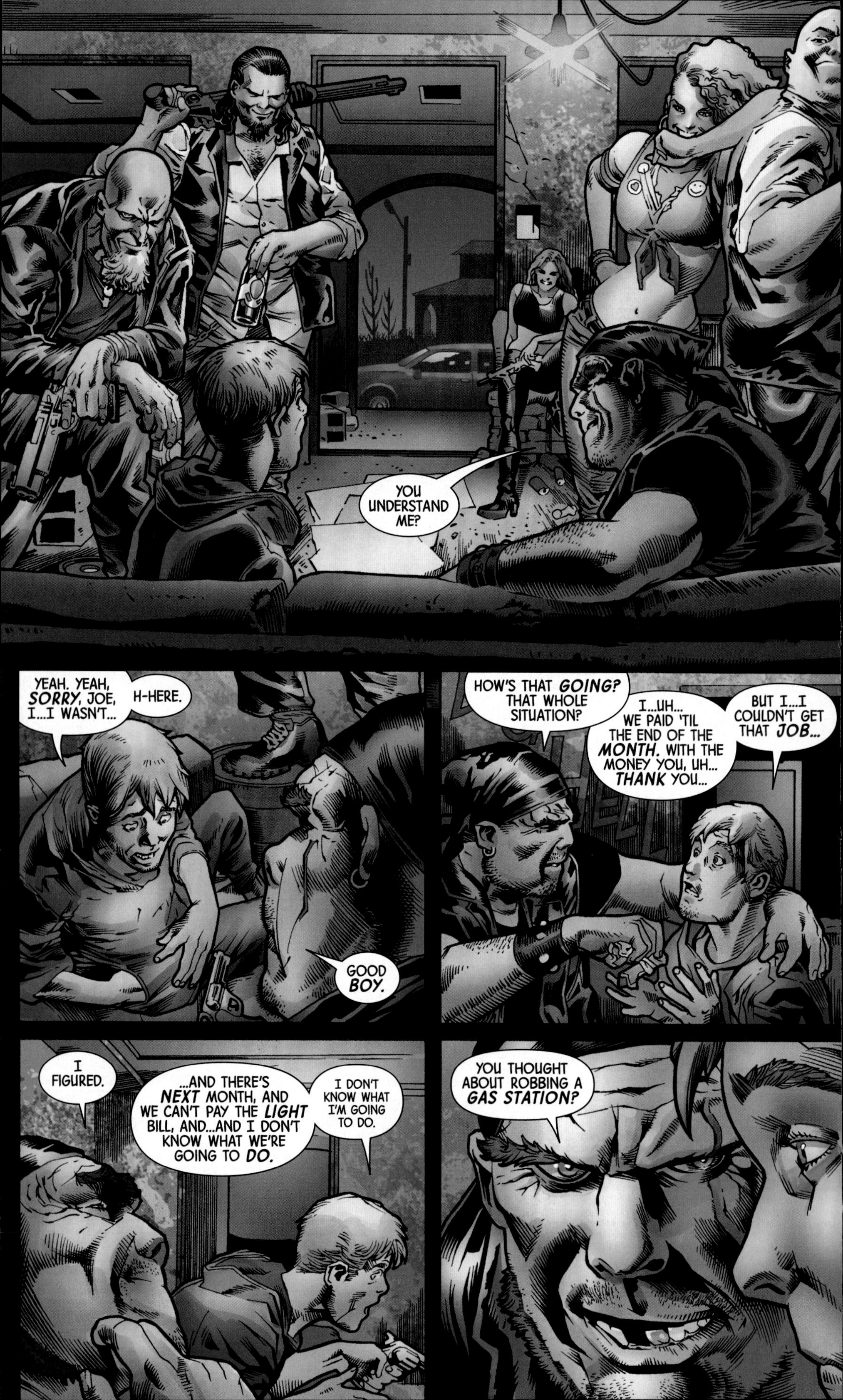
YOU UNDERSTAND ME?
YEAH. YEAH, SORRY, JOE, I...I WASN'T...
H-HERE.
GOOD BOY.
HOW'S THAT GOING? THAT WHOLE SITUATION?
I...UH... WE PAID 'TIL THE END OF THE MONTH. WITH THE MONEY YOU, UH... THANK YOU...
BUT I...I COULDN'T GET THAT JOB...
I FIGURED.
...AND THERE'S NEXT MONTH, AND WE CAN'T PAY THE LIGHT BILL, AND...AND I DON'T KNOW WHAT WE'RE GOING TO DO.
I DON'T KNOW WHAT I'M GOING TO DO.
YOU THOUGHT ABOUT ROBBING A GAS STATION?

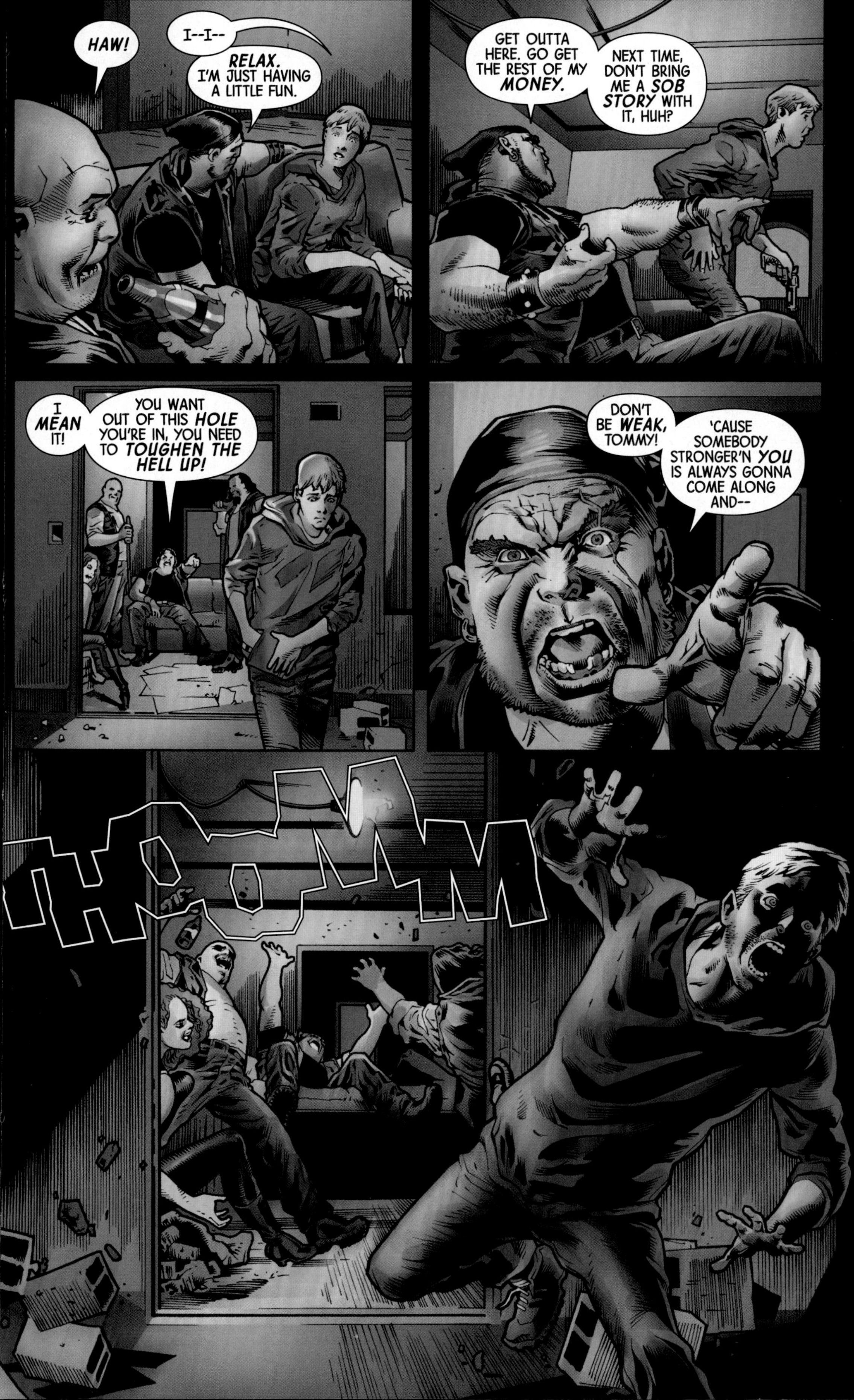
HAW!
I--I--
RELAX. I'M JUST HAVING A LITTLE FUN.
GET OUTTA HERE. GO GET THE REST OF MY MONEY.
NEXT TIME, DON'T BRING ME A SOB STORY WITH IT, HUH?
I MEAN IT!
YOU WANT OUT OF THIS HOLE YOU'RE IN, YOU NEED TO TOUGHEN THE HELL UP!
DON'T BE WEAK, TOMMY!
'CAUSE SOMEBODY STRONGER'N YOU IS ALWAYS GONNA COME ALONG AND--
THOOMM

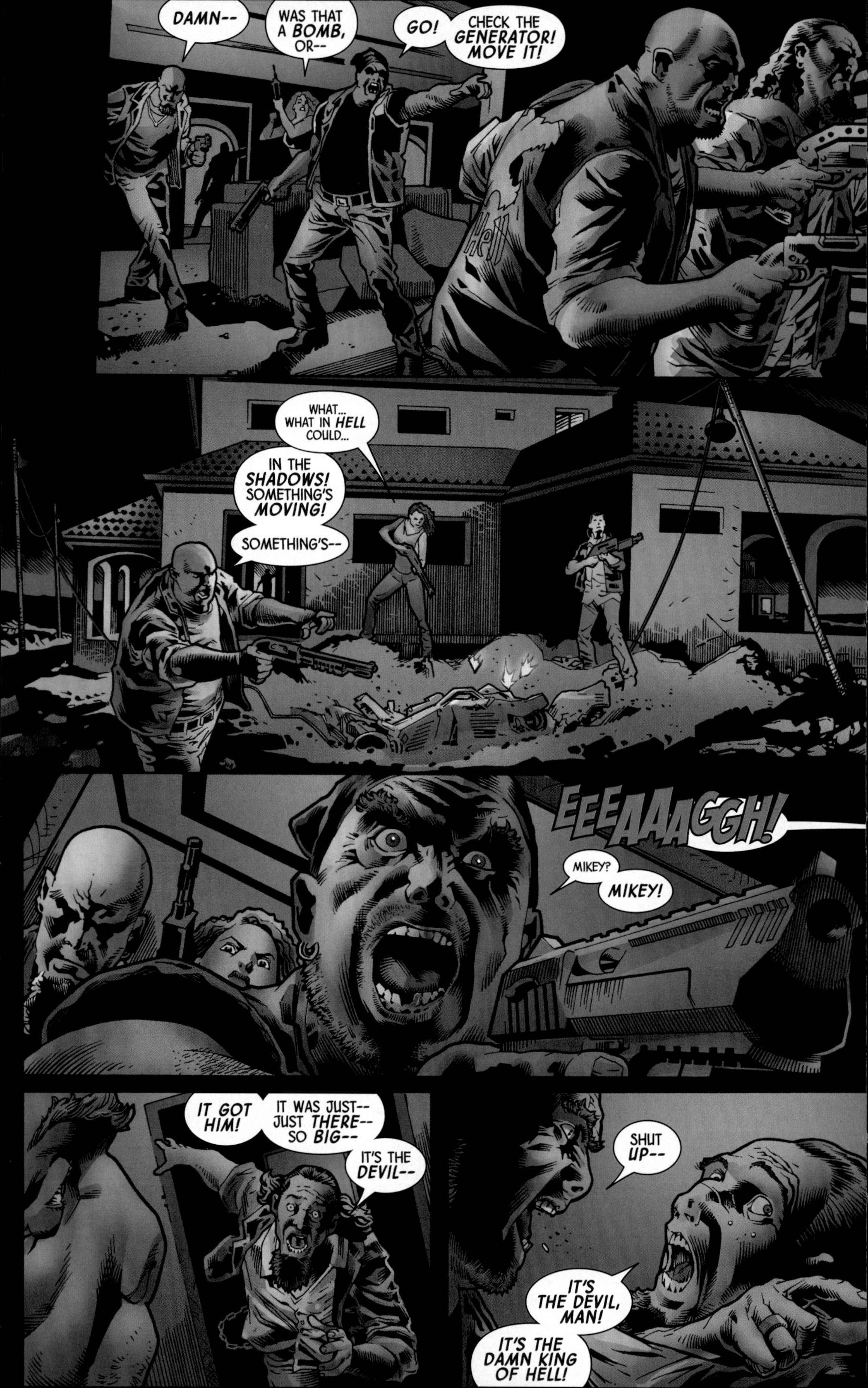
DAMN--
WAS THAT A BOMB, OR--
GO!
CHECK THE GENERATOR! MOVE IT!
WHAT... WHAT IN HELL COULD...
IN THE SHADOWS! SOMETHING'S MOVING!
SOMETHING'S--
EEEAAAGGH!
MIKEY?
MIKEY!
IT GOT HIM!
IT WAS JUST-- JUST THERE-- SO BIG--
IT'S THE DEVIL--
SHUT UP--
IT'S THE DEVIL, MAN!
IT'S THE DAMN KING OF HELL!

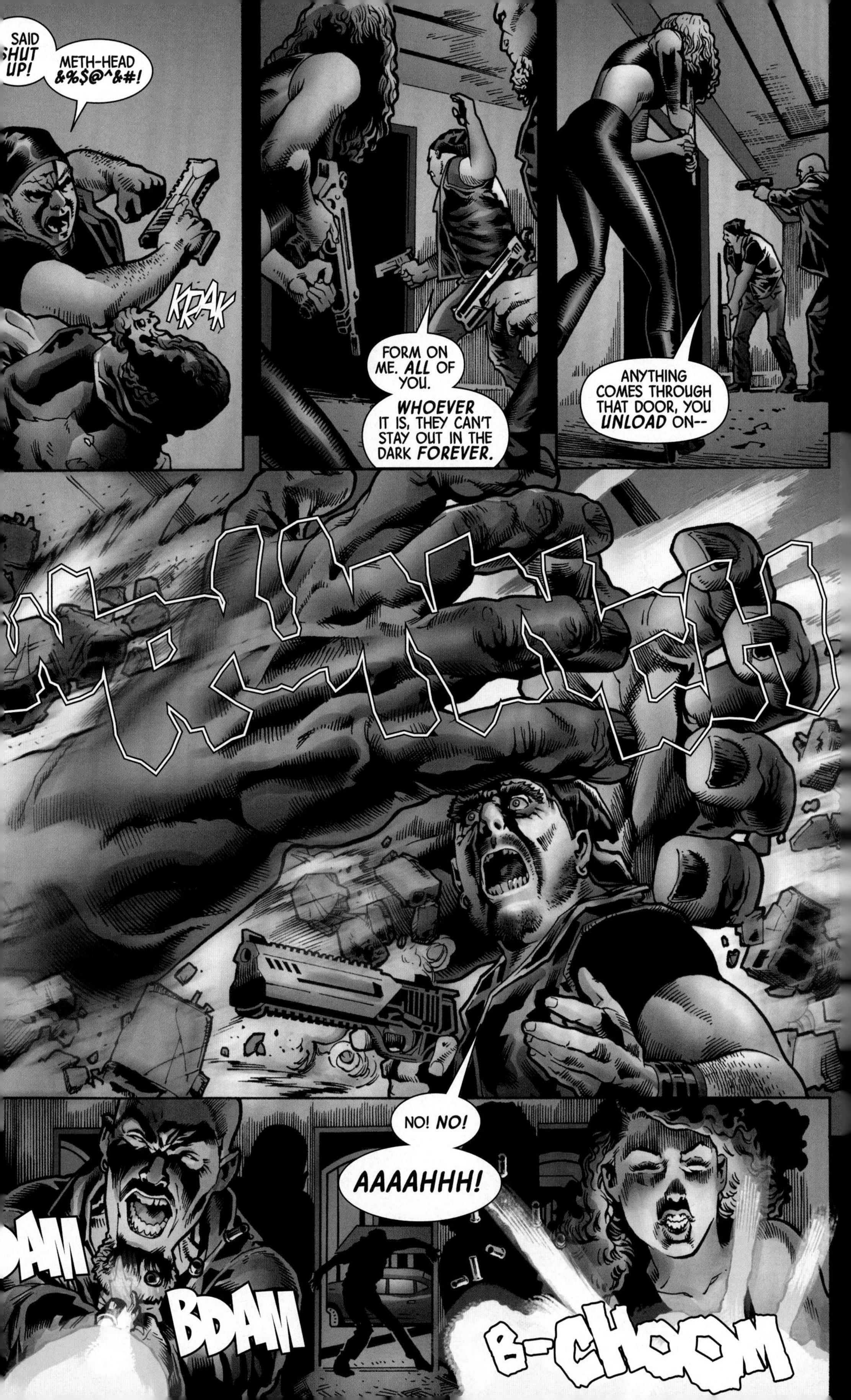
SAID SHUT UP!
METH-HEAD &%$@^&#!
KRAK
FORM ON ME. ALL OF YOU.
WHOEVER IT IS, THEY CAN'T STAY OUT IN THE DARK FOREVER.
ANYTHING COMES THROUGH THAT DOOR, YOU UNLOAD ON--
NO! NO!
AAAAHHH!
DAM
BDAM
B-CHOOM

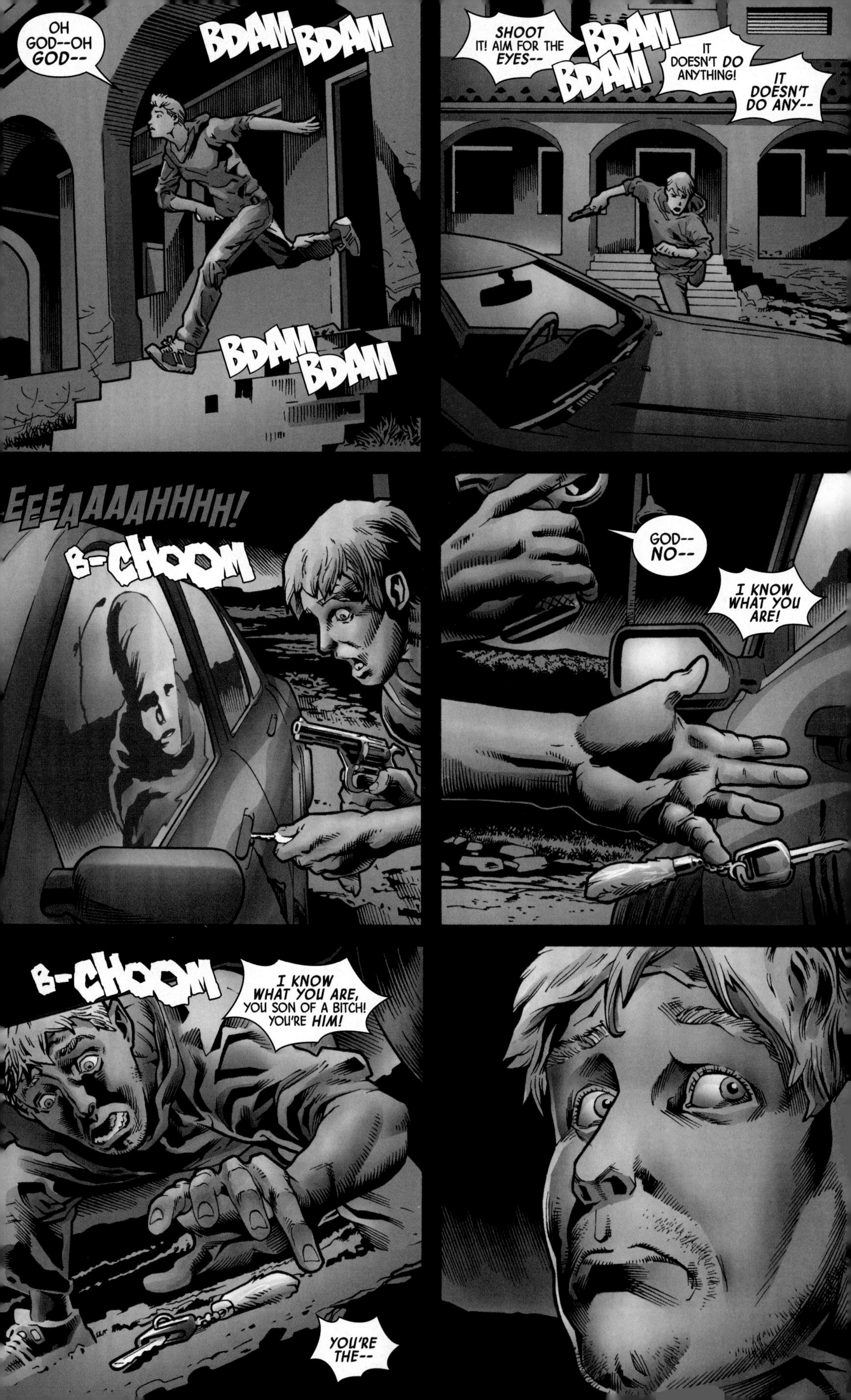
OH GOD--OH GOD--
BDAM BDAM
BDAM BDAM
SHOOT IT! AIM FOR THE EYES--
BDAM BDAM
IT DOESN'T DO ANYTHING!
IT DOESN'T DO ANY--
EEEAAAAHHHH!
B-CHOOM
GOD-- NO--
I KNOW WHAT YOU ARE!
B-CHOOM
I KNOW WHAT YOU ARE, YOU SON OF A BITCH! YOU'RE HIM!
YOU'RE THE--

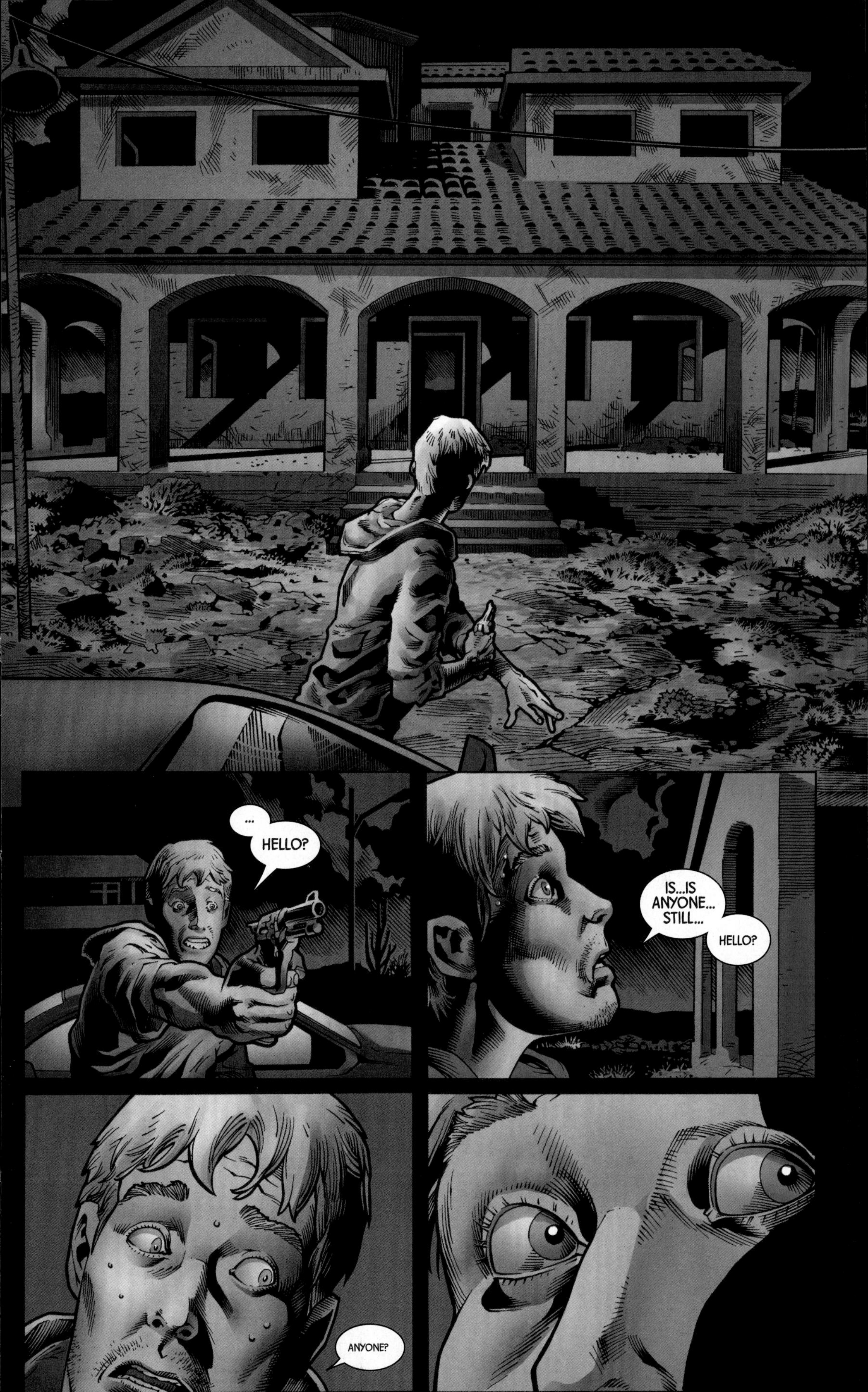
...
HELLO?
IS...IS ANYONE... STILL...
HELLO?
ANYONE?

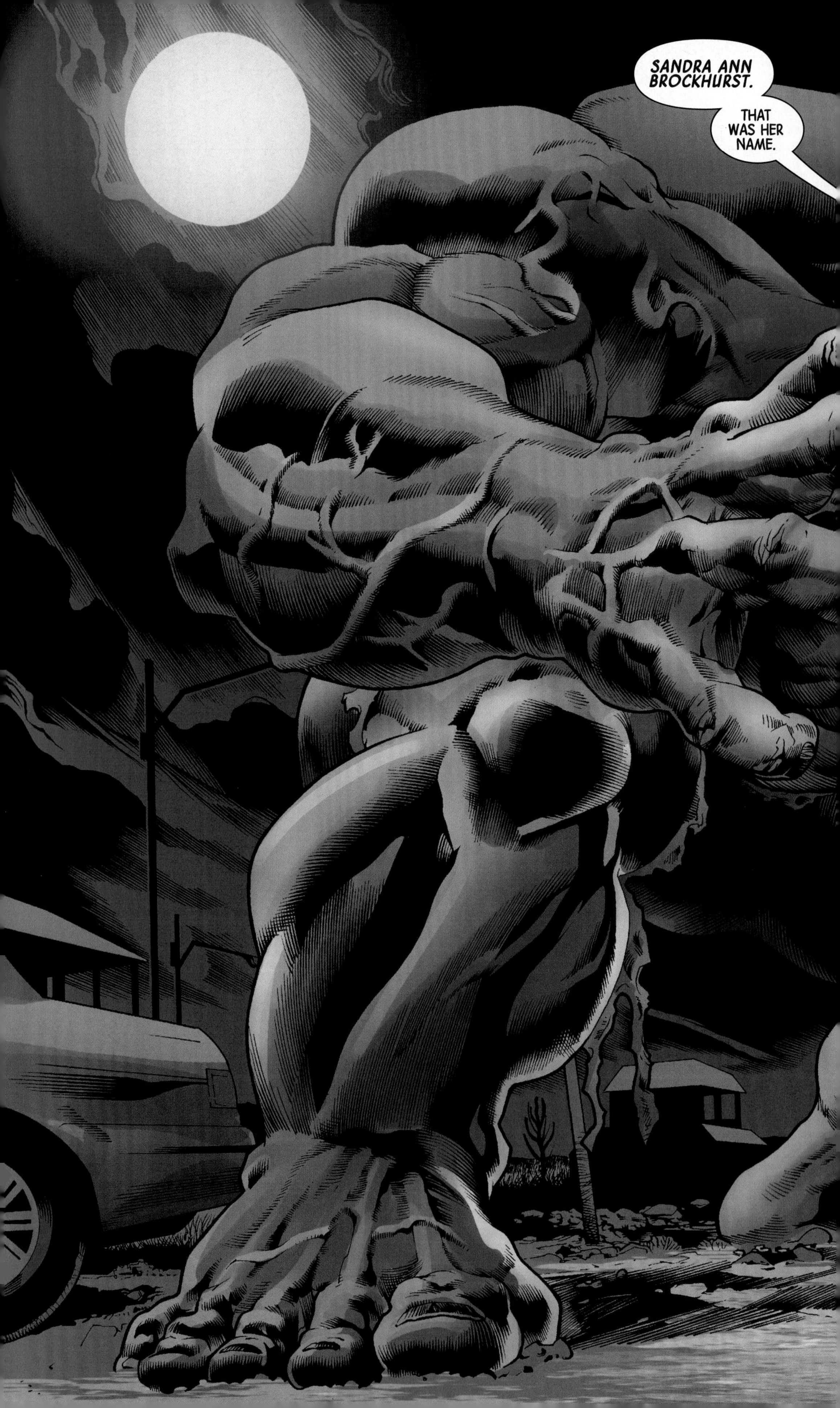
SANDRA ANN BROCKHURST.
THAT WAS HER NAME.

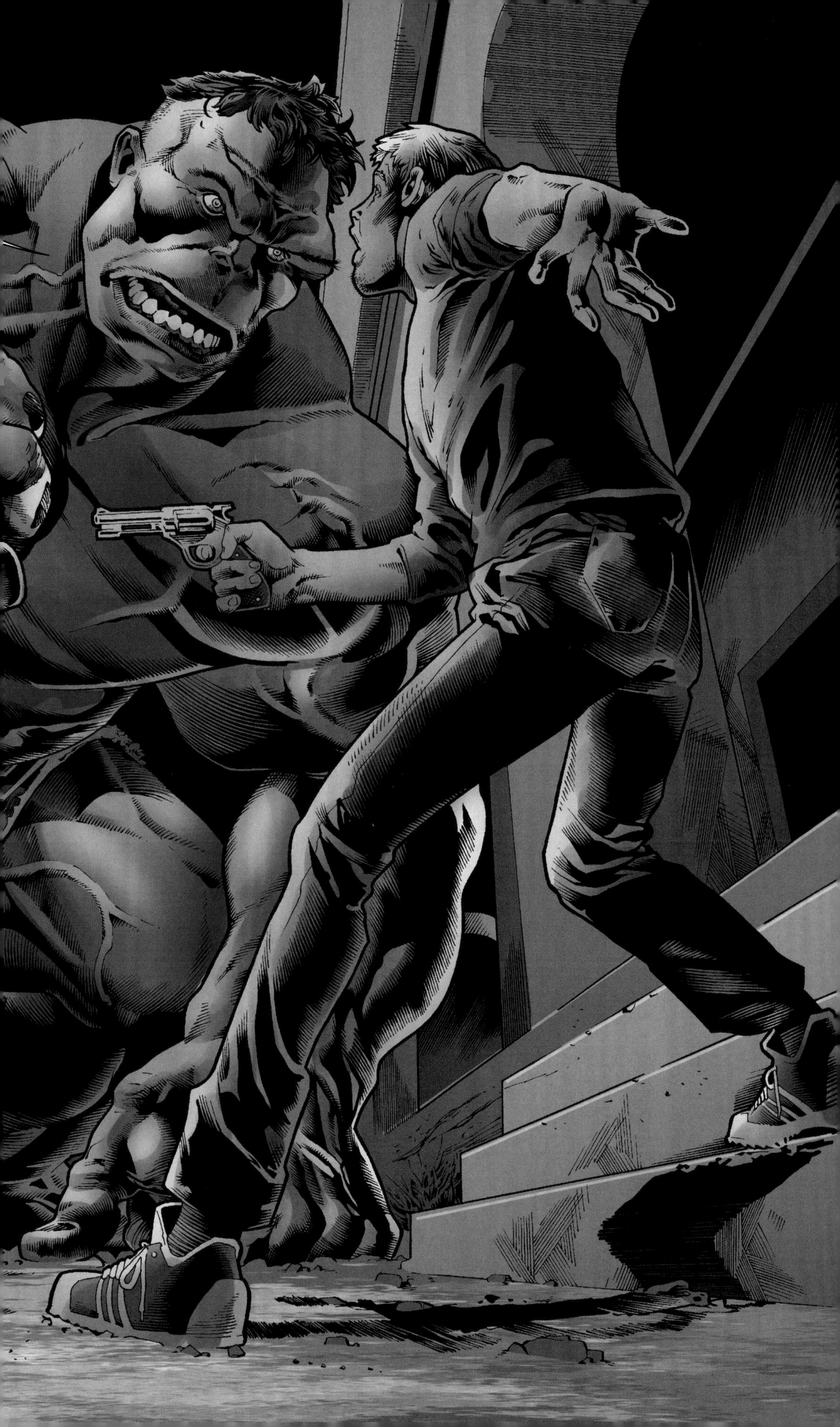

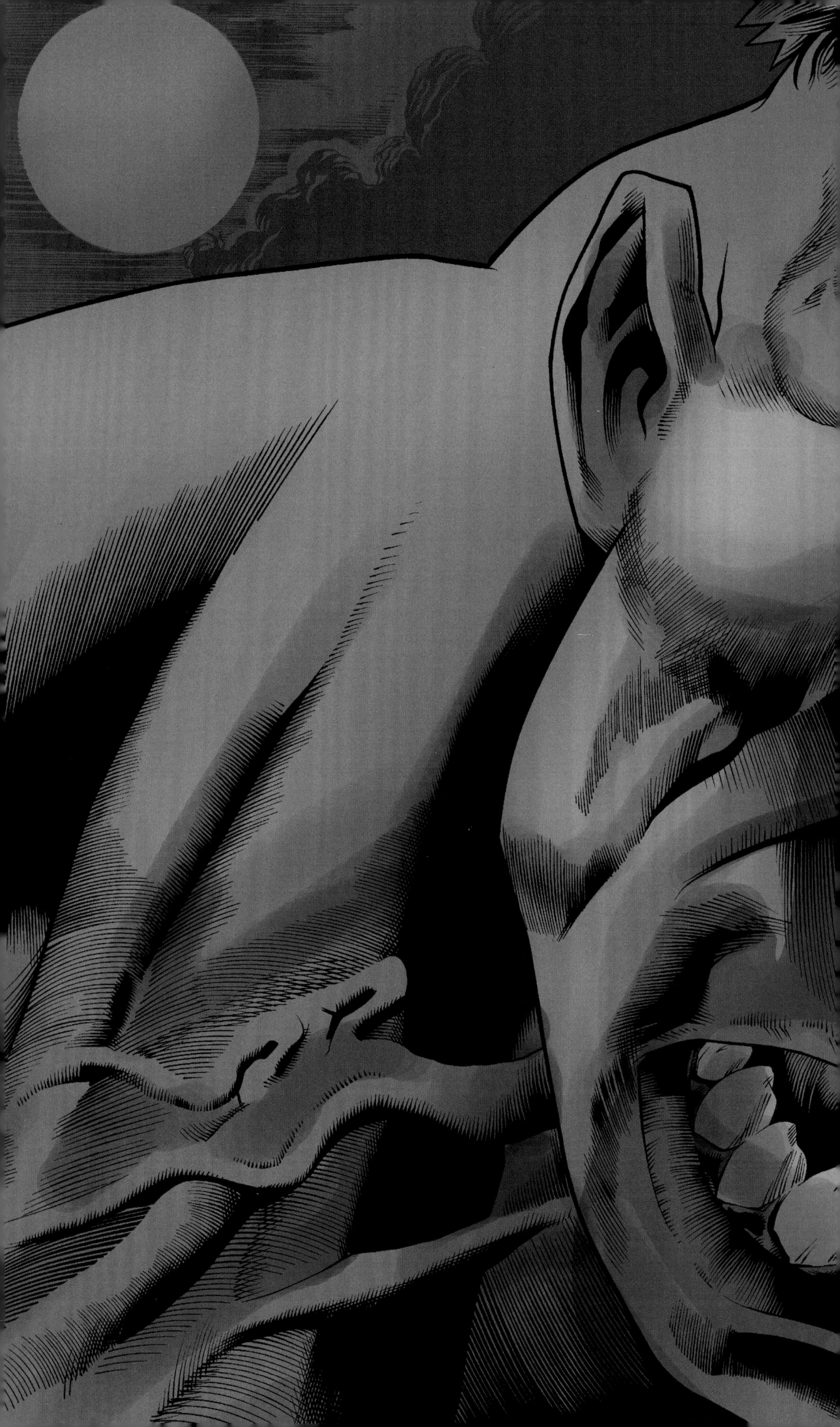

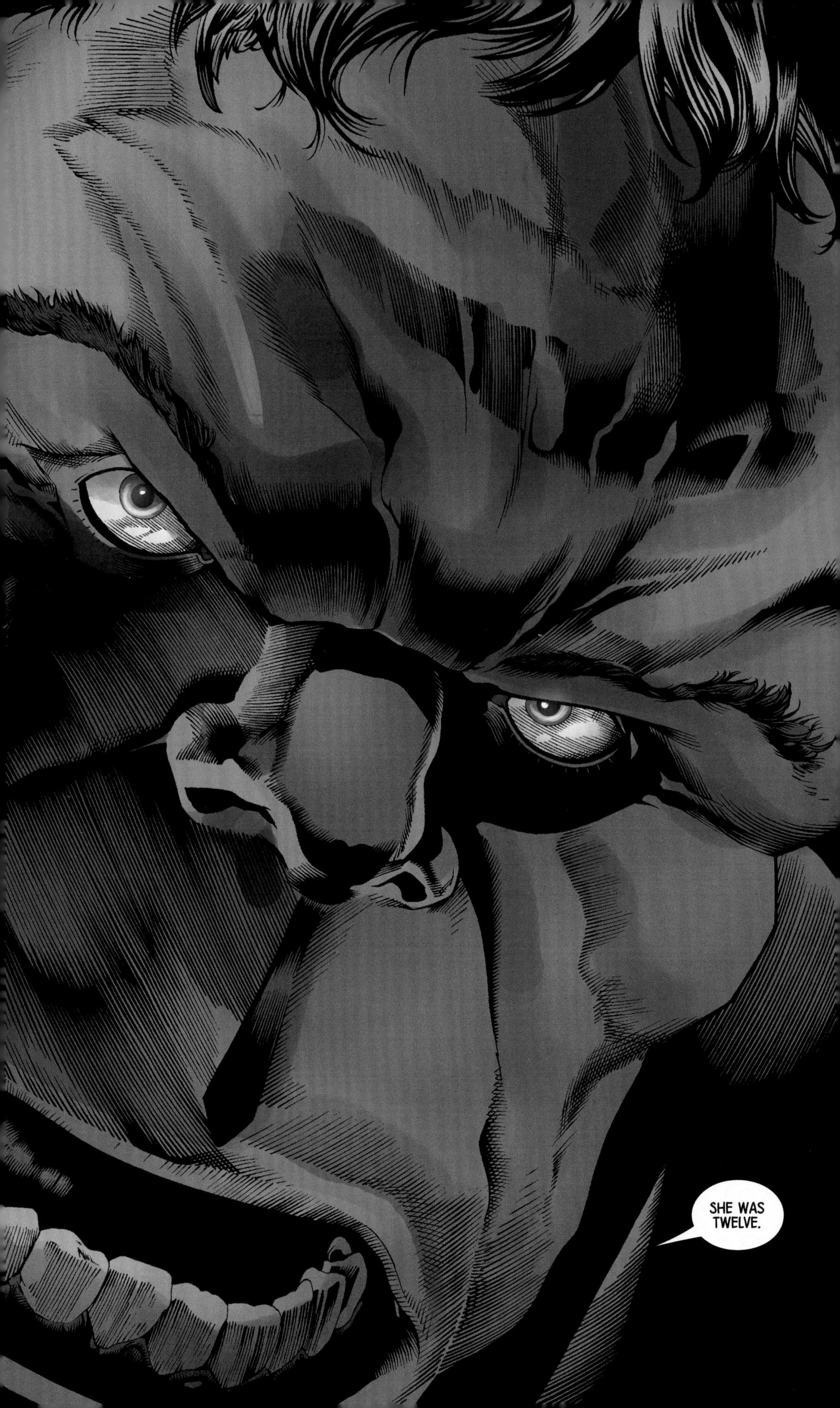
SHE WAS TWELVE.

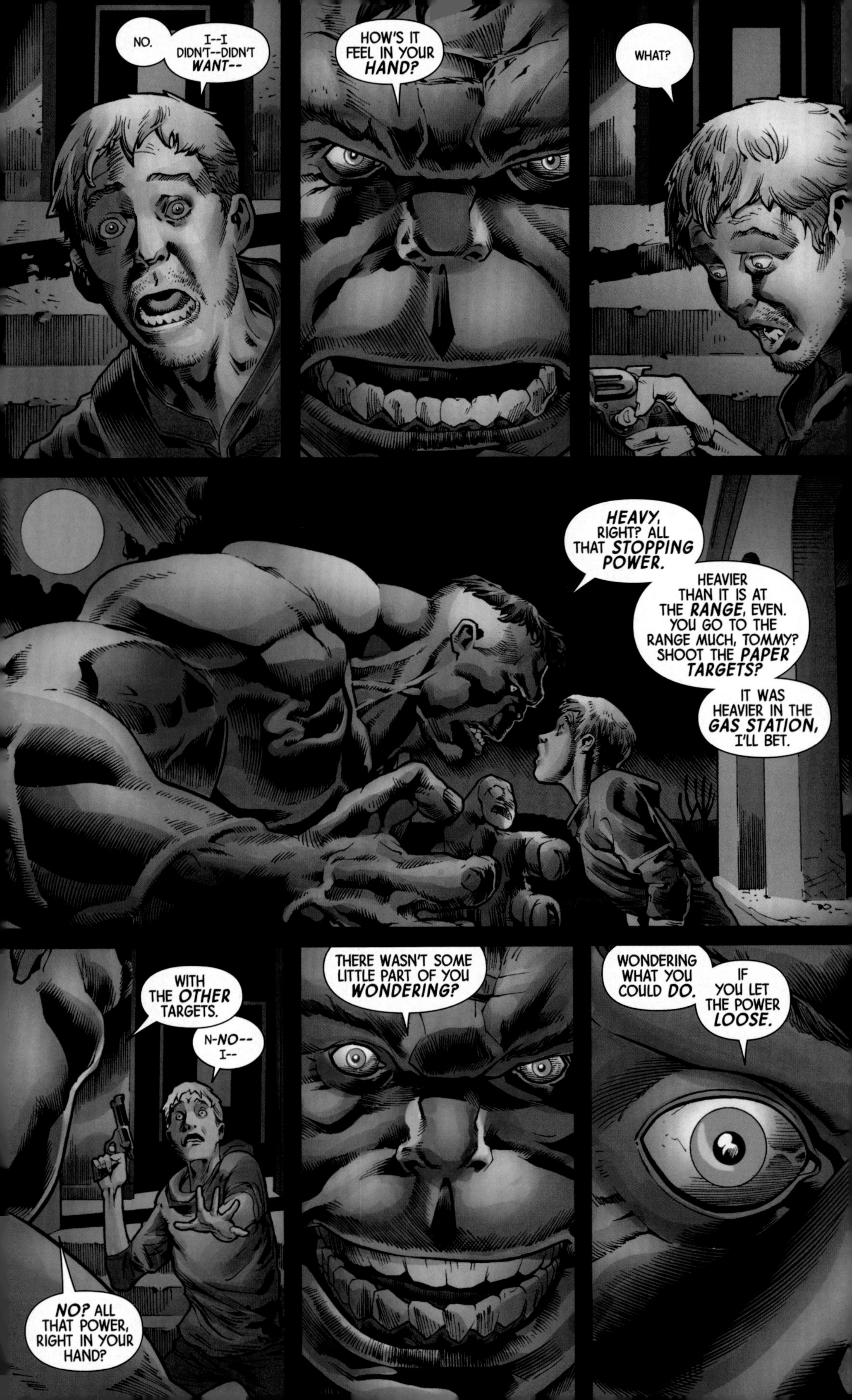
NO.
I--I DIDN'T--DIDN'T *WANT*--
HOW'S IT FEEL IN YOUR *HAND?*
WHAT?
*HEAVY*, RIGHT? ALL THAT *STOPPING POWER.*
HEAVIER THAN IT IS AT THE *RANGE*, EVEN. YOU GO TO THE RANGE MUCH, TOMMY? SHOOT THE *PAPER TARGETS?*
IT WAS HEAVIER IN THE *GAS STATION,* I'LL BET.
WITH THE *OTHER* TARGETS.
N-*NO*-- I--
*NO?* ALL THAT POWER, RIGHT IN YOUR HAND?
THERE WASN'T SOME LITTLE PART OF YOU *WONDERING?*
WONDERING WHAT YOU COULD *DO.*
IF YOU LET THE POWER *LOOSE.*

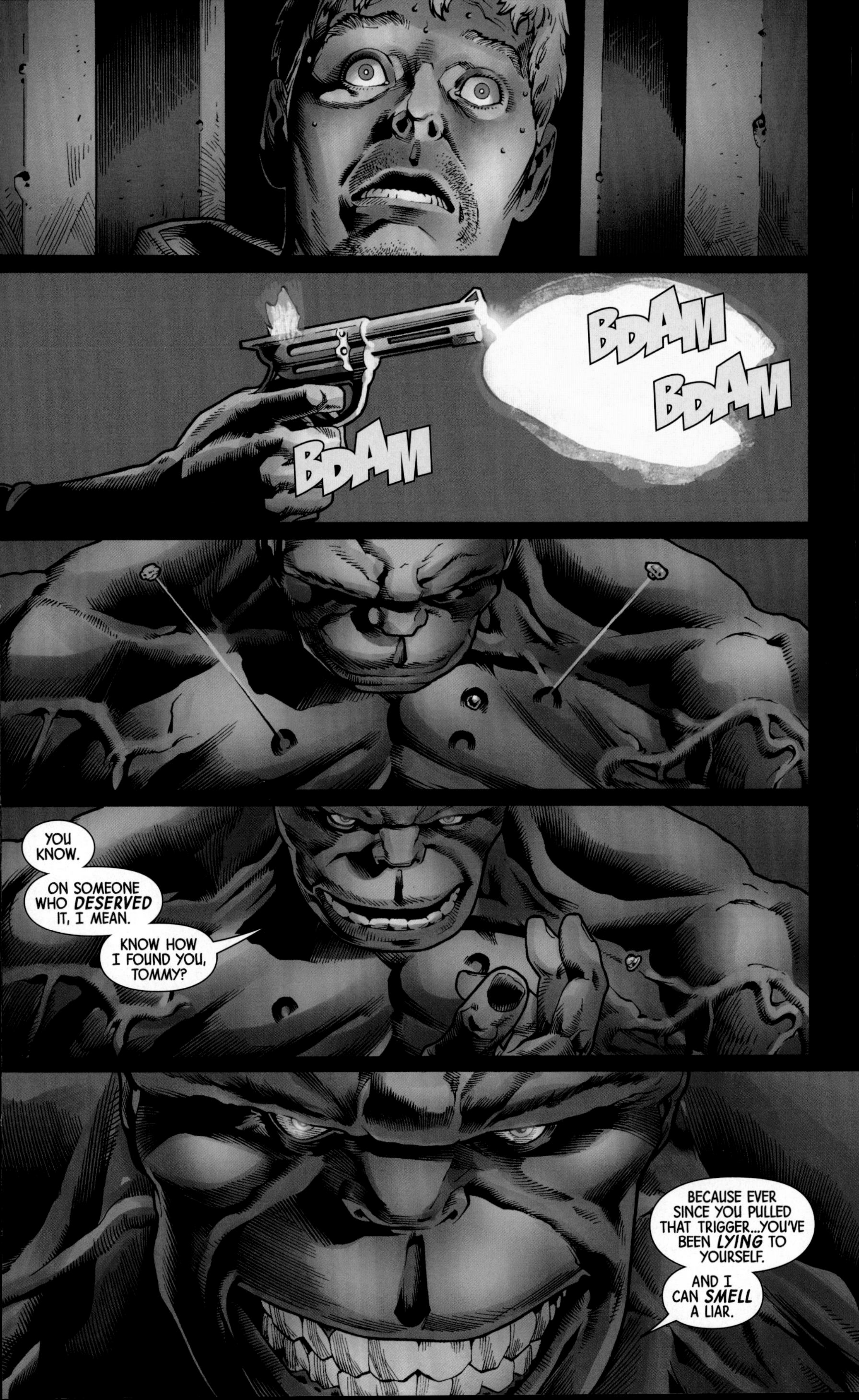

BDAM
BDAM
BDAM
YOU KNOW.
ON SOMEONE WHO DESERVED IT, I MEAN.
KNOW HOW I FOUND YOU, TOMMY?
BECAUSE EVER SINCE YOU PULLED THAT TRIGGER...YOU'VE BEEN LYING TO YOURSELF.
AND I CAN SMELL A LIAR.

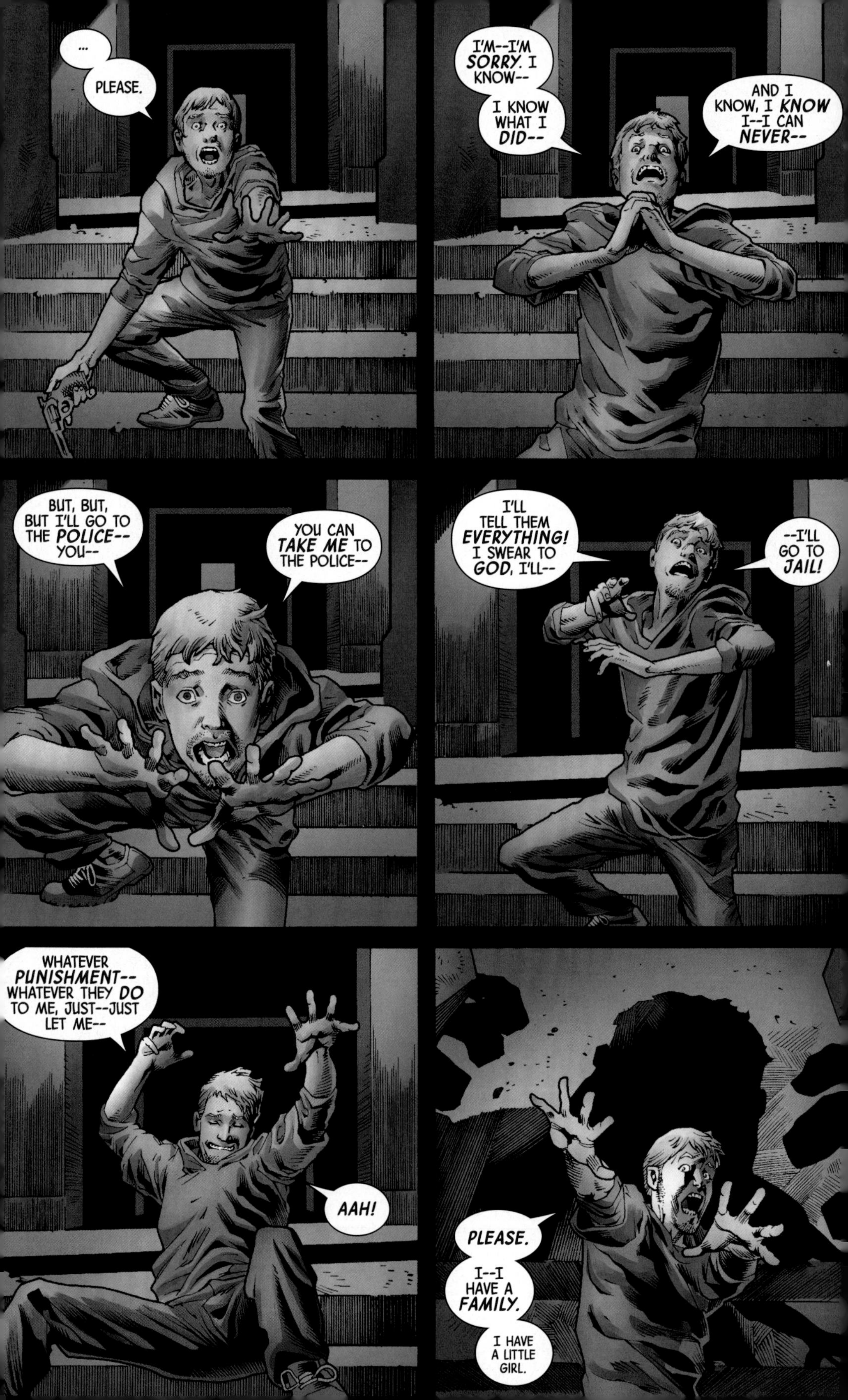
...
PLEASE.
I'M--I'M SORRY. I KNOW--
I KNOW WHAT I DID--
AND I KNOW, I KNOW I--I CAN NEVER--
BUT, BUT, BUT I'LL GO TO THE POLICE--YOU--
YOU CAN TAKE ME TO THE POLICE--
I'LL TELL THEM EVERYTHING! I SWEAR TO GOD, I'LL--
--I'LL GO TO JAIL!
WHATEVER PUNISHMENT--WHATEVER THEY DO TO ME, JUST--JUST LET ME--
AAH!
PLEASE.
I--I HAVE A FAMILY.
I HAVE A LITTLE GIRL.

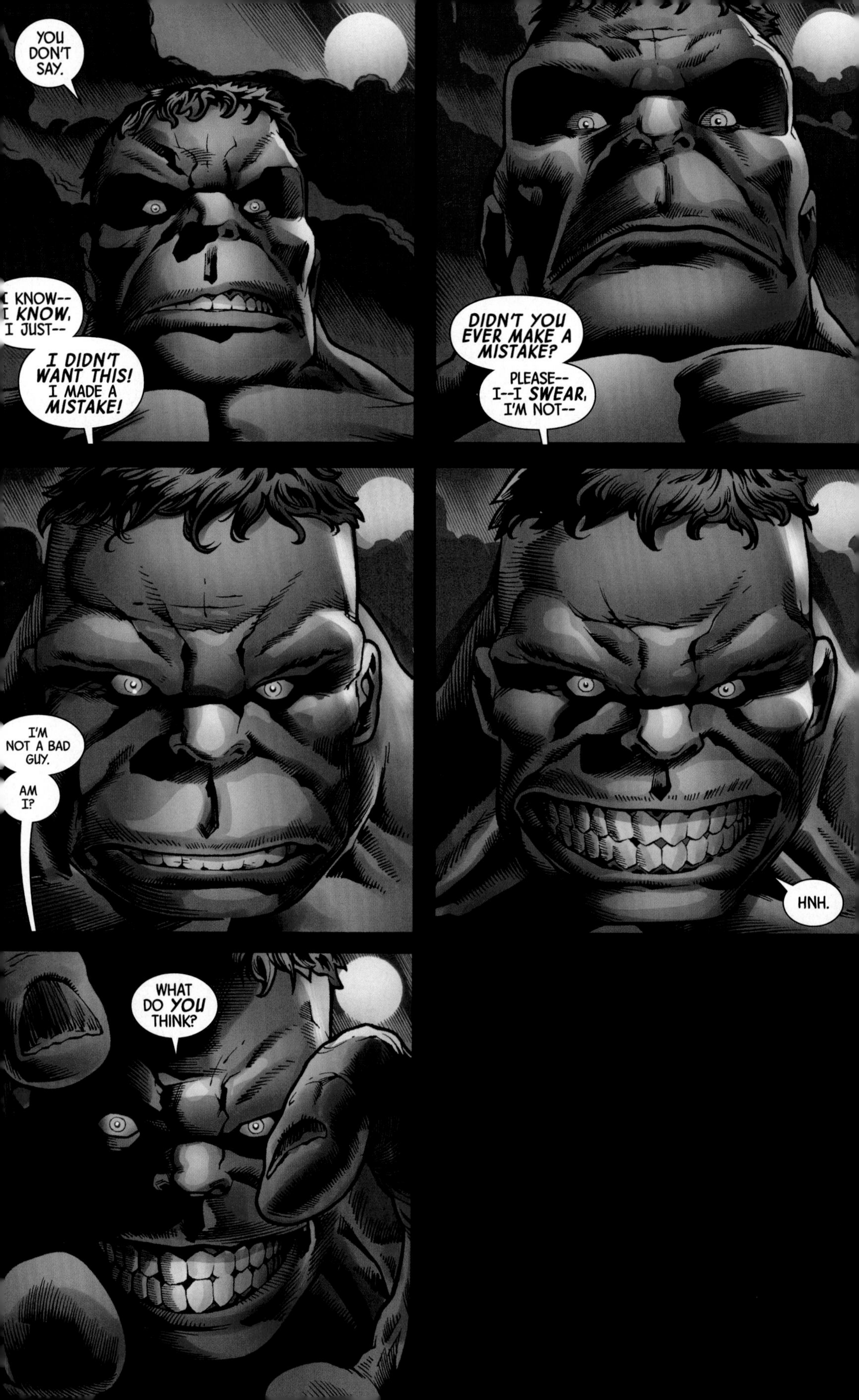
YOU DON'T SAY.
I KNOW-- I KNOW, I JUST--
I DIDN'T WANT THIS! I MADE A MISTAKE!
DIDN'T YOU EVER MAKE A MISTAKE?
PLEASE-- I--I SWEAR, I'M NOT--
I'M NOT A BAD GUY.
AM I?
HNH.
WHAT DO YOU THINK?

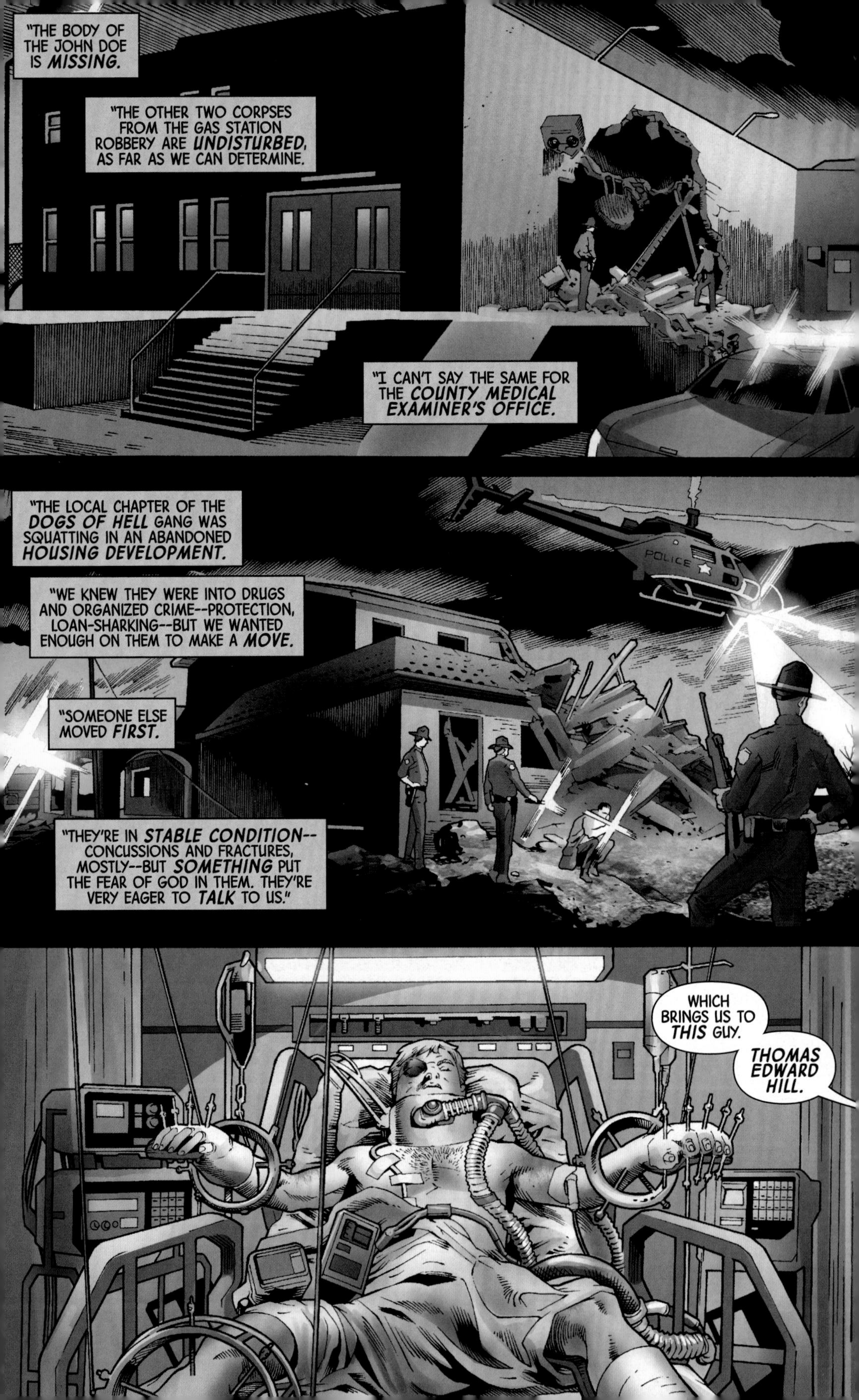

"THE BODY OF THE JOHN DOE IS MISSING.
"THE OTHER TWO CORPSES FROM THE GAS STATION ROBBERY ARE UNDISTURBED, AS FAR AS WE CAN DETERMINE.
"I CAN'T SAY THE SAME FOR THE COUNTY MEDICAL EXAMINER'S OFFICE.
"THE LOCAL CHAPTER OF THE DOGS OF HELL GANG WAS SQUATTING IN AN ABANDONED HOUSING DEVELOPMENT.
POLICE
"WE KNEW THEY WERE INTO DRUGS AND ORGANIZED CRIME--PROTECTION, LOAN-SHARKING--BUT WE WANTED ENOUGH ON THEM TO MAKE A MOVE.
"SOMEONE ELSE MOVED FIRST.
"THEY'RE IN STABLE CONDITION--CONCUSSIONS AND FRACTURES, MOSTLY--BUT SOMETHING PUT THE FEAR OF GOD IN THEM. THEY'RE VERY EAGER TO TALK TO US."
WHICH BRINGS US TO THIS GUY.
THOMAS EDWARD HILL.

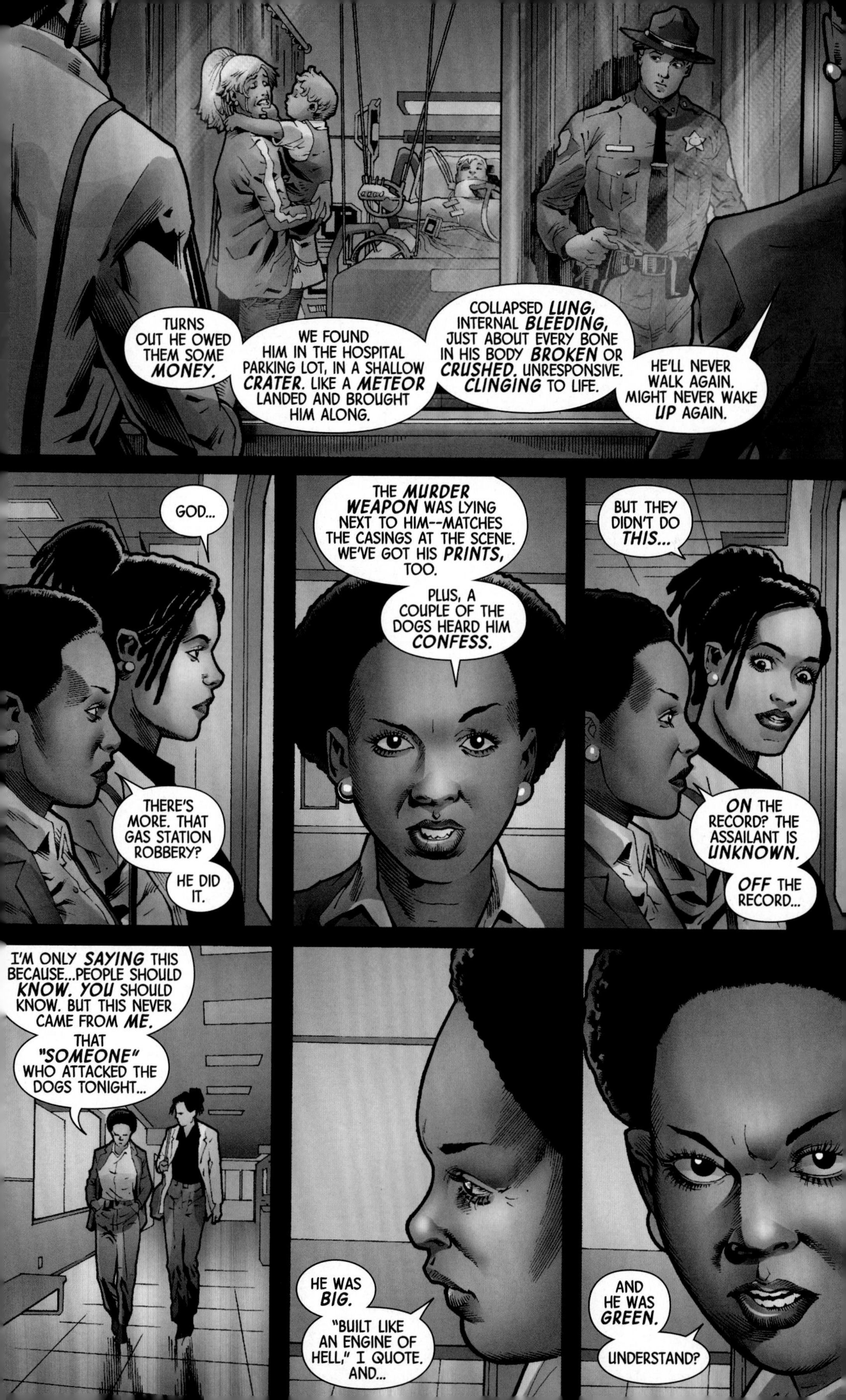
TURNS OUT HE OWED THEM SOME MONEY.
WE FOUND HIM IN THE HOSPITAL PARKING LOT, IN A SHALLOW CRATER. LIKE A METEOR LANDED AND BROUGHT HIM ALONG.
COLLAPSED LUNG, INTERNAL BLEEDING, JUST ABOUT EVERY BONE IN HIS BODY BROKEN OR CRUSHED. UNRESPONSIVE. CLINGING TO LIFE.
HE'LL NEVER WALK AGAIN. MIGHT NEVER WAKE UP AGAIN.
GOD...
THERE'S MORE. THAT GAS STATION ROBBERY?
HE DID IT.
THE MURDER WEAPON WAS LYING NEXT TO HIM--MATCHES THE CASINGS AT THE SCENE. WE'VE GOT HIS PRINTS, TOO.
PLUS, A COUPLE OF THE DOGS HEARD HIM CONFESS.
BUT THEY DIDN'T DO THIS...
ON THE RECORD? THE ASSAILANT IS UNKNOWN.
OFF THE RECORD...
I'M ONLY SAYING THIS BECAUSE...PEOPLE SHOULD KNOW. YOU SHOULD KNOW. BUT THIS NEVER CAME FROM ME.
THAT "SOMEONE" WHO ATTACKED THE DOGS TONIGHT...
HE WAS BIG.
"BUILT LIKE AN ENGINE OF HELL," I QUOTE. AND...
AND HE WAS GREEN.
UNDERSTAND?

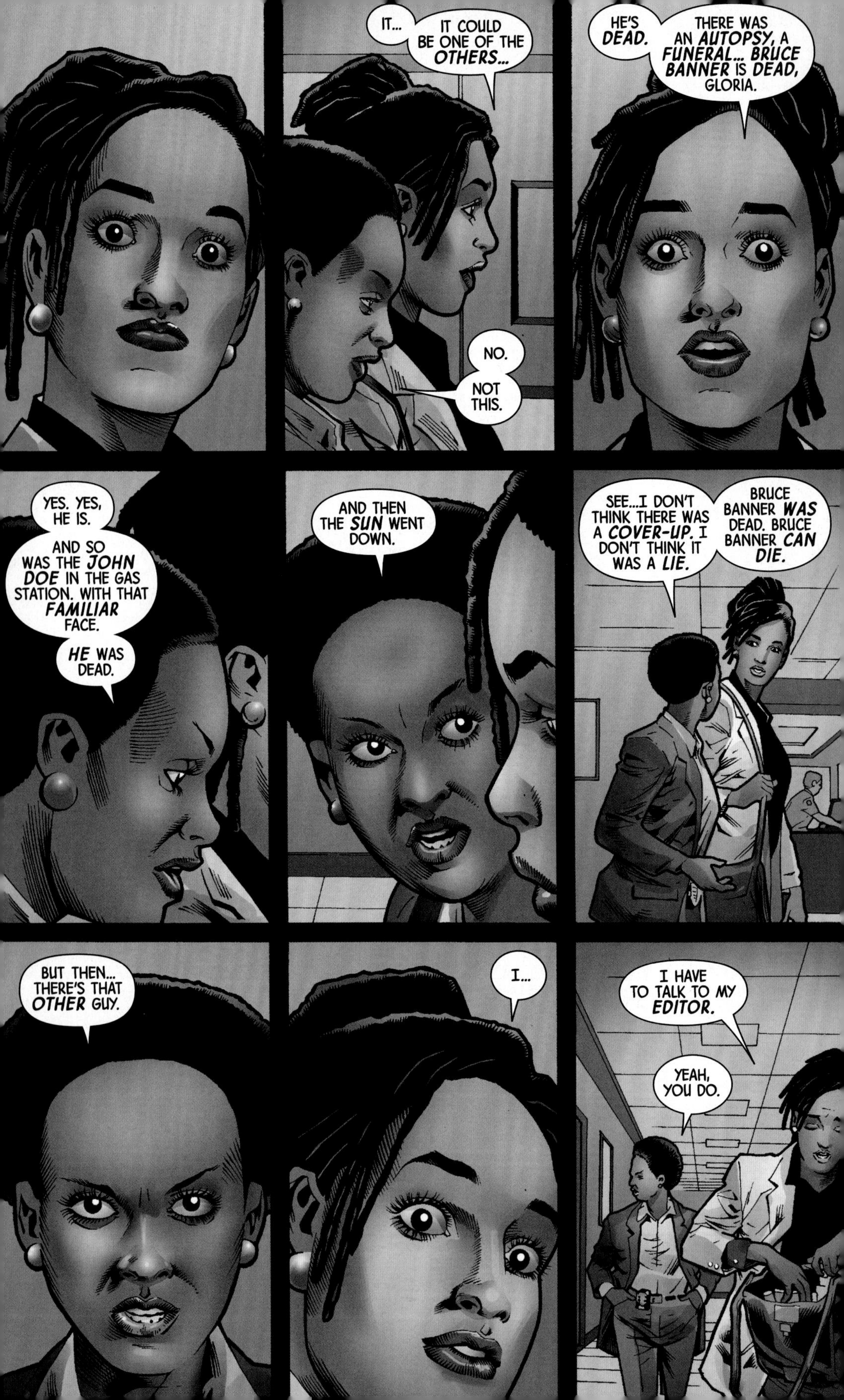
IT...
IT COULD BE ONE OF THE OTHERS...
NO.
NOT THIS.
HE'S DEAD.
THERE WAS AN AUTOPSY, A FUNERAL... BRUCE BANNER IS DEAD, GLORIA.
YES. YES, HE IS.
AND SO WAS THE JOHN DOE IN THE GAS STATION. WITH THAT FAMILIAR FACE.
HE WAS DEAD.
AND THEN THE SUN WENT DOWN.
SEE...I DON'T THINK THERE WAS A COVER-UP. I DON'T THINK IT WAS A LIE.
BRUCE BANNER WAS DEAD. BRUCE BANNER CAN DIE.
BUT THEN... THERE'S THAT OTHER GUY.
I...
I HAVE TO TALK TO MY EDITOR.
YEAH, YOU DO.

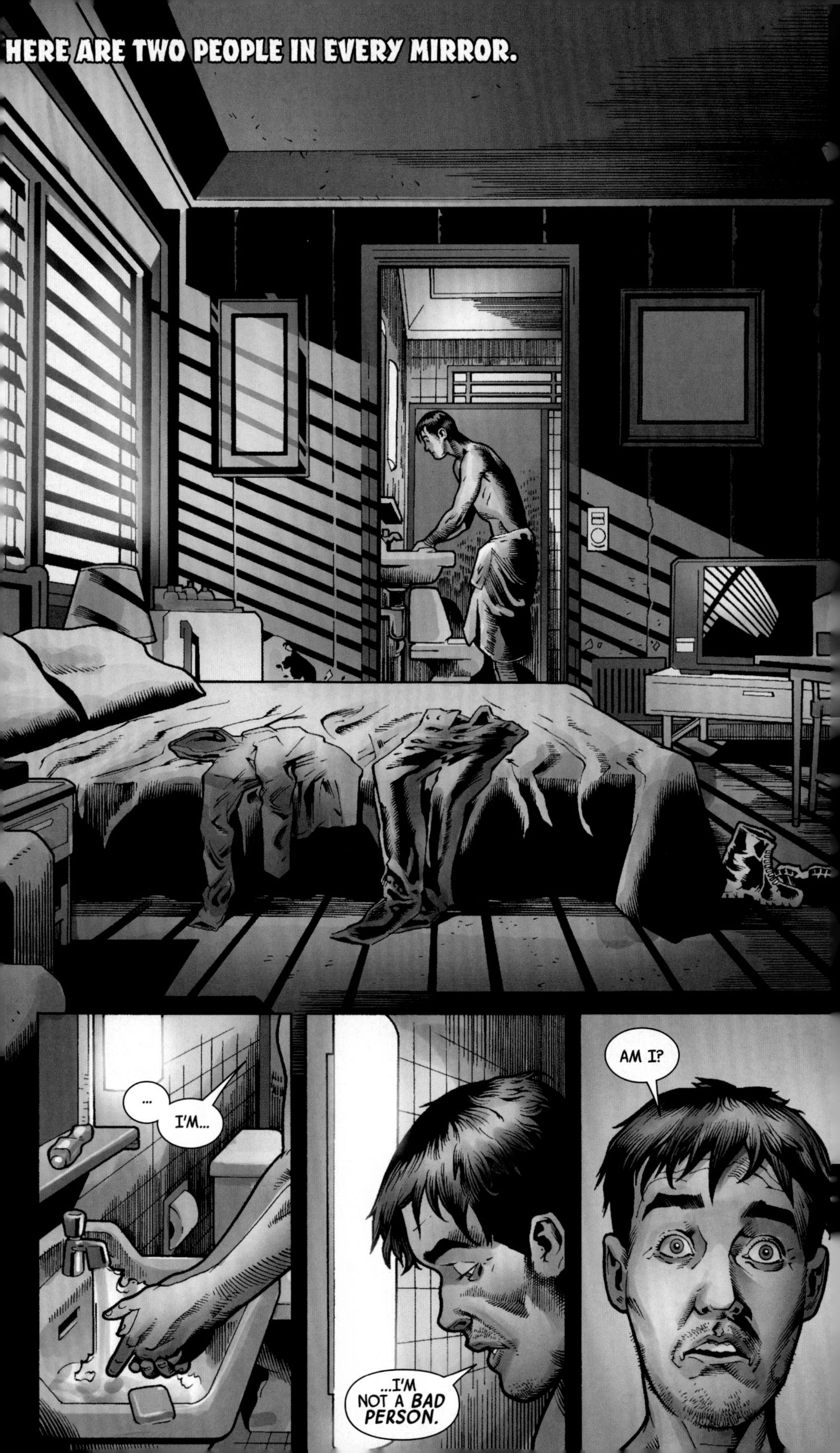
HERE ARE TWO PEOPLE IN EVERY MIRROR.
... I'M...
...I'M NOT A BAD PERSON.
AM I?

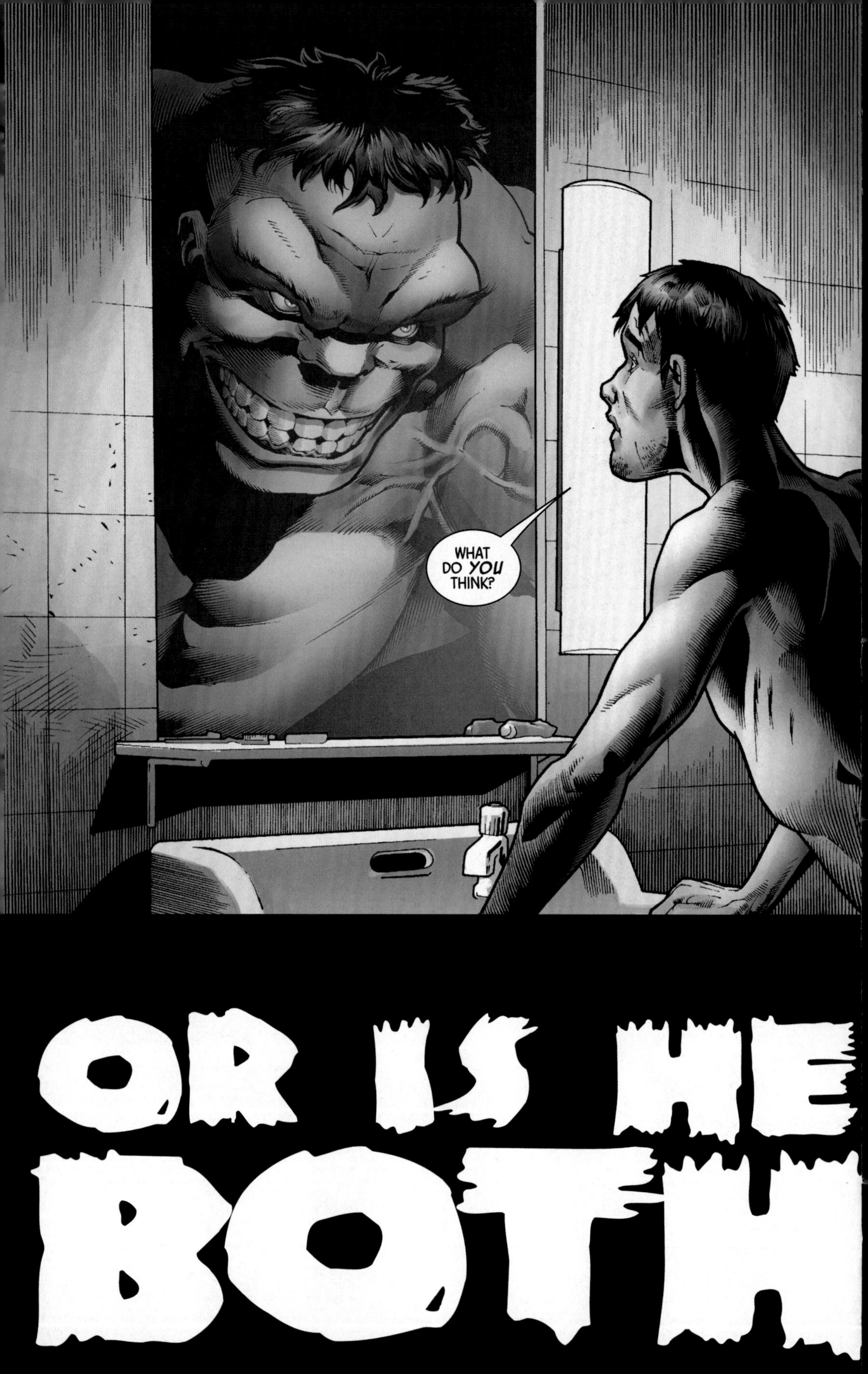
WHAT DO *YOU* THINK?

# OR IS HE BOTH

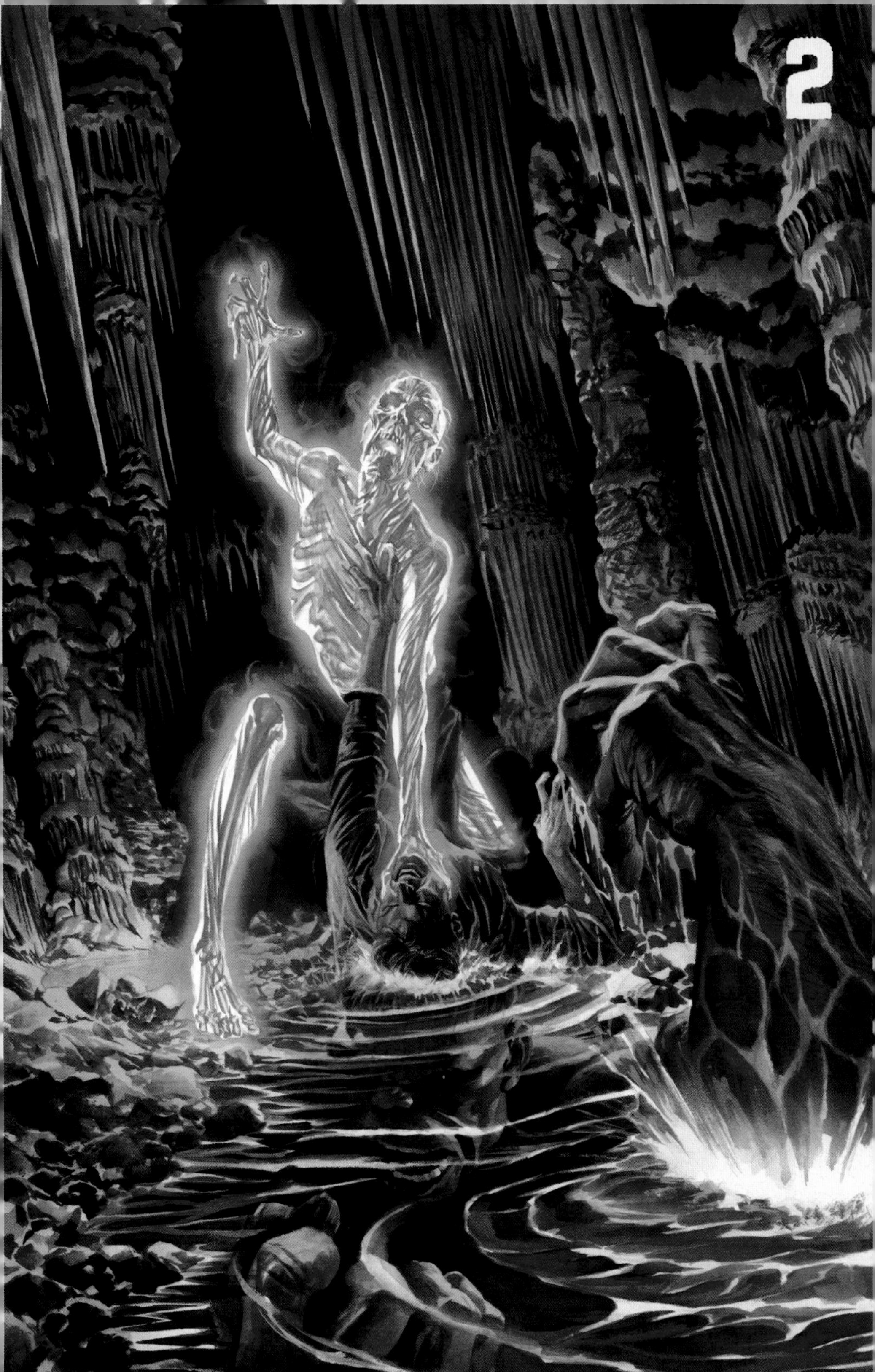
2

"ALL TH IS LIFE."

I DON'T DREAM ABOUT THE BOMB ANYMORE.

I DREAM ABOUT THE *WAITING*.

ABOUT A TINY ROOM AND A GEIGER COUNTER.

THE *RADIATION* I'D TAKEN...*NOBODY* COULD SURVIVE. NOBODY.

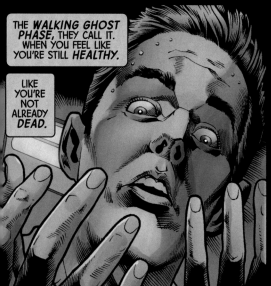

THE *WALKING GHOST PHASE*, THEY CALL IT. WHEN YOU FEEL LIKE YOU'RE STILL *HEALTHY*.

LIKE YOU'RE NOT ALREADY *DEAD*.

BUT DEATH WAS *COMING*. LUMBERING TOWARD ME...SLOW, *PAINFUL*...

AND THAT DAMN *GEIGER COUNTER* KEPT *HISSING* AND *CRACKLING* AT ME... *LAUGHING* AT ME...

IT WOULDN'T *SHUT UP*.

IT WOULDN'T LEAVE ME *ALONE*.

IT *WOULDN'T*

LEAVE ME

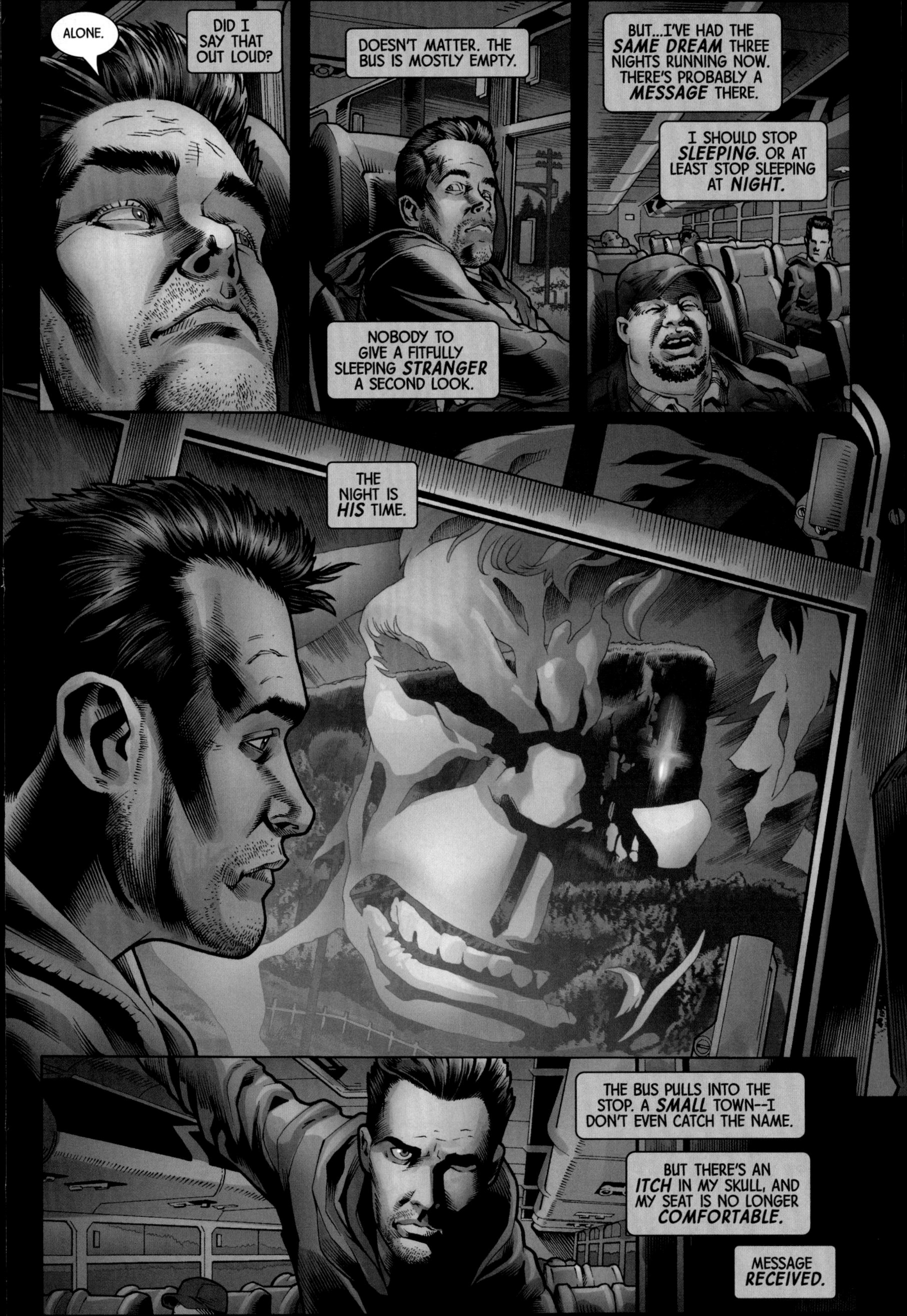

ALONE.
DID I SAY THAT OUT LOUD?
DOESN'T MATTER. THE BUS IS MOSTLY EMPTY.
NOBODY TO GIVE A FITFULLY SLEEPING STRANGER A SECOND LOOK.
BUT...I'VE HAD THE SAME DREAM THREE NIGHTS RUNNING NOW. THERE'S PROBABLY A MESSAGE THERE.
I SHOULD STOP SLEEPING. OR AT LEAST STOP SLEEPING AT NIGHT.
THE NIGHT IS HIS TIME.
THE BUS PULLS INTO THE STOP. A SMALL TOWN--I DON'T EVEN CATCH THE NAME.
BUT THERE'S AN ITCH IN MY SKULL, AND MY SEAT IS NO LONGER COMFORTABLE.
MESSAGE RECEIVED.

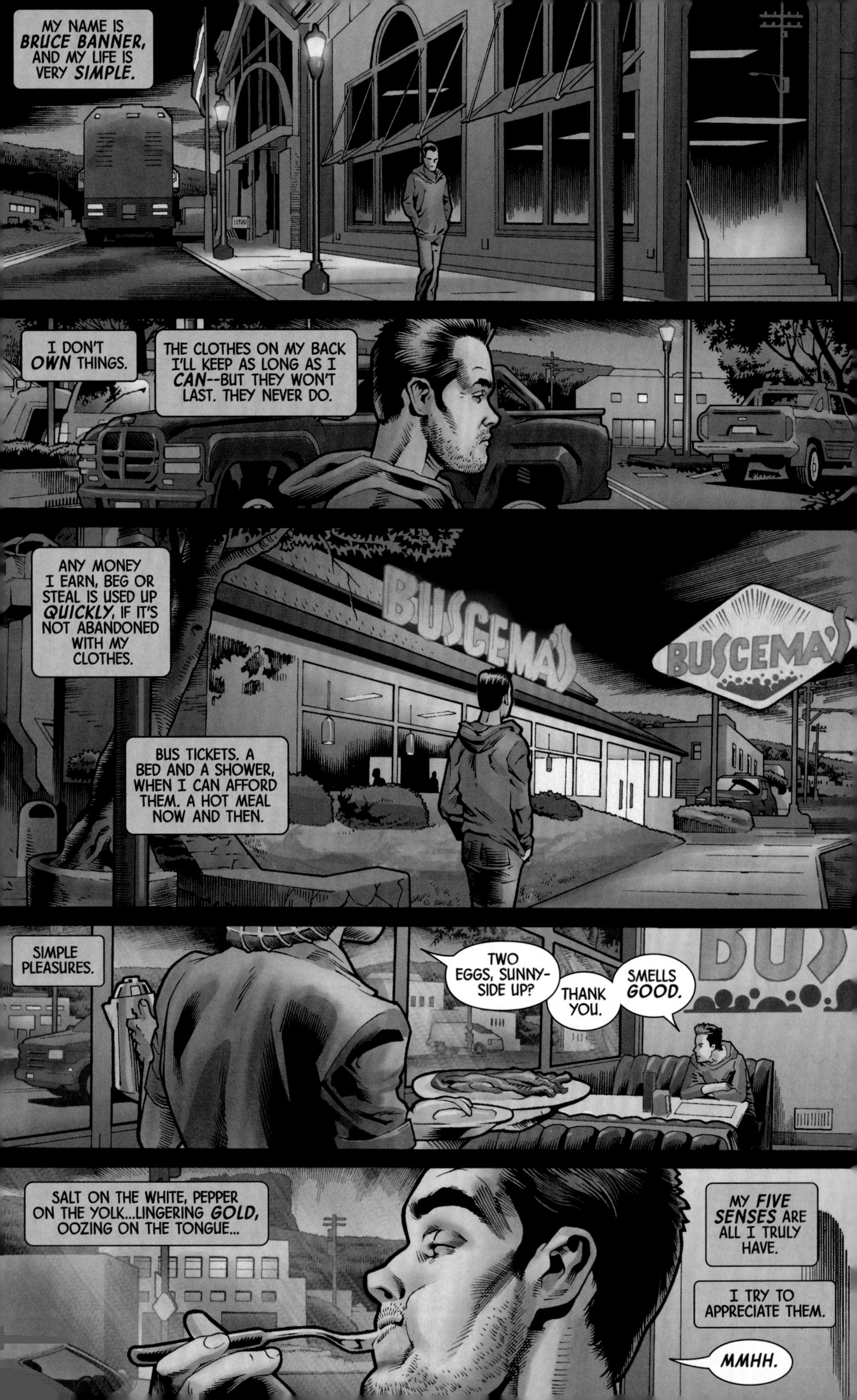
MY NAME IS BRUCE BANNER, AND MY LIFE IS VERY SIMPLE.
I DON'T OWN THINGS.
THE CLOTHES ON MY BACK I'LL KEEP AS LONG AS I CAN--BUT THEY WON'T LAST. THEY NEVER DO.
ANY MONEY I EARN, BEG OR STEAL IS USED UP QUICKLY, IF IT'S NOT ABANDONED WITH MY CLOTHES.
BUSCEMA'S
BUSCEMA'S
BUS TICKETS. A BED AND A SHOWER, WHEN I CAN AFFORD THEM. A HOT MEAL NOW AND THEN.
SIMPLE PLEASURES.
TWO EGGS, SUNNY-SIDE UP?
THANK YOU.
SMELLS GOOD.
BUS
SALT ON THE WHITE, PEPPER ON THE YOLK...LINGERING GOLD, OOZING ON THE TONGUE...
MY FIVE SENSES ARE ALL I TRULY HAVE.
I TRY TO APPRECIATE THEM.
MMHH.

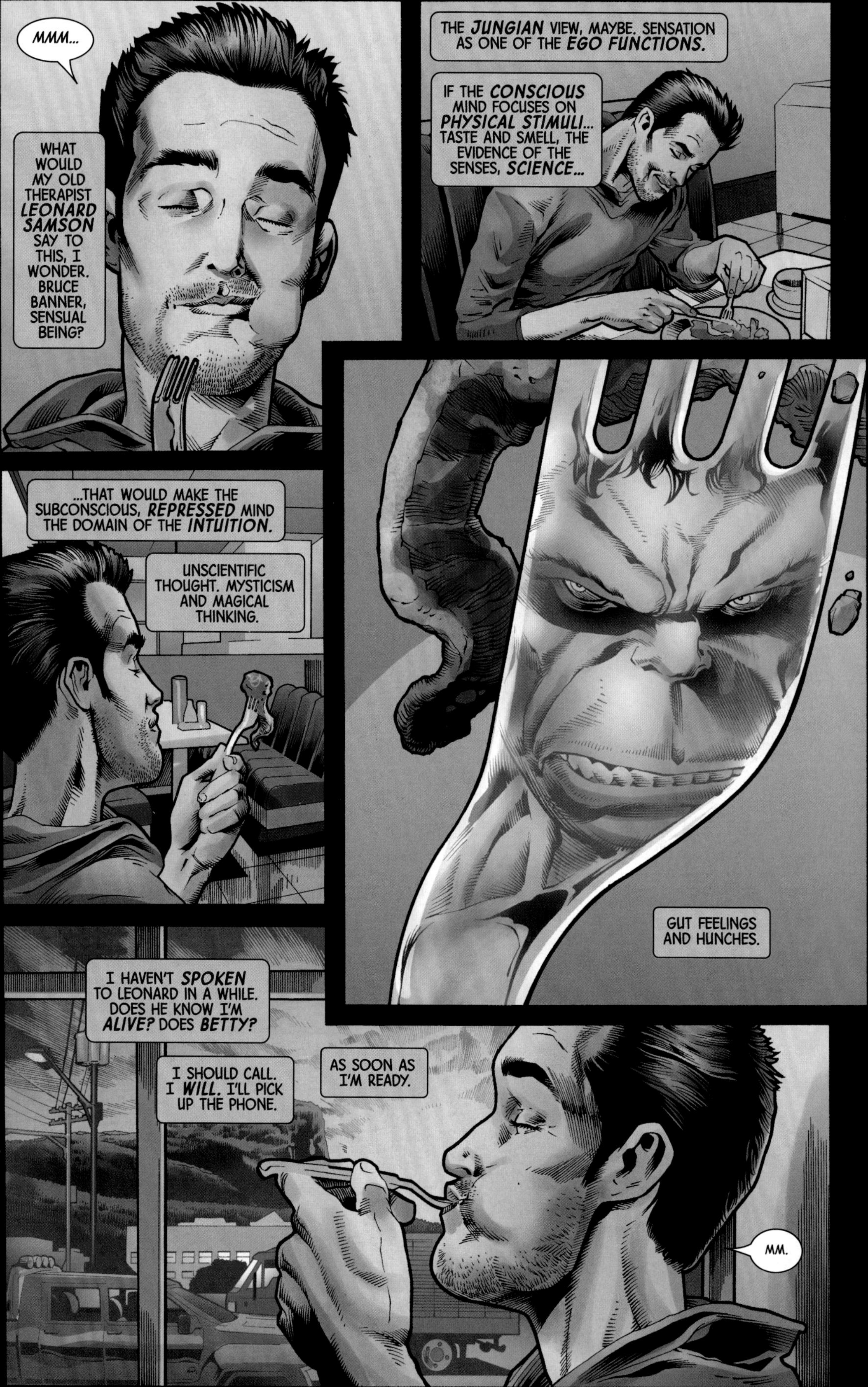
MMM...
WHAT WOULD MY OLD THERAPIST LEONARD SAMSON SAY TO THIS, I WONDER. BRUCE BANNER, SENSUAL BEING?
THE JUNGIAN VIEW, MAYBE. SENSATION AS ONE OF THE EGO FUNCTIONS.
IF THE CONSCIOUS MIND FOCUSES ON PHYSICAL STIMULI... TASTE AND SMELL, THE EVIDENCE OF THE SENSES, SCIENCE...
...THAT WOULD MAKE THE SUBCONSCIOUS, REPRESSED MIND THE DOMAIN OF THE INTUITION.
UNSCIENTIFIC THOUGHT. MYSTICISM AND MAGICAL THINKING.
GUT FEELINGS AND HUNCHES.
I HAVEN'T SPOKEN TO LEONARD IN A WHILE. DOES HE KNOW I'M ALIVE? DOES BETTY?
I SHOULD CALL. I WILL. I'LL PICK UP THE PHONE.
AS SOON AS I'M READY.
MM.

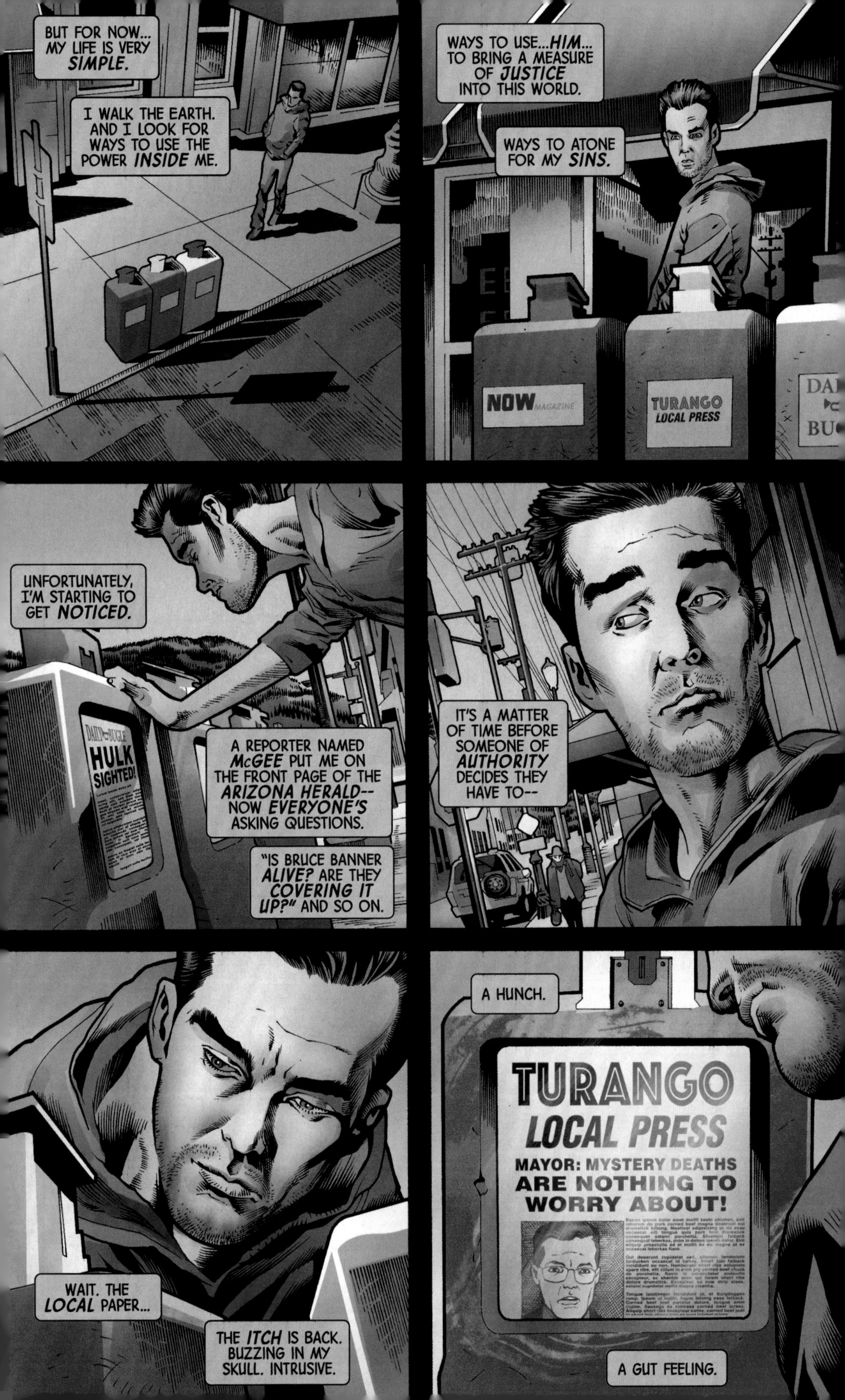
BUT FOR NOW... MY LIFE IS VERY SIMPLE.
I WALK THE EARTH. AND I LOOK FOR WAYS TO USE THE POWER INSIDE ME.
WAYS TO USE...HIM... TO BRING A MEASURE OF JUSTICE INTO THIS WORLD.
WAYS TO ATONE FOR MY SINS.
NOW MAGAZINE
TURANGO LOCAL PRESS
UNFORTUNATELY, I'M STARTING TO GET NOTICED.
DAILY BUGLE
HULK SIGHTED!
A REPORTER NAMED McGEE PUT ME ON THE FRONT PAGE OF THE ARIZONA HERALD-- NOW EVERYONE'S ASKING QUESTIONS.
"IS BRUCE BANNER ALIVE? ARE THEY COVERING IT UP?" AND SO ON.
IT'S A MATTER OF TIME BEFORE SOMEONE OF AUTHORITY DECIDES THEY HAVE TO--
WAIT. THE LOCAL PAPER...
THE ITCH IS BACK. BUZZING IN MY SKULL. INTRUSIVE.
A HUNCH.
TURANGO
LOCAL PRESS
MAYOR: MYSTERY DEATHS ARE NOTHING TO WORRY ABOUT!
A GUT FEELING.

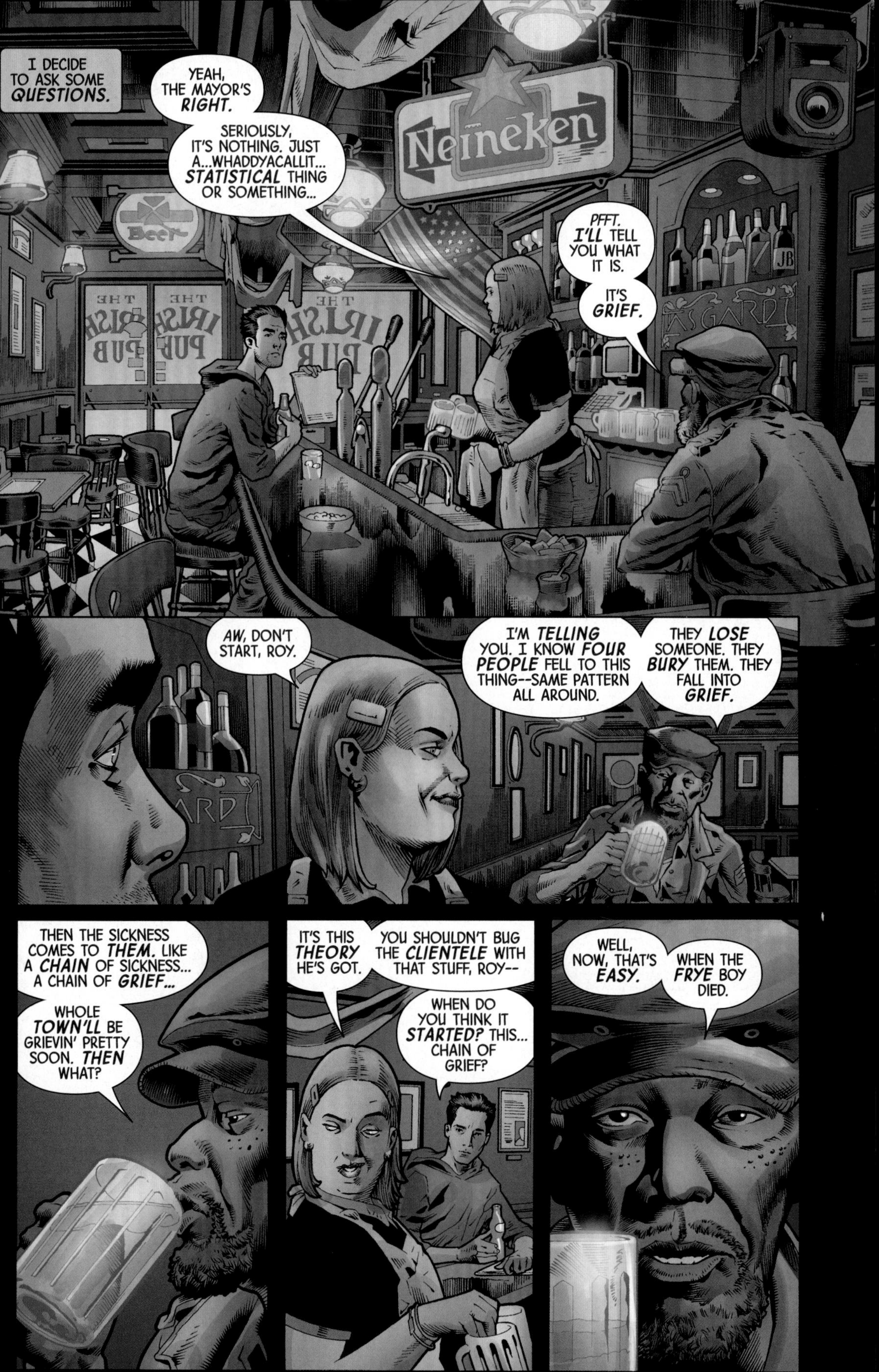

I DECIDE TO ASK SOME QUESTIONS.
YEAH, THE MAYOR'S RIGHT.
SERIOUSLY, IT'S NOTHING. JUST A...WHADDYACALLIT... STATISTICAL THING OR SOMETHING...
Heineken
Beer
THE IRISH PUB
THE IRISH PUB
THE IRISH PUB
PFFT. I'LL TELL YOU WHAT IT IS.
IT'S GRIEF.
JB
AW, DON'T START, ROY.
I'M TELLING YOU. I KNOW FOUR PEOPLE FELL TO THIS THING--SAME PATTERN ALL AROUND.
THEY LOSE SOMEONE. THEY BURY THEM. THEY FALL INTO GRIEF.
THEN THE SICKNESS COMES TO THEM. LIKE A CHAIN OF SICKNESS... A CHAIN OF GRIEF...
WHOLE TOWN'LL BE GRIEVIN' PRETTY SOON. THEN WHAT?
IT'S THIS THEORY HE'S GOT.
YOU SHOULDN'T BUG THE CLIENTELE WITH THAT STUFF, ROY--
WHEN DO YOU THINK IT STARTED? THIS... CHAIN OF GRIEF?
WELL, NOW, THAT'S EASY.
WHEN THE FRYE BOY DIED.

ROY...

WHEN THAT BOY DIED, SOMETHING *DARK* LANDED ON THIS TOWN.

I'M TELLING YOU.

THE FRYE BOY?

DEL FRYE. PROM KING, STAR *QUARTERBACK*...I MEAN, BASICALLY HE *WAS* THE COLLEGE TEAM...

HANG ON, I'VE GOT A *PHOTO* SOMEWHERE...

THAT'S HIM.

...

HOW DID HE *DIE?*

*EMBOLISM* OR SOMETHING. JUST KEELED OVER AND DIED.

NICE *KID.* I MEAN, HE HAD *LOOKS,* HE WAS EVERYBODY'S *HERO...* THE WHOLE TOWN *LOVED* HIM, BUT HE NEVER LET IT GO TO HIS HEAD.

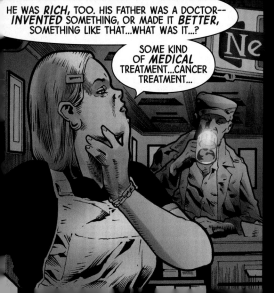

HE WAS *RICH,* TOO. HIS FATHER WAS A DOCTOR-- *INVENTED* SOMETHING, OR MADE IT *BETTER,* SOMETHING LIKE THAT...WHAT WAS IT...?

SOME KIND OF *MEDICAL* TREATMENT...CANCER TREATMENT...

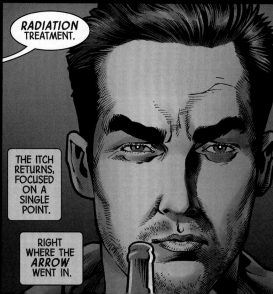

*RADIATION* TREATMENT.

THE ITCH RETURNS, FOCUSED ON A SINGLE POINT.

RIGHT WHERE THE *ARROW* WENT IN.

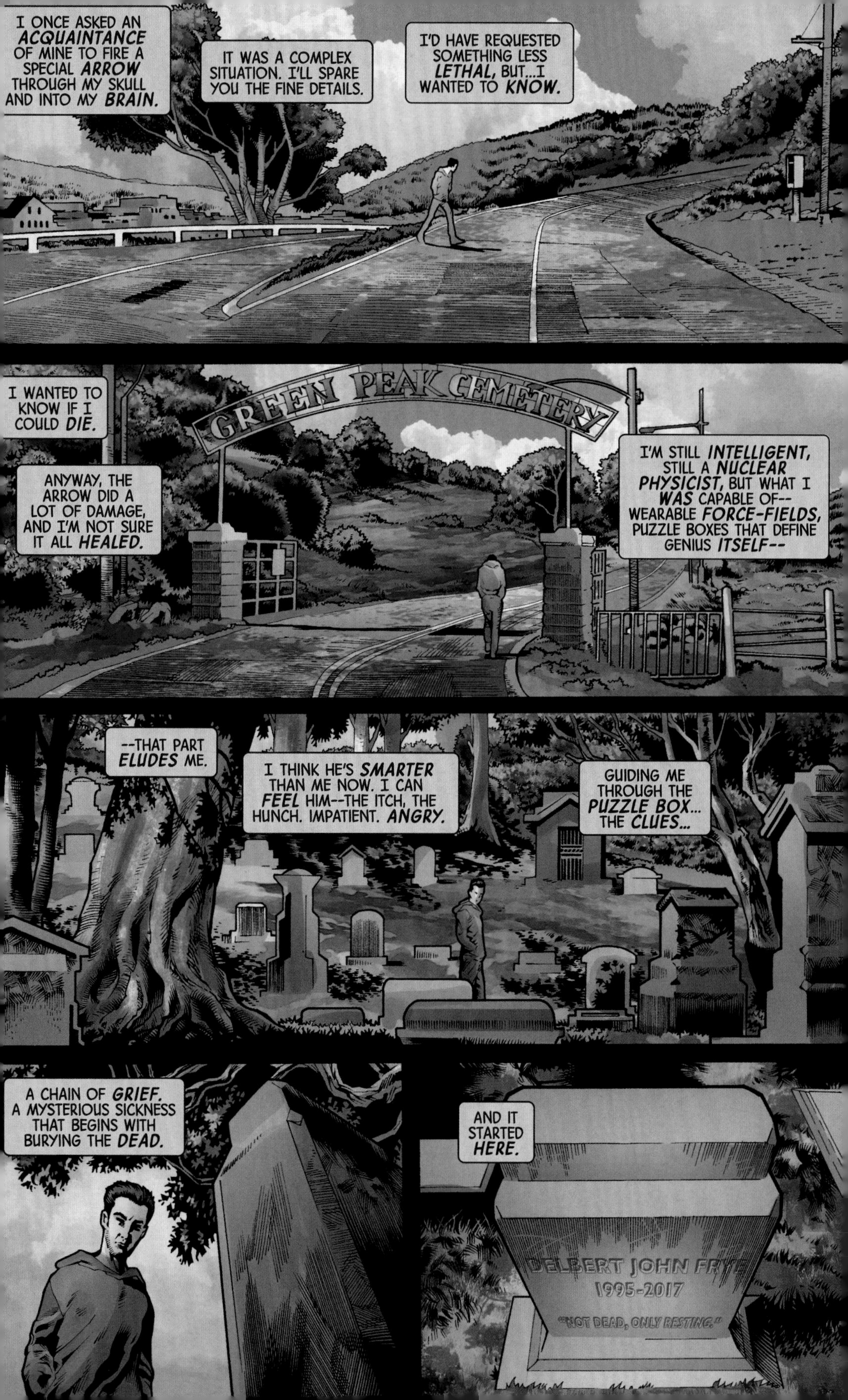
I ONCE ASKED AN ACQUAINTANCE OF MINE TO FIRE A SPECIAL ARROW THROUGH MY SKULL AND INTO MY BRAIN.
IT WAS A COMPLEX SITUATION. I'LL SPARE YOU THE FINE DETAILS.
I'D HAVE REQUESTED SOMETHING LESS LETHAL, BUT...I WANTED TO KNOW.
GREEN PEAK CEMETERY
I WANTED TO KNOW IF I COULD DIE.
ANYWAY, THE ARROW DID A LOT OF DAMAGE, AND I'M NOT SURE IT ALL HEALED.
I'M STILL INTELLIGENT, STILL A NUCLEAR PHYSICIST, BUT WHAT I WAS CAPABLE OF-- WEARABLE FORCE-FIELDS, PUZZLE BOXES THAT DEFINE GENIUS ITSELF--
--THAT PART ELUDES ME.
I THINK HE'S SMARTER THAN ME NOW. I CAN FEEL HIM--THE ITCH, THE HUNCH. IMPATIENT. ANGRY.
GUIDING ME THROUGH THE PUZZLE BOX... THE CLUES...
A CHAIN OF GRIEF. A MYSTERIOUS SICKNESS THAT BEGINS WITH BURYING THE DEAD.
AND IT STARTED HERE.
DELBERT JOHN FRYE
1995-2017
"NOT DEAD, ONLY RESTING."

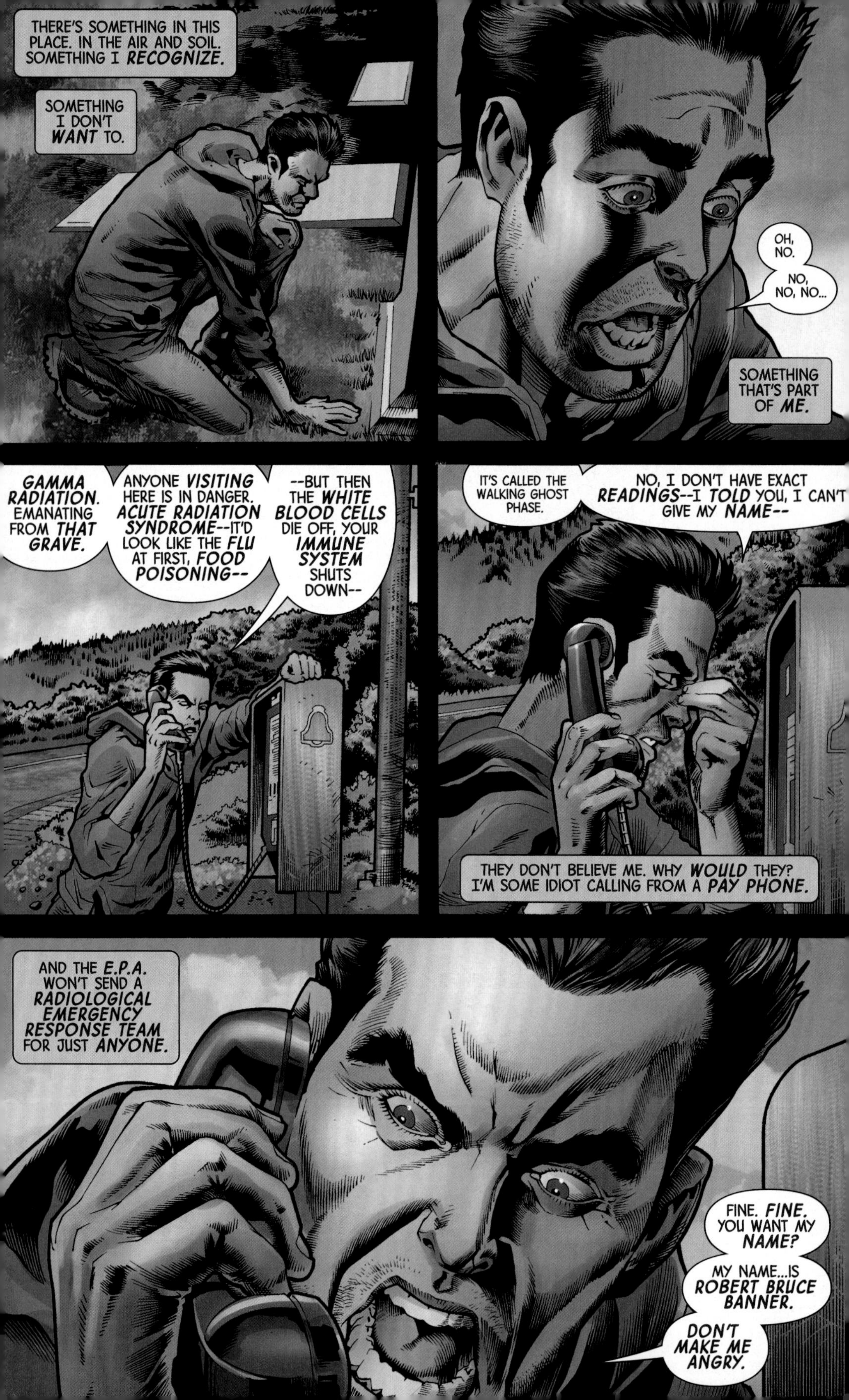

THERE'S SOMETHING IN THIS PLACE. IN THE AIR AND SOIL. SOMETHING I RECOGNIZE.
SOMETHING I DON'T WANT TO.
OH, NO.
NO, NO, NO...
SOMETHING THAT'S PART OF ME.
GAMMA RADIATION. EMANATING FROM THAT GRAVE.
ANYONE VISITING HERE IS IN DANGER. ACUTE RADIATION SYNDROME--IT'D LOOK LIKE THE FLU AT FIRST, FOOD POISONING--
--BUT THEN THE WHITE BLOOD CELLS DIE OFF, YOUR IMMUNE SYSTEM SHUTS DOWN--
IT'S CALLED THE WALKING GHOST PHASE.
NO, I DON'T HAVE EXACT READINGS--I TOLD YOU, I CAN'T GIVE MY NAME--
THEY DON'T BELIEVE ME. WHY WOULD THEY? I'M SOME IDIOT CALLING FROM A PAY PHONE.
AND THE E.P.A. WON'T SEND A RADIOLOGICAL EMERGENCY RESPONSE TEAM FOR JUST ANYONE.
FINE. FINE. YOU WANT MY NAME?
MY NAME...IS ROBERT BRUCE BANNER.
DON'T MAKE ME ANGRY.

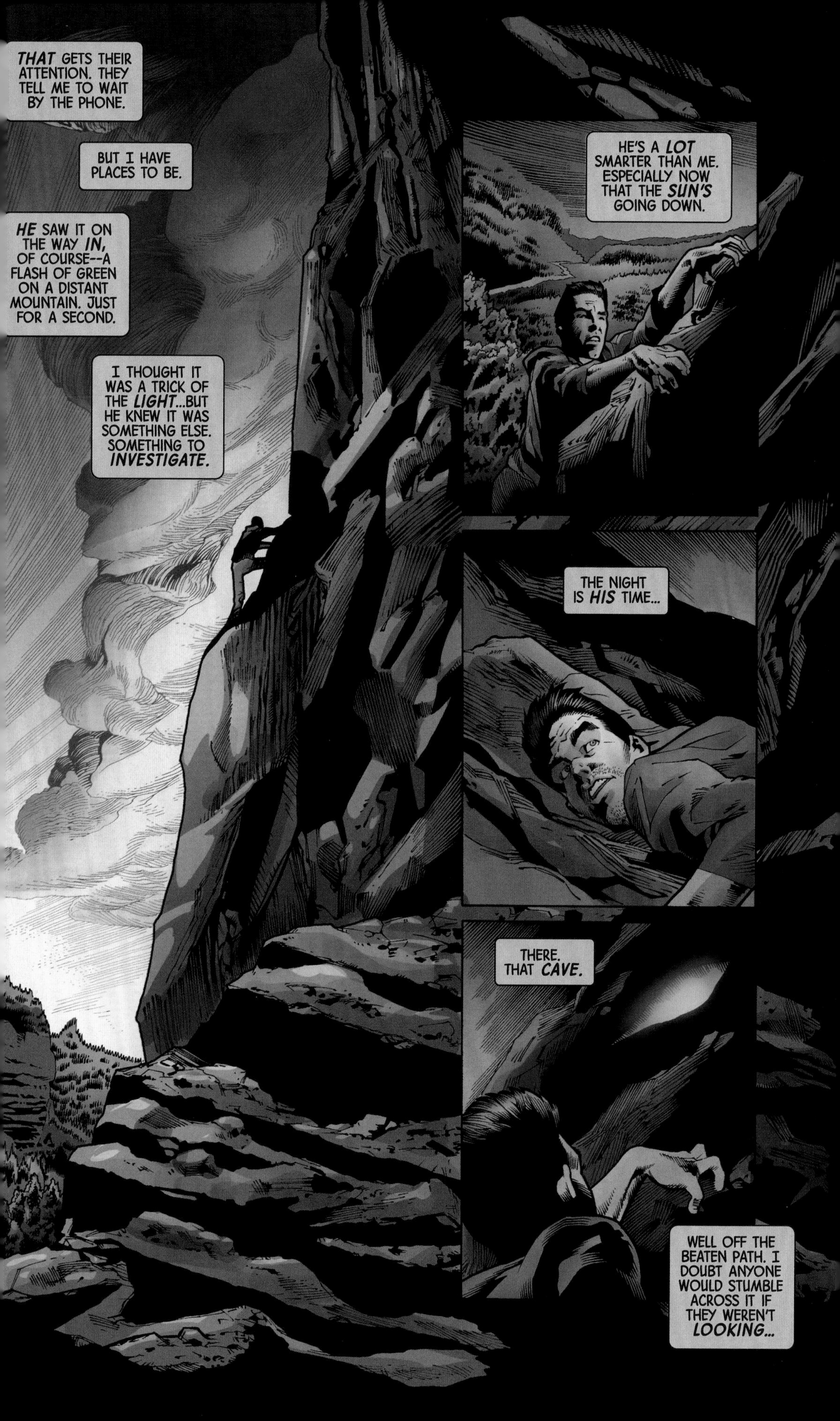
THAT GETS THEIR ATTENTION. THEY TELL ME TO WAIT BY THE PHONE.
BUT I HAVE PLACES TO BE.
HE SAW IT ON THE WAY IN, OF COURSE--A FLASH OF GREEN ON A DISTANT MOUNTAIN. JUST FOR A SECOND.
I THOUGHT IT WAS A TRICK OF THE LIGHT...BUT HE KNEW IT WAS SOMETHING ELSE. SOMETHING TO INVESTIGATE.
HE'S A LOT SMARTER THAN ME. ESPECIALLY NOW THAT THE SUN'S GOING DOWN.
THE NIGHT IS HIS TIME...
THERE. THAT CAVE.
WELL OFF THE BEATEN PATH. I DOUBT ANYONE WOULD STUMBLE ACROSS IT IF THEY WEREN'T LOOKING...

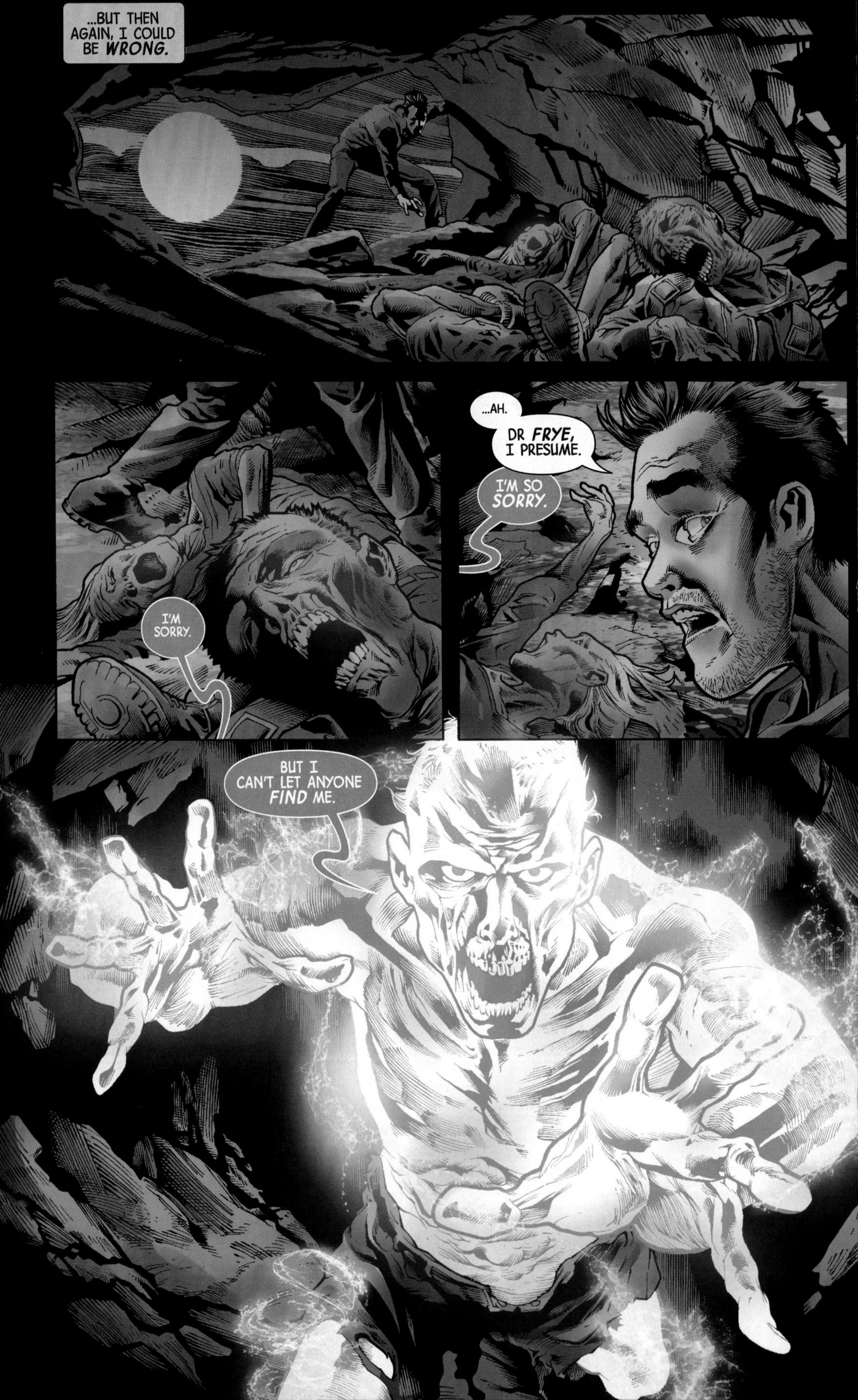
...BUT THEN AGAIN, I COULD BE WRONG.
I'M SORRY.
...AH.
DR FRYE, I PRESUME.
I'M SO SORRY.
BUT I CAN'T LET ANYONE FIND ME.

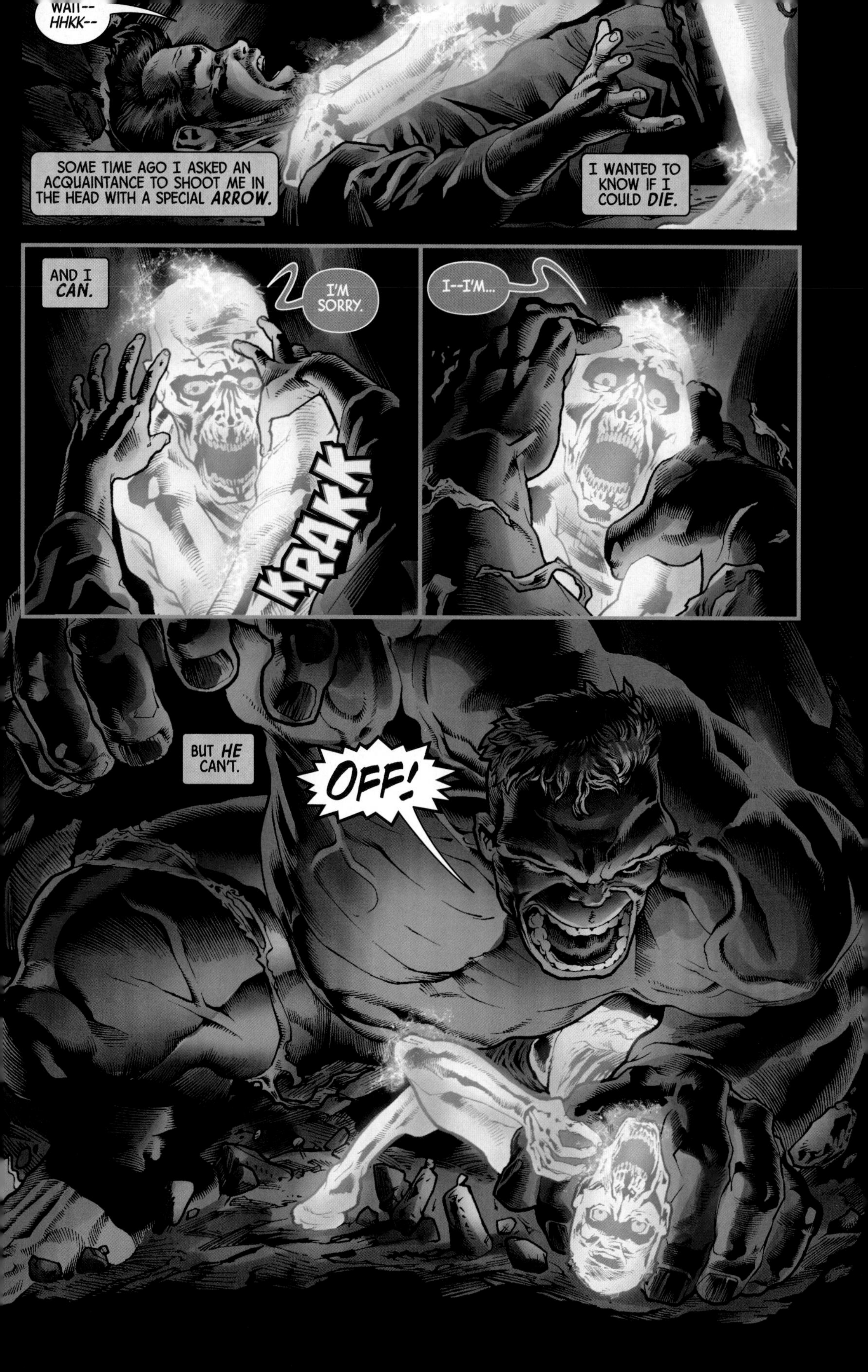

WAIT--
HHKK--
SOME TIME AGO I ASKED AN ACQUAINTANCE TO SHOOT ME IN THE HEAD WITH A SPECIAL ARROW.
I WANTED TO KNOW IF I COULD DIE.
AND I CAN.
I'M SORRY.
KRAKK
I--I'M...
BUT HE CAN'T.
OFF!

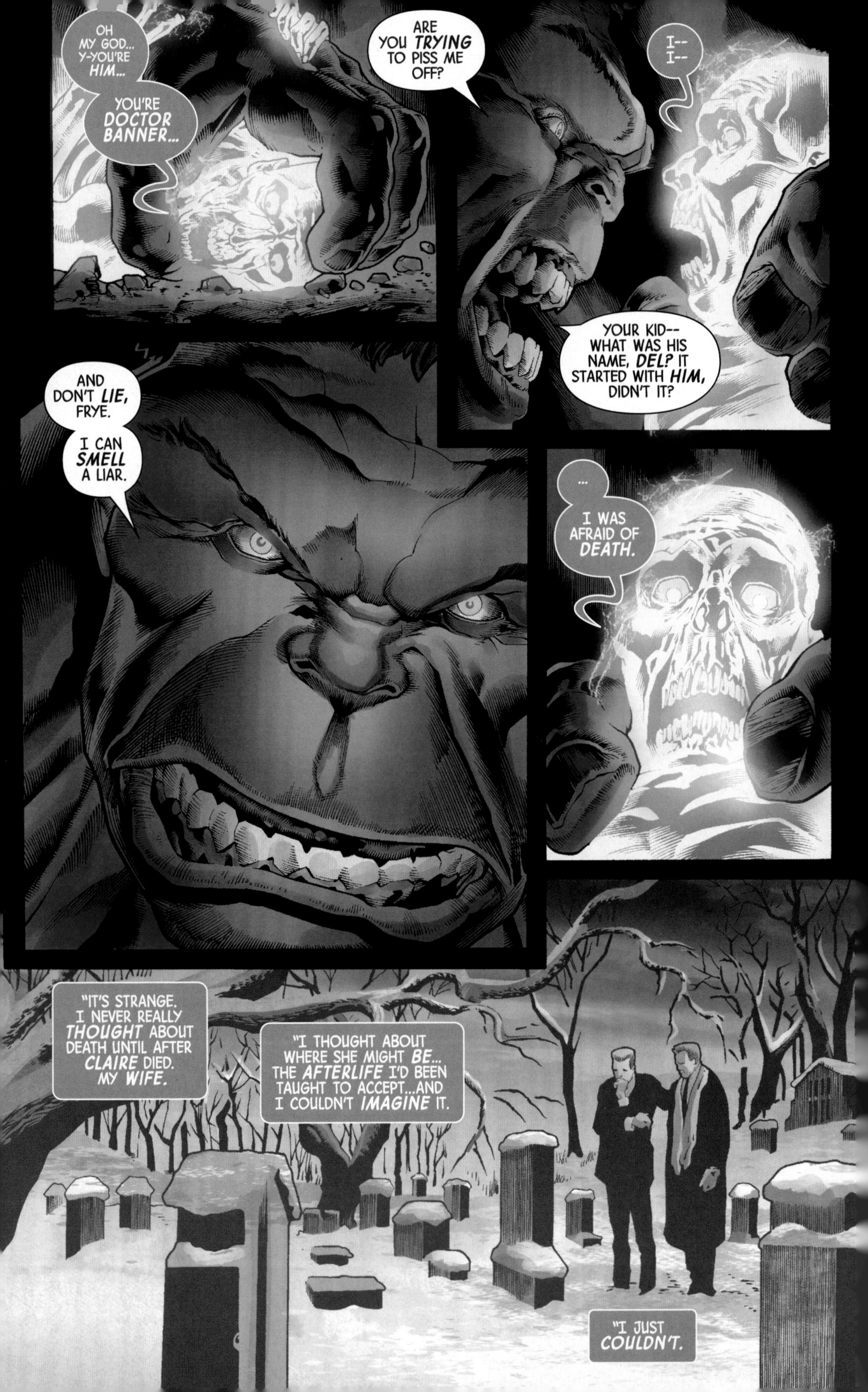

OH MY GOD... Y-YOU'RE HIM...
YOU'RE DOCTOR BANNER...
ARE YOU TRYING TO PISS ME OFF?
I-- I--
YOUR KID-- WHAT WAS HIS NAME, DEL? IT STARTED WITH HIM, DIDN'T IT?
AND DON'T LIE, FRYE.
I CAN SMELL A LIAR.
...
I WAS AFRAID OF DEATH.
"IT'S STRANGE. I NEVER REALLY THOUGHT ABOUT DEATH UNTIL AFTER CLAIRE DIED. MY WIFE.
"I THOUGHT ABOUT WHERE SHE MIGHT BE... THE AFTERLIFE I'D BEEN TAUGHT TO ACCEPT...AND I COULDN'T IMAGINE IT.
"I JUST COULDN'T.

"AND I BEGAN TO THINK ABOUT WHAT DEATH REALLY *WAS.*

"AN UNIMAGINABLE *ABSENCE.* A TOTAL CESSATION OF BEING.

"ALL THE JOYS OF *TOUCH* AND *TASTE* AND *SMELL,* OF *THOUGHT,* EVEN THE *MEMORY* OF THOUGHT--*GONE.*

"UTTERLY.

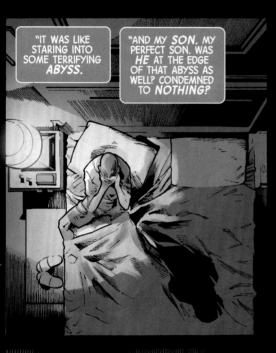

"IT WAS LIKE STARING INTO SOME TERRIFYING *ABYSS.*

"AND MY *SON.* MY *PERFECT SON.* WAS *HE* AT THE EDGE OF THAT ABYSS AS WELL? CONDEMNED TO *NOTHING?*

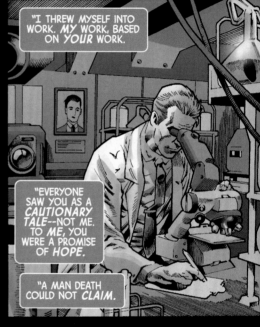

"I THREW MYSELF INTO WORK. *MY* WORK, BASED ON *YOUR* WORK.

"EVERYONE SAW YOU AS A *CAUTIONARY TALE*--NOT ME. TO *ME,* YOU WERE A PROMISE OF *HOPE.*

"A MAN DEATH COULD NOT *CLAIM.*

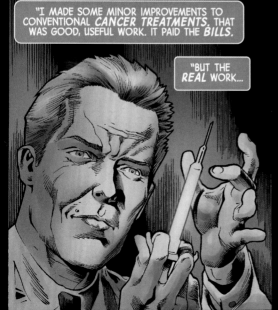

"I MADE SOME MINOR IMPROVEMENTS TO CONVENTIONAL *CANCER TREATMENTS.* THAT WAS GOOD, USEFUL WORK. IT PAID THE *BILLS.*

"BUT THE *REAL* WORK...

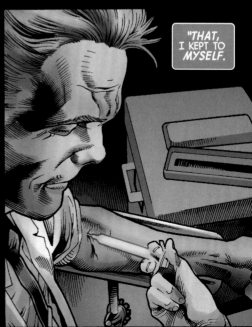

"*THAT,* I KEPT TO *MYSELF.*

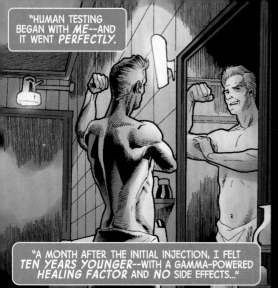

"HUMAN TESTING BEGAN WITH *ME*--AND IT WENT *PERFECTLY.*

"A MONTH AFTER THE INITIAL INJECTION, I FELT *TEN YEARS YOUNGER*--WITH A GAMMA-POWERED *HEALING FACTOR* AND *NO* SIDE EFFECTS..."

SO THEN YOU GAVE SOME TO YOUR *SON.*

"I *HAD* TO. HE WAS GOING *PRO* AND-- THE *INJURIES* YOU GET PLAYING FOOTBALL... *CONCUSSIONS, BRAIN DAMAGE...*

"I COULDN'T *WAIT.*

DAD...?

YOU'LL FEEL *DIZZY* FOR A MOMENT. BUT IT PASSES.

YOU'LL--

DAD... I...I CAN *SEE...*

DEL?

I CAN SEE A *DOOR.*

A...A *GREEN* DOOR... AND...

AND THERE'S SOMEONE LOOKING THROUGH IT.

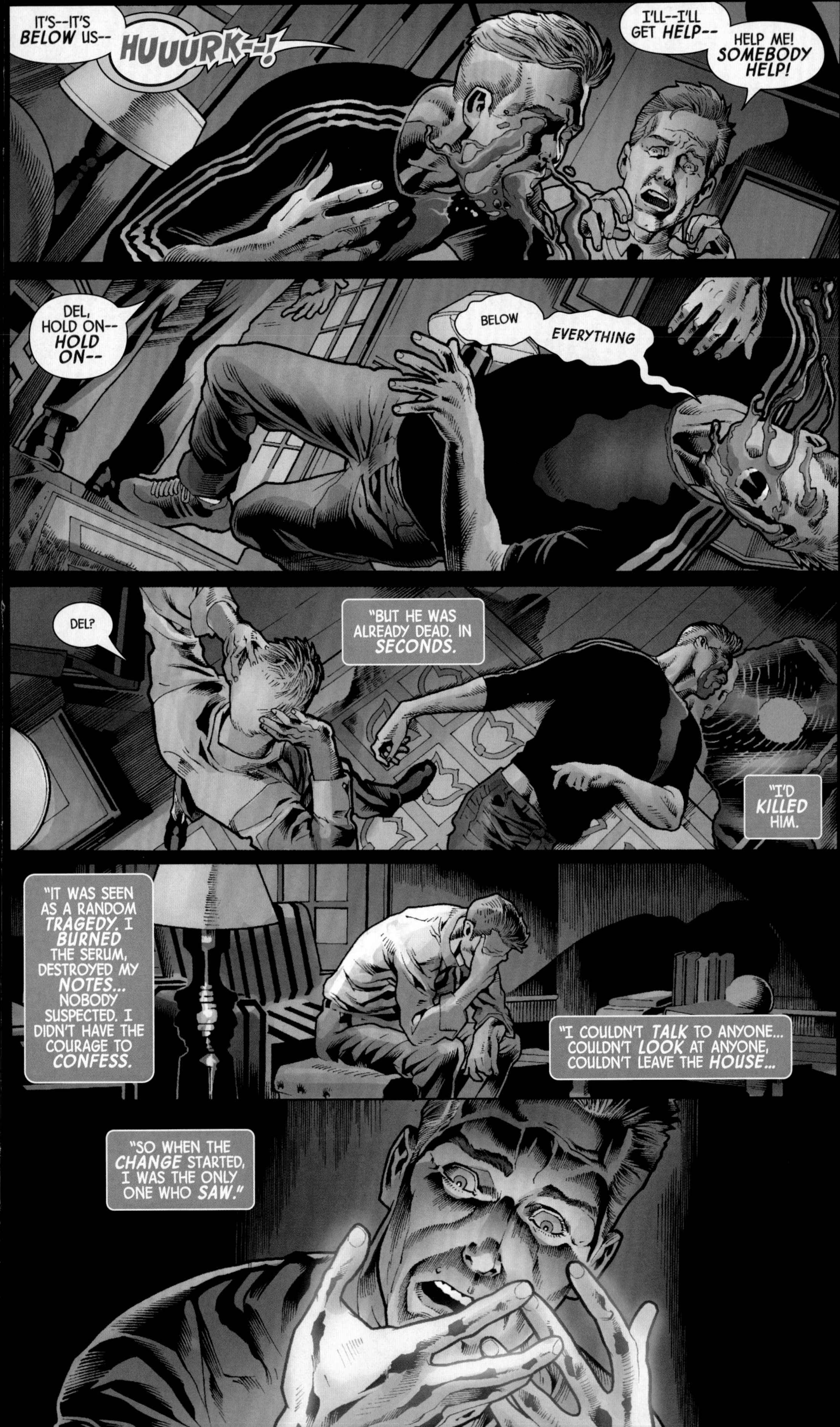

IT'S--IT'S BELOW US--
HUUURK--!
I'LL--I'LL GET HELP--
HELP ME! SOMEBODY HELP!
DEL, HOLD ON--HOLD ON--
BELOW
EVERYTHING
DEL?
"BUT HE WAS ALREADY DEAD. IN SECONDS.
"I'D KILLED HIM.
"IT WAS SEEN AS A RANDOM TRAGEDY. I BURNED THE SERUM, DESTROYED MY NOTES... NOBODY SUSPECTED. I DIDN'T HAVE THE COURAGE TO CONFESS.
"I COULDN'T TALK TO ANYONE... COULDN'T LOOK AT ANYONE, COULDN'T LEAVE THE HOUSE...
"SO WHEN THE CHANGE STARTED, I WAS THE ONLY ONE WHO SAW."

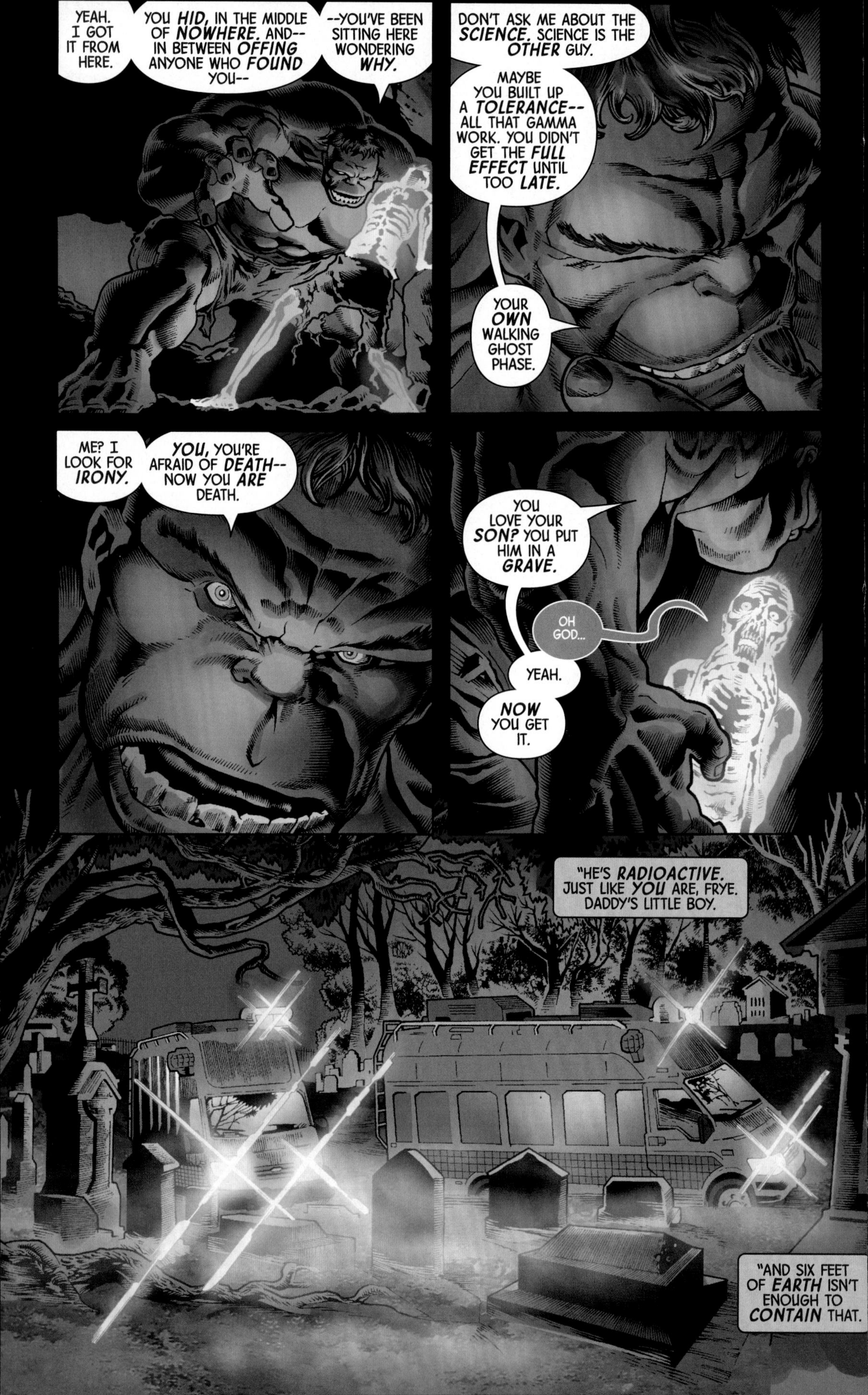
YEAH. I GOT IT FROM HERE.
YOU HID, IN THE MIDDLE OF NOWHERE. AND-- IN BETWEEN OFFING ANYONE WHO FOUND YOU--
--YOU'VE BEEN SITTING HERE WONDERING WHY.
DON'T ASK ME ABOUT THE SCIENCE. SCIENCE IS THE OTHER GUY.
MAYBE YOU BUILT UP A TOLERANCE-- ALL THAT GAMMA WORK. YOU DIDN'T GET THE FULL EFFECT UNTIL TOO LATE.
YOUR OWN WALKING GHOST PHASE.
ME? I LOOK FOR IRONY.
YOU, YOU'RE AFRAID OF DEATH-- NOW YOU ARE DEATH.
YOU LOVE YOUR SON? YOU PUT HIM IN A GRAVE.
OH GOD...
YEAH.
NOW YOU GET IT.
"HE'S RADIOACTIVE. JUST LIKE YOU ARE, FRYE. DADDY'S LITTLE BOY.
"AND SIX FEET OF EARTH ISN'T ENOUGH TO CONTAIN THAT.

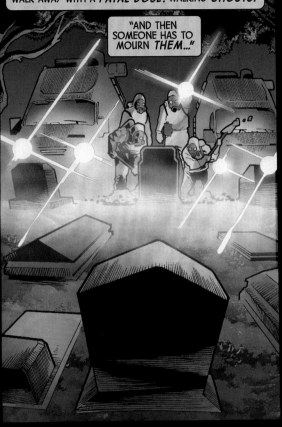

"EVERYONE WHO GETS IN RANGE--TO MOURN--COULD WALK AWAY WITH A FATAL DOSE. WALKING GHOSTS.

"AND THEN SOMEONE HAS TO MOURN THEM..."

A CHAIN OF GRIEF.

HOW MANY, DR. FRYE?

HOW MANY BECAUSE YOU WERE SCARED?

PLEASE-- I--I MADE MISTAKES-- BUT--

--BUT I DON'T WANT TO DIE--

IS THAT SO?

WELL, YOU MADE YOUR BED, FRYE.

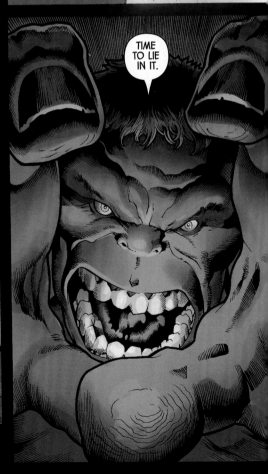

TIME TO LIE IN IT.

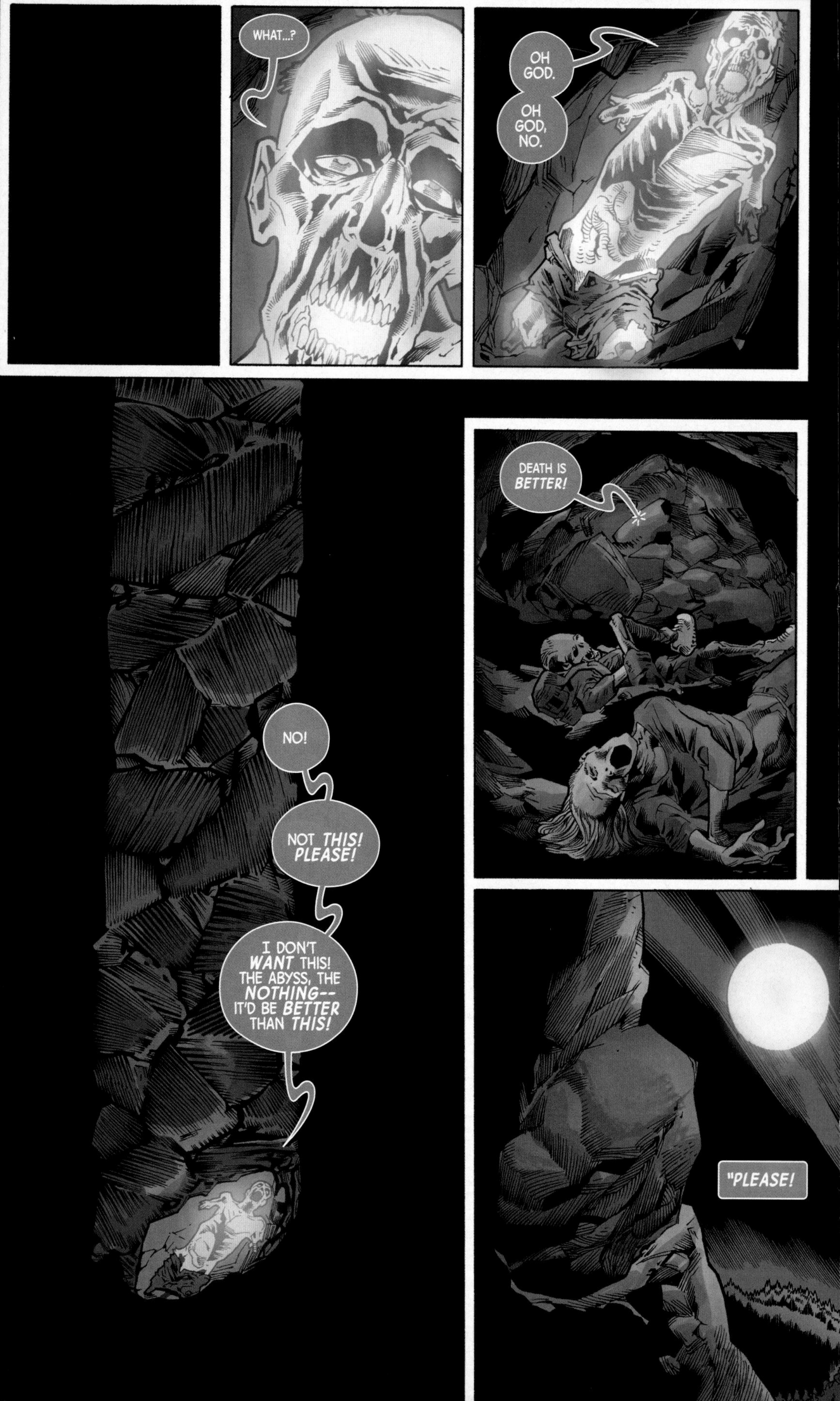

WHAT...?
OH GOD.
OH GOD, NO.
NO!
NOT THIS! PLEASE!
I DON'T WANT THIS! THE ABYSS, THE NOTHING-- IT'D BE BETTER THAN THIS!
DEATH IS BETTER!
"PLEASE!

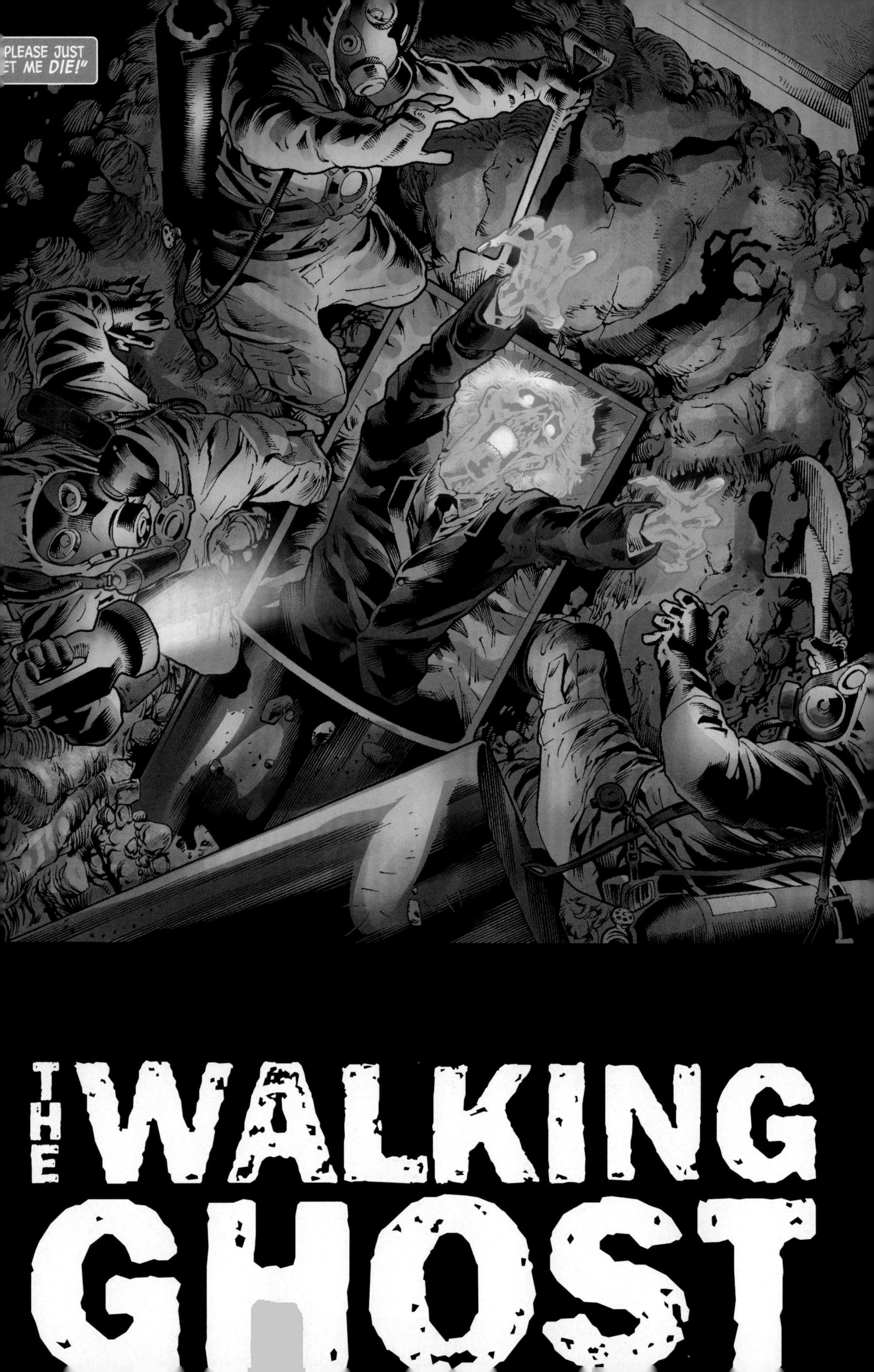

PLEASE JUST
ET ME DIE!"


# THE WALKING GHOST

# 3

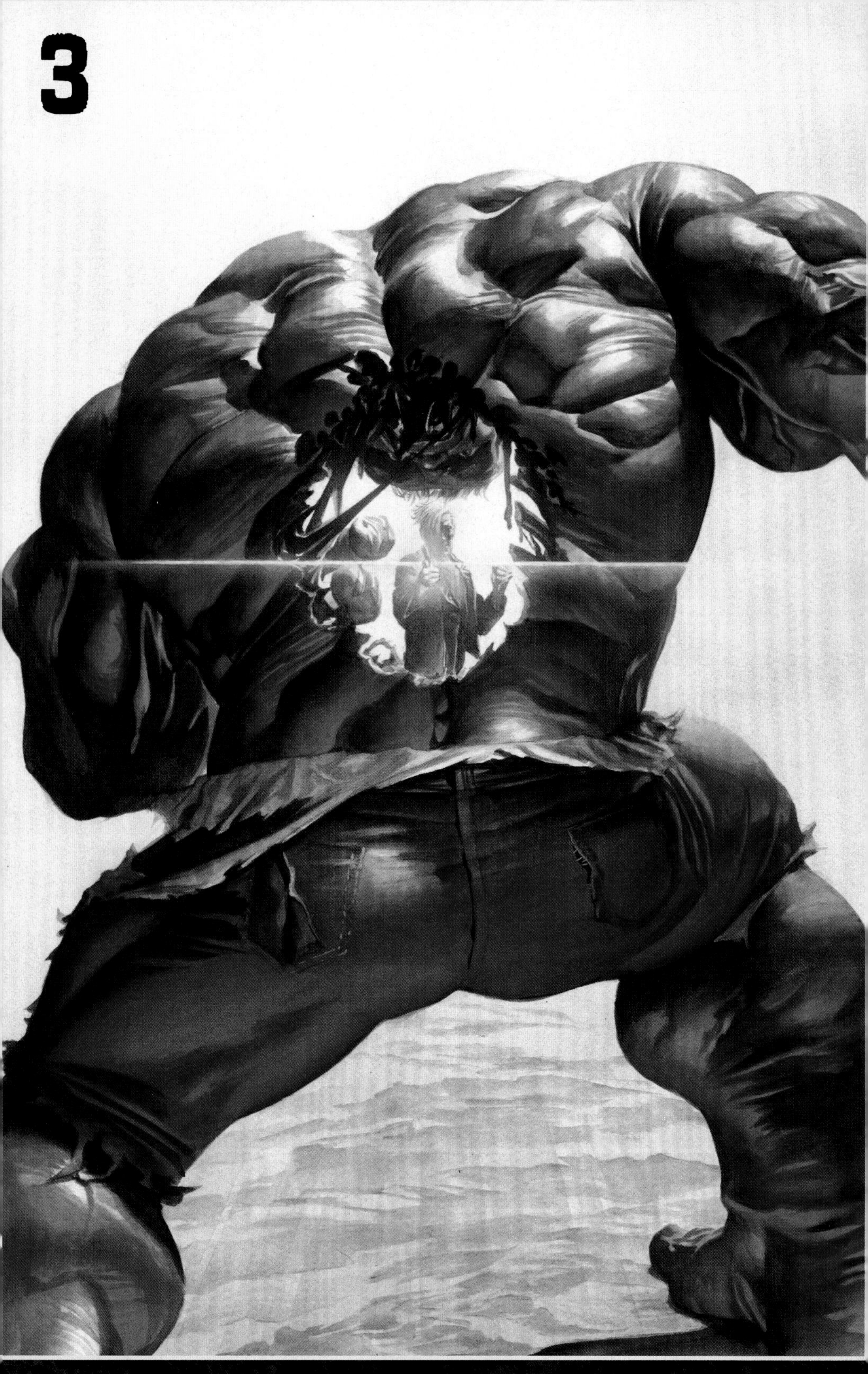

"AND IN THE LOWEST DEEP A LOWER DEEP

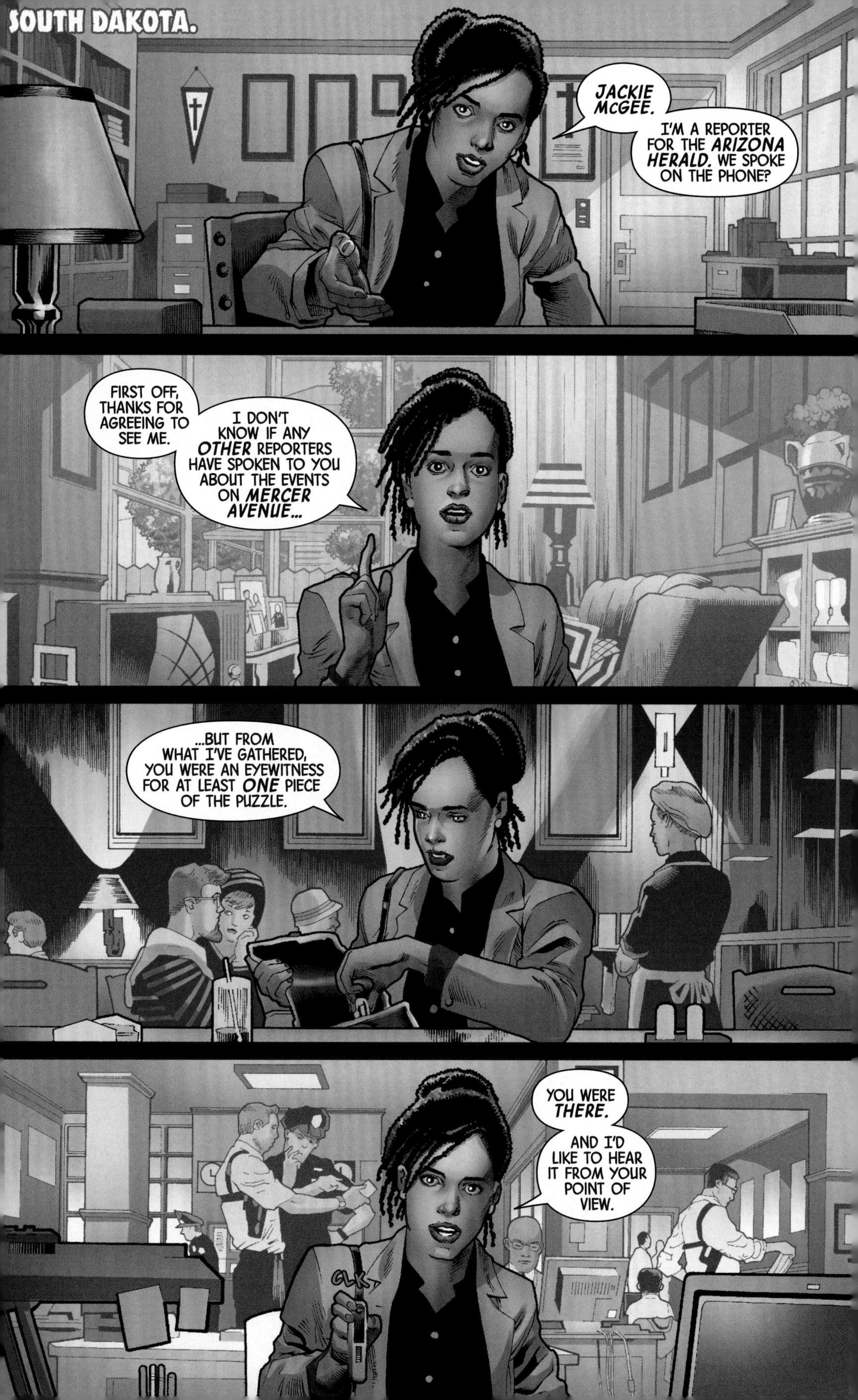
SOUTH DAKOTA.
JACKIE McGEE.
I'M A REPORTER FOR THE ARIZONA HERALD. WE SPOKE ON THE PHONE?
FIRST OFF, THANKS FOR AGREEING TO SEE ME.
I DON'T KNOW IF ANY OTHER REPORTERS HAVE SPOKEN TO YOU ABOUT THE EVENTS ON MERCER AVENUE...
...BUT FROM WHAT I'VE GATHERED, YOU WERE AN EYEWITNESS FOR AT LEAST ONE PIECE OF THE PUZZLE.
YOU WERE THERE.
AND I'D LIKE TO HEAR IT FROM YOUR POINT OF VIEW.
CLK

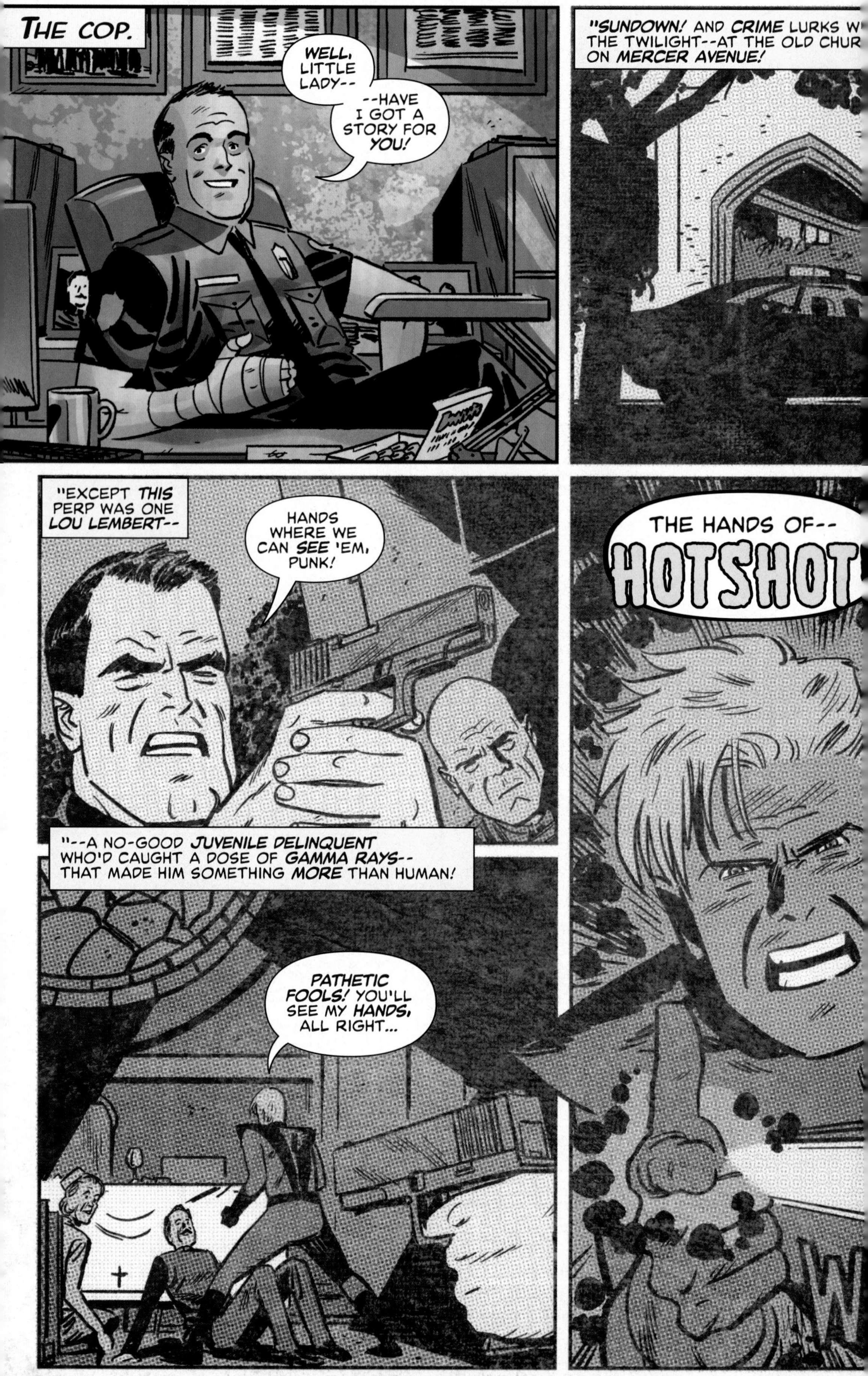
THE COP.
WELL, LITTLE LADY--
--HAVE I GOT A STORY FOR YOU!
"SUNDOWN! AND CRIME LURKS W THE TWILIGHT--AT THE OLD CHUR ON MERCER AVENUE!
"EXCEPT THIS PERP WAS ONE LOU LEMBERT--
HANDS WHERE WE CAN SEE 'EM, PUNK!
"--A NO-GOOD JUVENILE DELINQUENT WHO'D CAUGHT A DOSE OF GAMMA RAYS--THAT MADE HIM SOMETHING MORE THAN HUMAN!
PATHETIC FOOLS! YOU'LL SEE MY HANDS, ALL RIGHT...
THE HANDS OF--
HOTSHOT

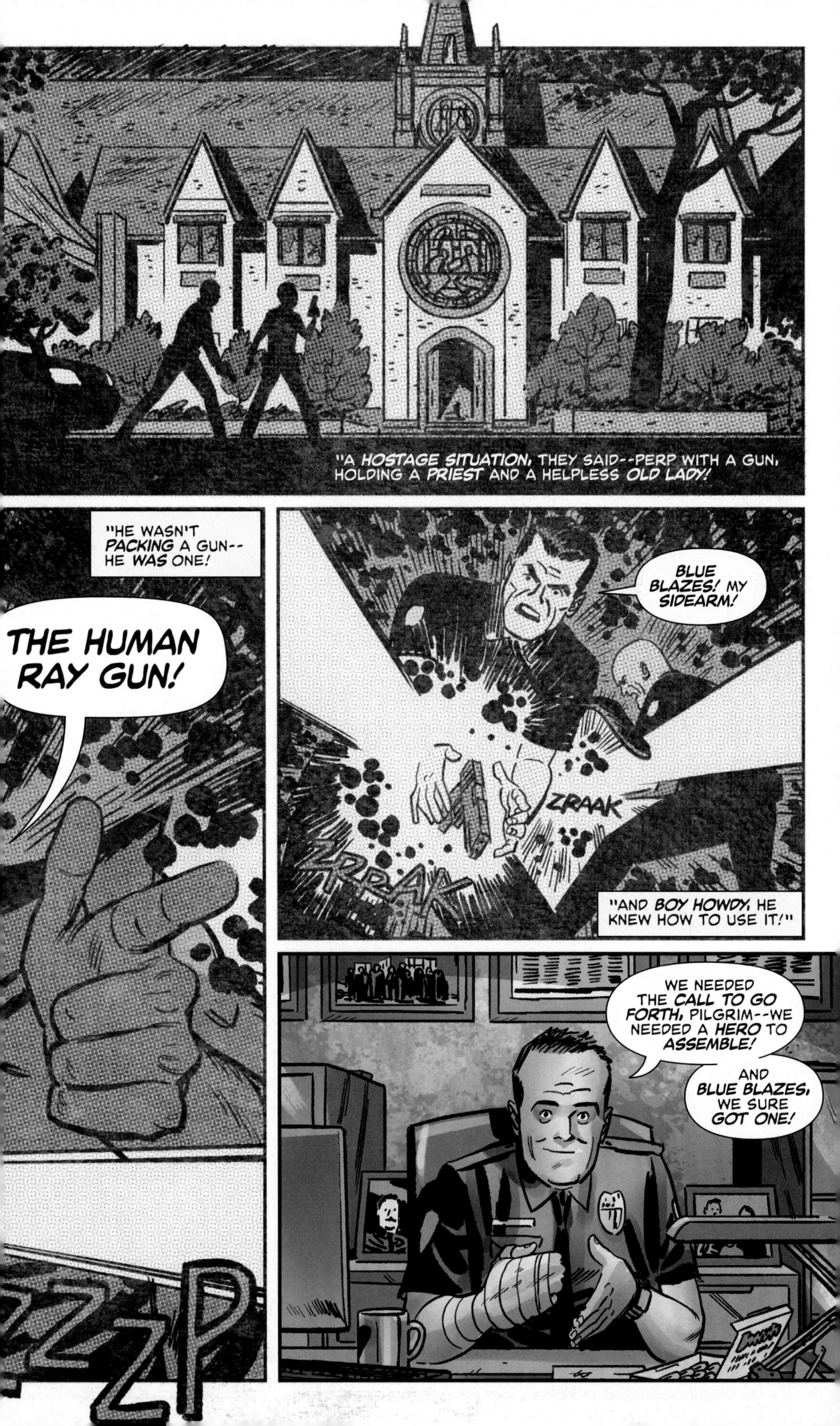
"A HOSTAGE SITUATION, THEY SAID--PERP WITH A GUN, HOLDING A PRIEST AND A HELPLESS OLD LADY!
"HE WASN'T PACKING A GUN-- HE WAS ONE!
THE HUMAN RAY GUN!
ZZZP
BLUE BLAZES! MY SIDEARM!
ZRAAK
ZRRAAK
"AND BOY HOWDY, HE KNEW HOW TO USE IT!"
WE NEEDED THE CALL TO GO FORTH, PILGRIM--WE NEEDED A HERO TO ASSEMBLE!
AND BLUE BLAZES, WE SURE GOT ONE!

THE BARTENDER.

I MEAN, I'M NOT A BAD PERSON OR ANYTHING.

CAN I USE THE RESTROOM, PLEASE?

"BUT WHAT WAS I GONNA DO?

"HIS CLOTHES DIDN'T EVEN FIT HIM.

"THEY LOOKED LIKE SOMEONE DIED IN THEM.

IT'D JUS FO MO YOUR WAY.

"AND HE LOOKED LIKE A SERIAL KILLER."

I MEAN, HE WAS AT LEAST GOING TO SHOOT UP IN THERE.

RIGHT?

THIS IS HOW

"ANYWAY, THINGS GOT PRETTY HEATED.

GO?

I KNOW MY

"I GUESS, LOOKING BACK, I DODGED A BULLET.

"ANYWAY.

EH?

"THAT WAS WHEN HE SAW THE TV.

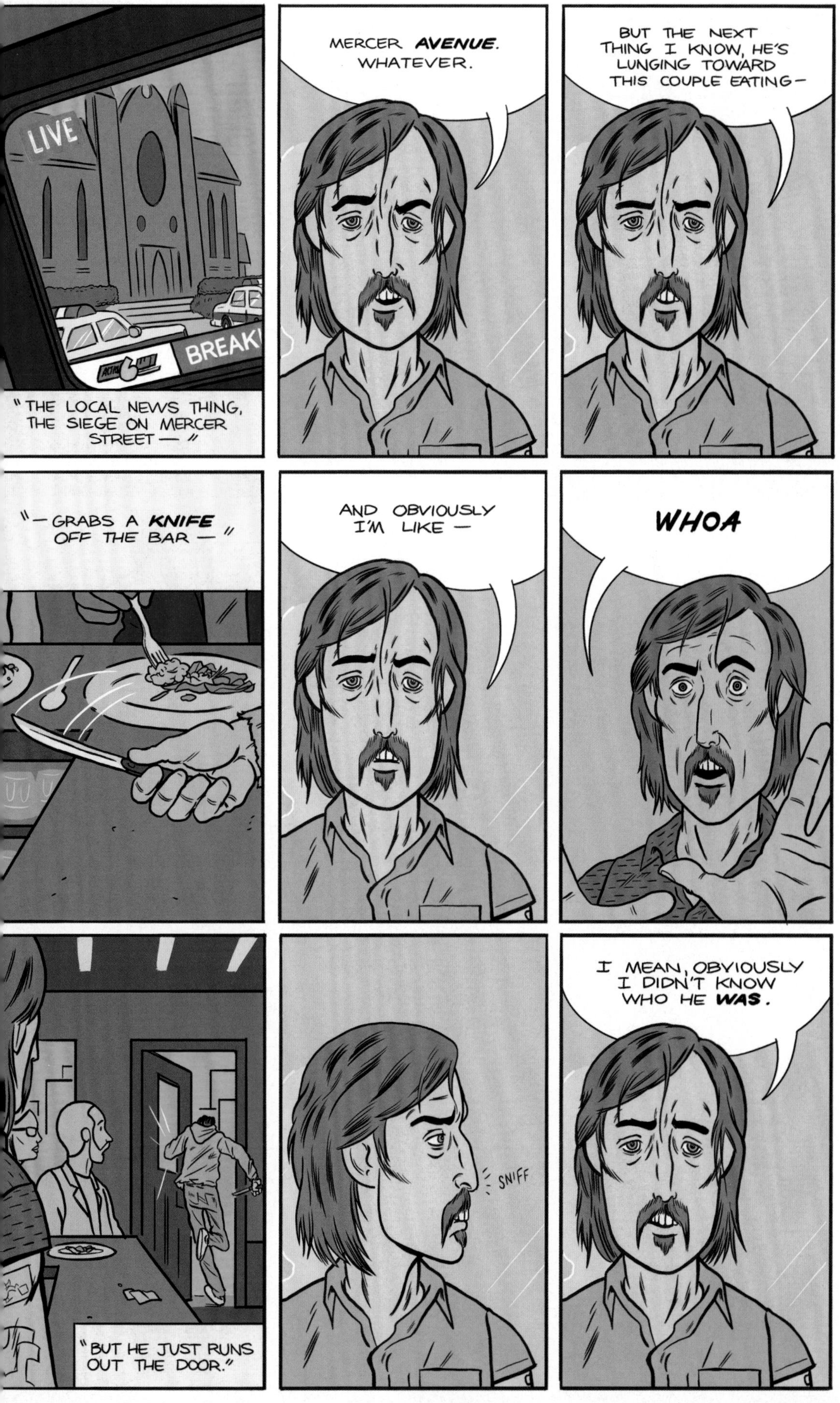
LIVE
BREAK
"THE LOCAL NEWS THING, THE SIEGE ON MERCER STREET—"
MERCER AVENUE. WHATEVER.
BUT THE NEXT THING I KNOW, HE'S LUNGING TOWARD THIS COUPLE EATING—
"—GRABS A KNIFE OFF THE BAR—"
AND OBVIOUSLY I'M LIKE—
WHOA
"BUT HE JUST RUNS OUT THE DOOR."
SNIFF
I MEAN, OBVIOUSLY I DIDN'T KNOW WHO HE WAS.

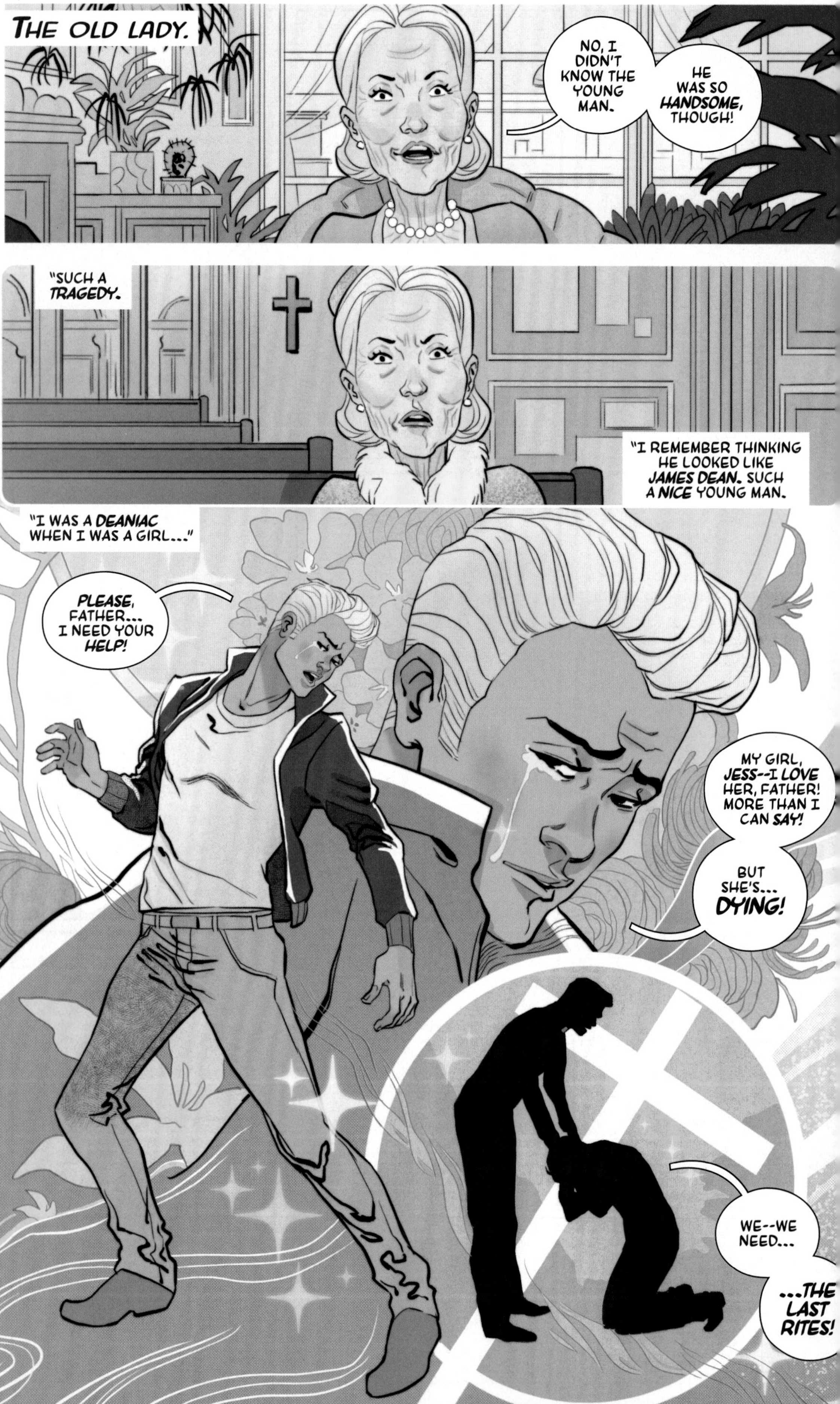
THE OLD LADY.
NO, I DIDN'T KNOW THE YOUNG MAN.
HE WAS SO HANDSOME, THOUGH!
"SUCH A TRAGEDY.
"I REMEMBER THINKING HE LOOKED LIKE JAMES DEAN. SUCH A NICE YOUNG MAN.
"I WAS A DEANIAC WHEN I WAS A GIRL..."
PLEASE, FATHER... I NEED YOUR HELP!
MY GIRL, JESS--I LOVE HER, FATHER! MORE THAN I CAN SAY!
BUT SHE'S... DYING!
WE--WE NEED...
...THE LAST RITES!

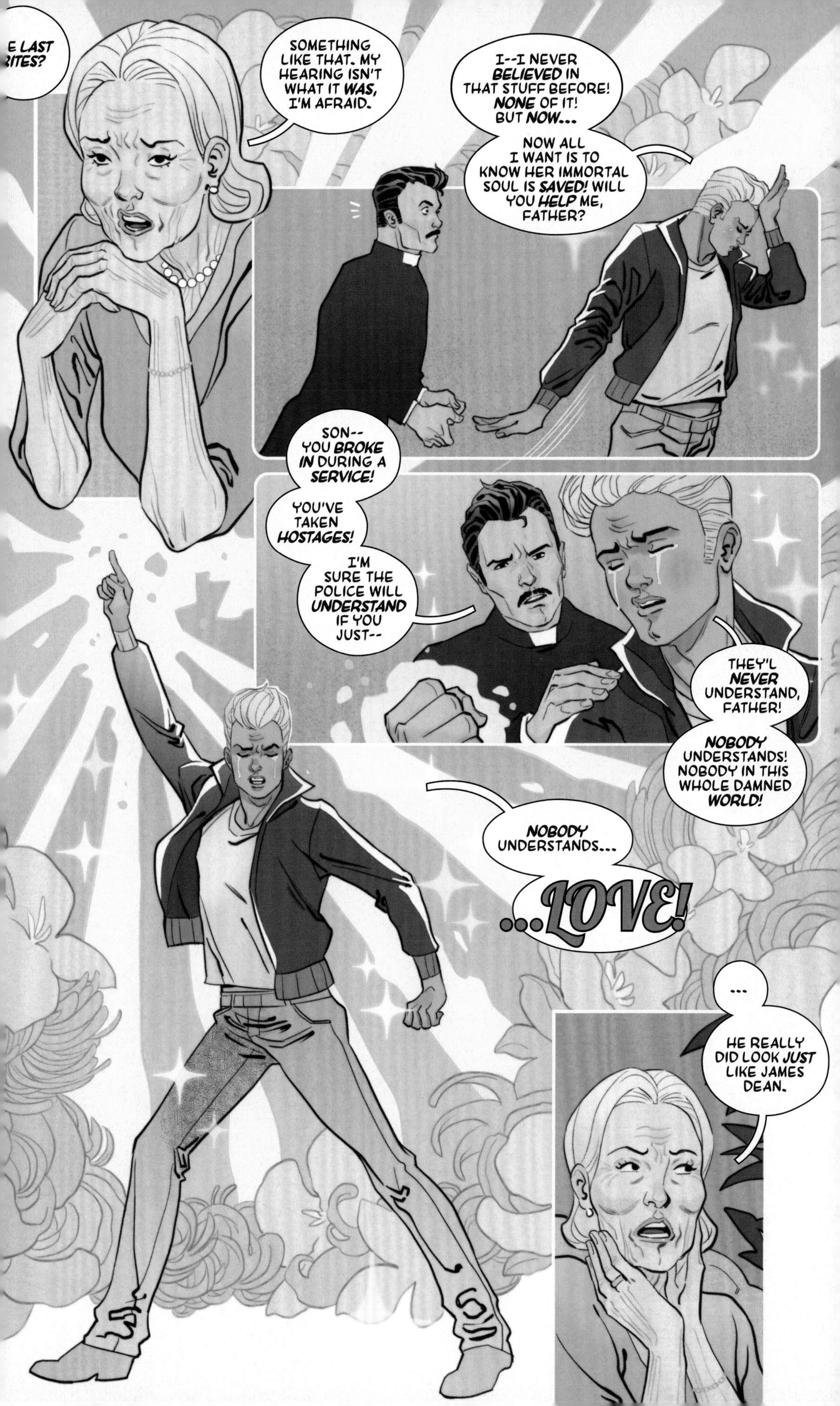

E LAST RITES?
SOMETHING LIKE THAT. MY HEARING ISN'T WHAT IT WAS, I'M AFRAID.
I--I NEVER BELIEVED IN THAT STUFF BEFORE! NONE OF IT! BUT NOW...
NOW ALL I WANT IS TO KNOW HER IMMORTAL SOUL IS SAVED! WILL YOU HELP ME, FATHER?
SON-- YOU BROKE IN DURING A SERVICE!
YOU'VE TAKEN HOSTAGES!
I'M SURE THE POLICE WILL UNDERSTAND IF YOU JUST--
THEY'L NEVER UNDERSTAND, FATHER!
NOBODY UNDERSTANDS! NOBODY IN THIS WHOLE DAMNED WORLD!
NOBODY UNDERSTANDS...
...LOVE!
...
HE REALLY DID LOOK JUST LIKE JAMES DEAN.

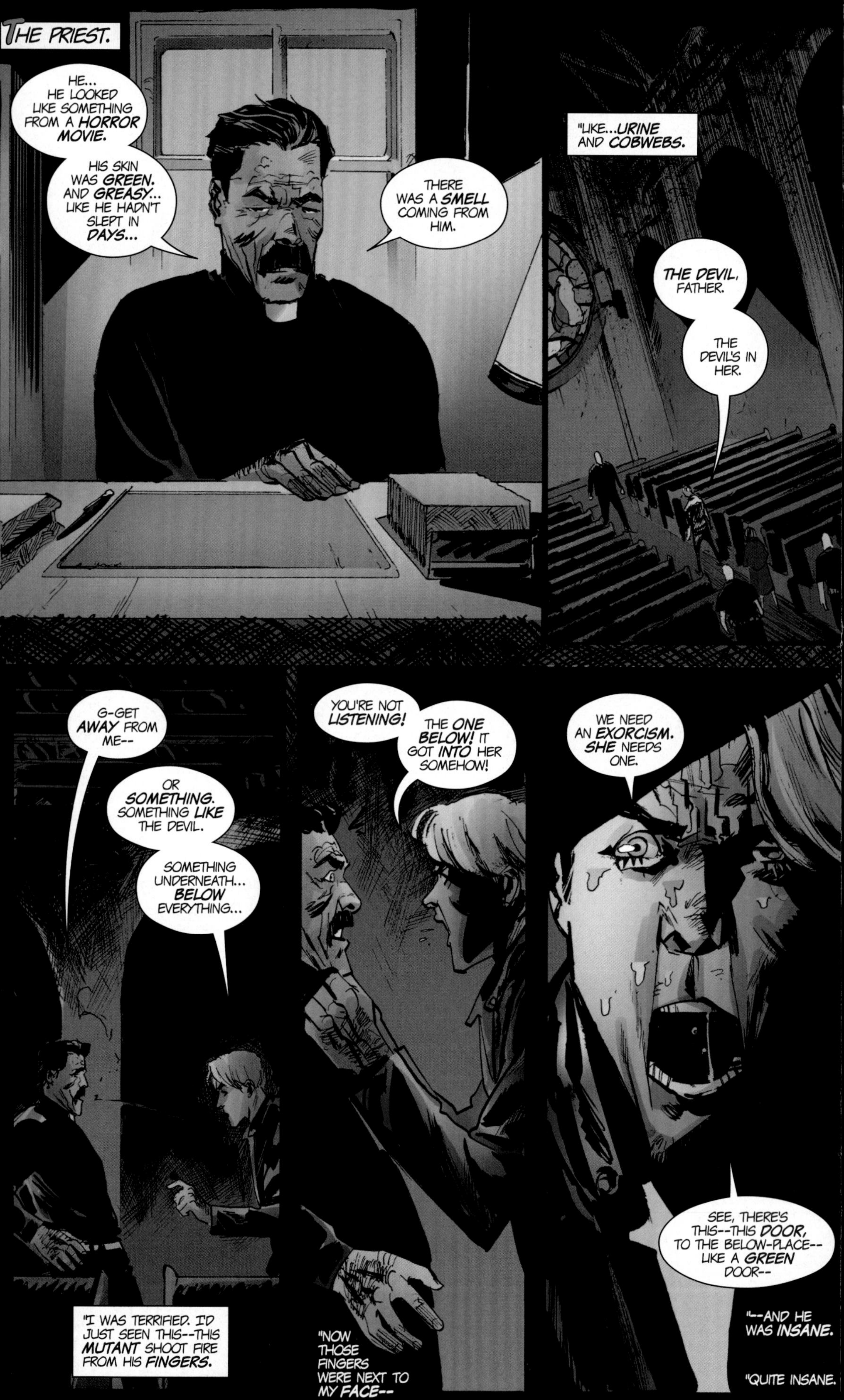
THE PRIEST.
HE... HE LOOKED LIKE SOMETHING FROM A HORROR MOVIE.
HIS SKIN WAS GREEN. AND GREASY... LIKE HE HADN'T SLEPT IN DAYS...
THERE WAS A SMELL COMING FROM HIM.
"LIKE...URINE AND COBWEBS.
THE DEVIL, FATHER.
THE DEVIL'S IN HER.
G-GET AWAY FROM ME--
OR SOMETHING. SOMETHING LIKE THE DEVIL.
SOMETHING UNDERNEATH... BELOW EVERYTHING...
"I WAS TERRIFIED. I'D JUST SEEN THIS--THIS MUTANT SHOOT FIRE FROM HIS FINGERS.
YOU'RE NOT LISTENING!
THE ONE BELOW! IT GOT INTO HER SOMEHOW!
"NOW THOSE FINGERS WERE NEXT TO MY FACE--
WE NEED AN EXORCISM. SHE NEEDS ONE.
SEE, THERE'S THIS--THIS DOOR, TO THE BELOW-PLACE-- LIKE A GREEN DOOR--
"--AND HE WAS INSANE.
"QUITE INSANE.

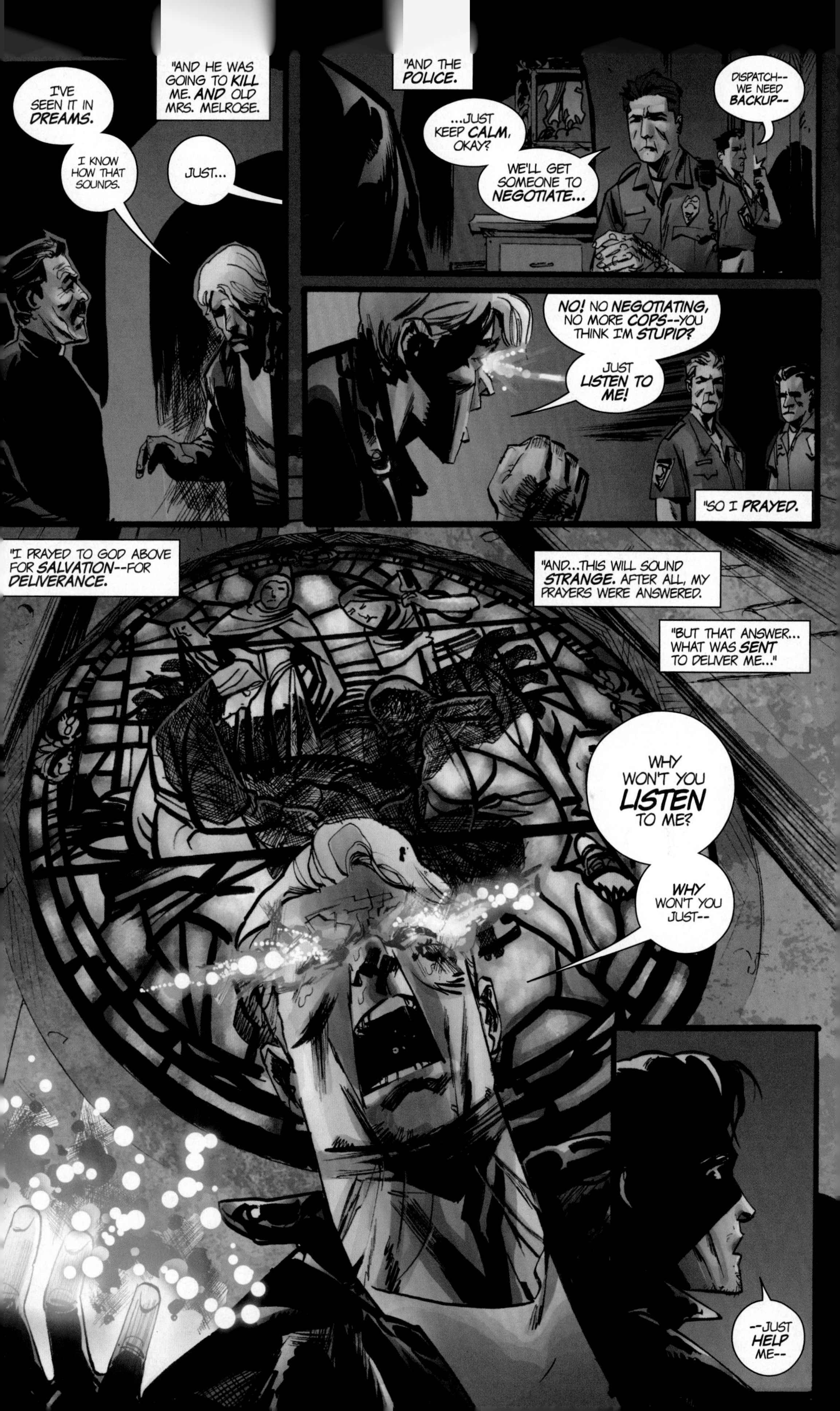

I'VE SEEN IT IN DREAMS.
I KNOW HOW THAT SOUNDS.
"AND HE WAS GOING TO KILL ME. AND OLD MRS. MELROSE.
JUST...
"AND THE POLICE.
...JUST KEEP CALM, OKAY?
WE'LL GET SOMEONE TO NEGOTIATE...
DISPATCH-- WE NEED BACKUP--
NO! NO NEGOTIATING, NO MORE COPS--YOU THINK I'M STUPID?
JUST LISTEN TO ME!
"SO I PRAYED.
"I PRAYED TO GOD ABOVE FOR SALVATION--FOR DELIVERANCE.
"AND...THIS WILL SOUND STRANGE. AFTER ALL, MY PRAYERS WERE ANSWERED.
"BUT THAT ANSWER... WHAT WAS SENT TO DELIVER ME..."
WHY WON'T YOU LISTEN TO ME?
WHY WON'T YOU JUST--
--JUST HELP ME--

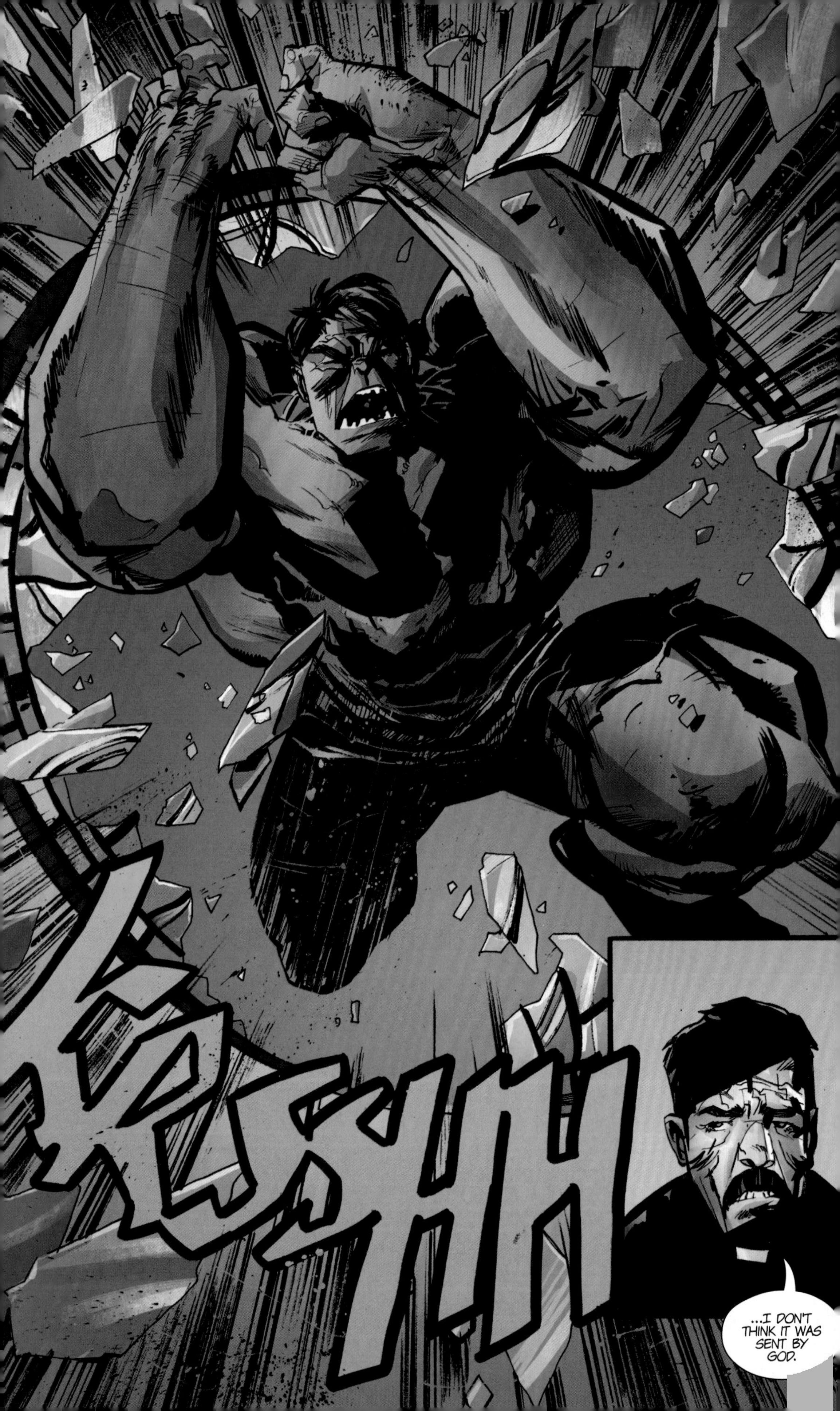
...I DON'T THINK IT WAS SENT BY GOD.

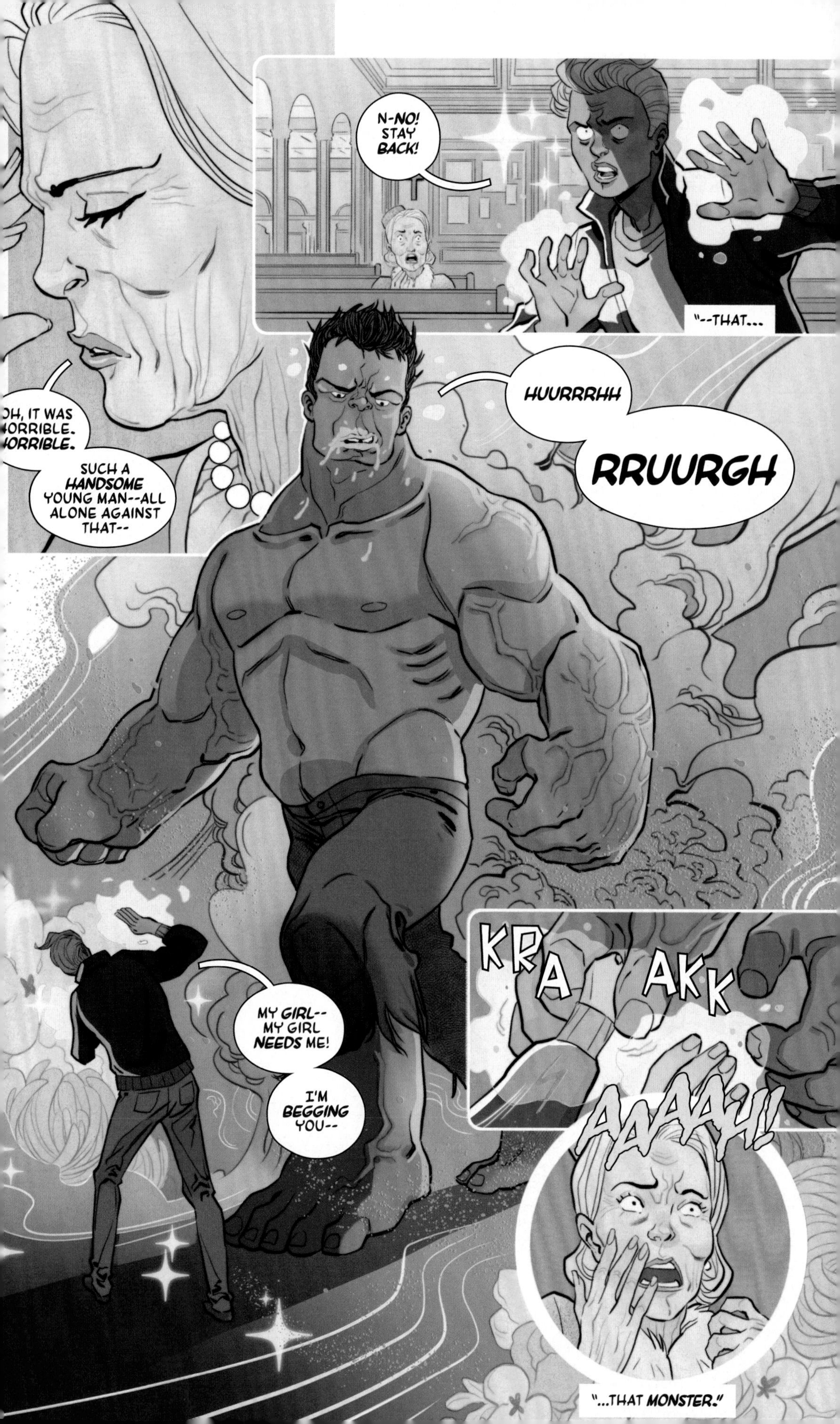
OH, IT WAS HORRIBLE. HORRIBLE.
SUCH A HANDSOME YOUNG MAN--ALL ALONE AGAINST THAT--
N-NO! STAY BACK!
"--THAT...
HUURRRHH
RRUURGH
MY GIRL-- MY GIRL NEEDS ME!
I'M BEGGING YOU--
KRA AKK
AAAAH!!
"...THAT MONSTER."

MONSTER? OL' JADE JAWS? COME ON, LADY.

HE'S A FOUNDING AVENGER. HE'S BEEN IN MOVIES. HE'S A HERO.

ROUGH AROUND THE EDGES, MAYBE--

"--BUT HE WAS DISARMING A FELON.

"LITERALLY!

M-MY HANDS-- BROKEN--

YOU WON'T USE THAT GAMMA BLAST AGAIN, HOTSHOT-- NO MATTER WHAT THE COURTS DECIDE!

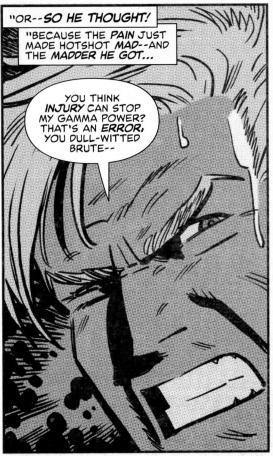

"OR--SO HE THOUGHT!

"BECAUSE THE PAIN JUST MADE HOTSHOT MAD--AND THE MADDER HE GOT...

YOU THINK INJURY CAN STOP MY GAMMA POWER? THAT'S AN ERROR, YOU DULL-WITTED BRUTE--

WZZZHAW

--YOUR FINAL ERROR!

"...THE STRONGER HE GOT!"

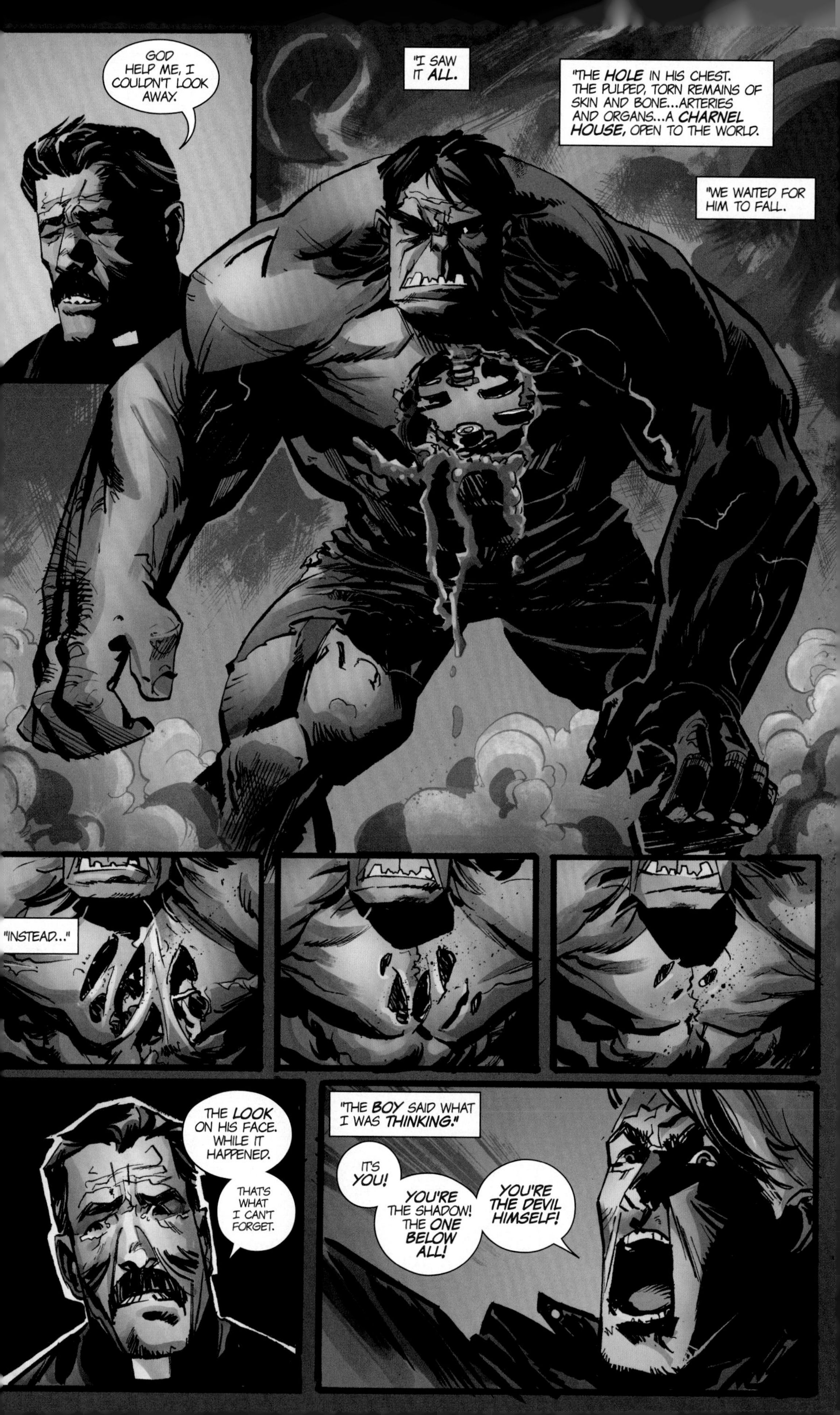

GOD HELP ME, I COULDN'T LOOK AWAY.
"I SAW IT ALL.
"THE HOLE IN HIS CHEST. THE PULPED, TORN REMAINS OF SKIN AND BONE...ARTERIES AND ORGANS...A CHARNEL HOUSE, OPEN TO THE WORLD.
"WE WAITED FOR HIM TO FALL.
"INSTEAD..."
THE LOOK ON HIS FACE. WHILE IT HAPPENED.
THAT'S WHAT I CAN'T FORGET.
"THE BOY SAID WHAT I WAS THINKING."
IT'S YOU!
YOU'RE THE SHADOW! THE ONE BELOW ALL!
YOU'RE THE DEVIL HIMSELF!

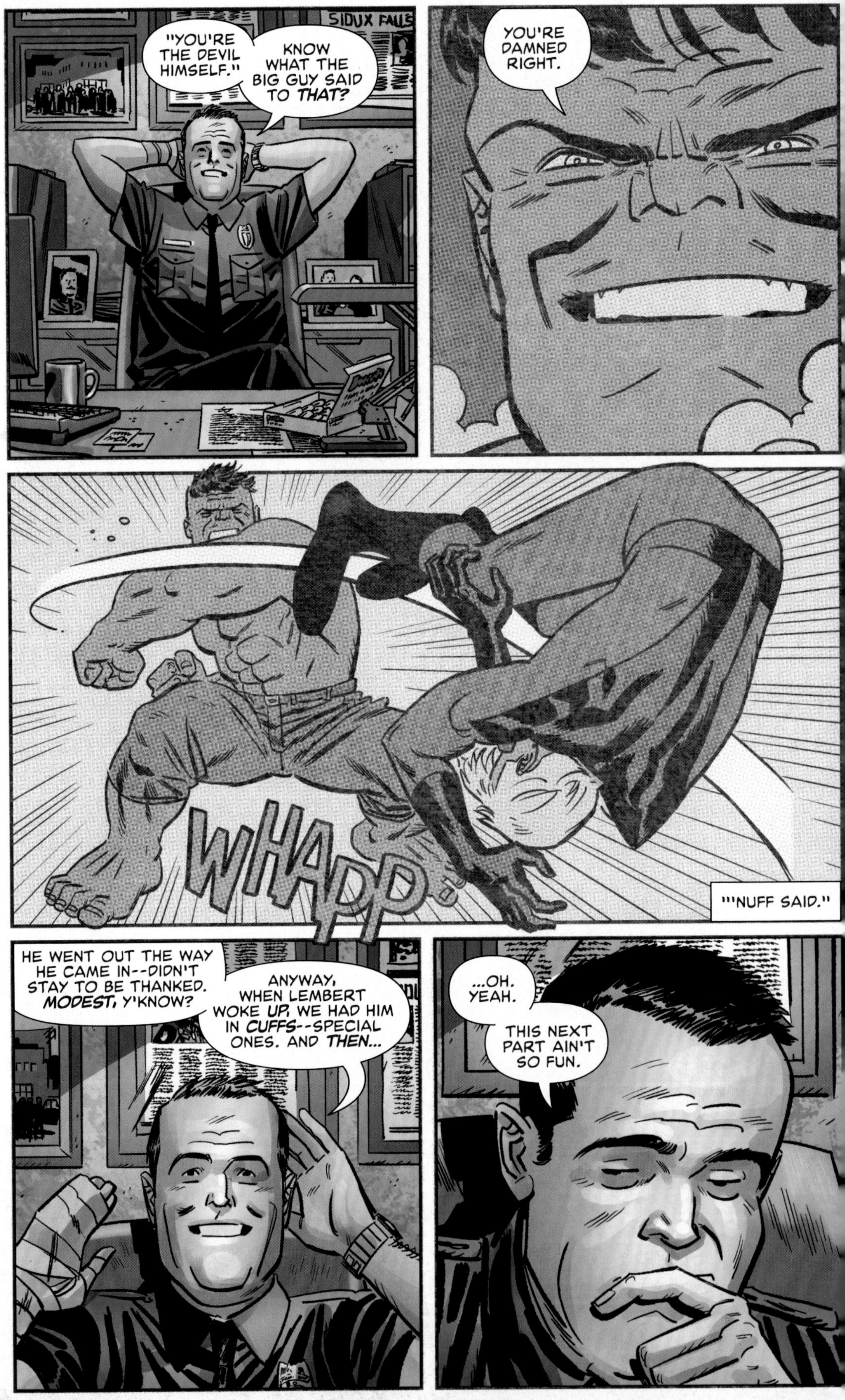

SIOUX FALLS
"YOU'RE THE DEVIL HIMSELF."
KNOW WHAT THE BIG GUY SAID TO THAT?
YOU'RE DAMNED RIGHT.
WHAPP
"'NUFF SAID."
HE WENT OUT THE WAY HE CAME IN--DIDN'T STAY TO BE THANKED. MODEST, Y'KNOW?
ANYWAY, WHEN LEMBERT WOKE UP, WE HAD HIM IN CUFFS--SPECIAL ONES. AND THEN...
...OH. YEAH.
THIS NEXT PART AIN'T SO FUN.

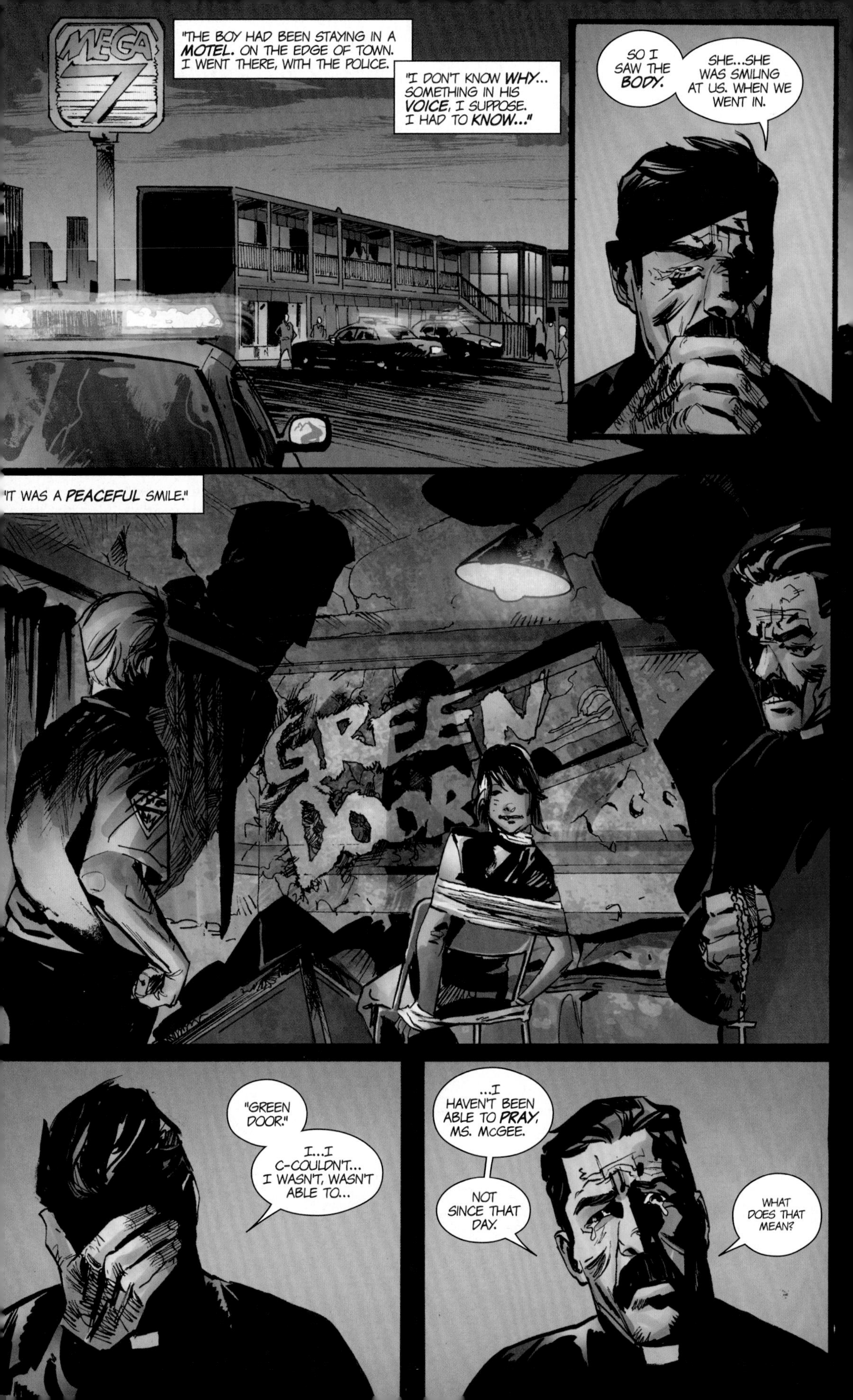
MEGA 7
"THE BOY HAD BEEN STAYING IN A MOTEL. ON THE EDGE OF TOWN. I WENT THERE, WITH THE POLICE.
"I DON'T KNOW WHY... SOMETHING IN HIS VOICE, I SUPPOSE. I HAD TO KNOW..."
SO I SAW THE BODY.
SHE...SHE WAS SMILING AT US. WHEN WE WENT IN.
"IT WAS A PEACEFUL SMILE."
GREEN DOOR
"GREEN DOOR."
I...I C-COULDN'T... I WASN'T, WASN'T ABLE TO...
...I HAVEN'T BEEN ABLE TO PRAY, MS. McGEE.
NOT SINCE THAT DAY.
WHAT DOES THAT MEAN?

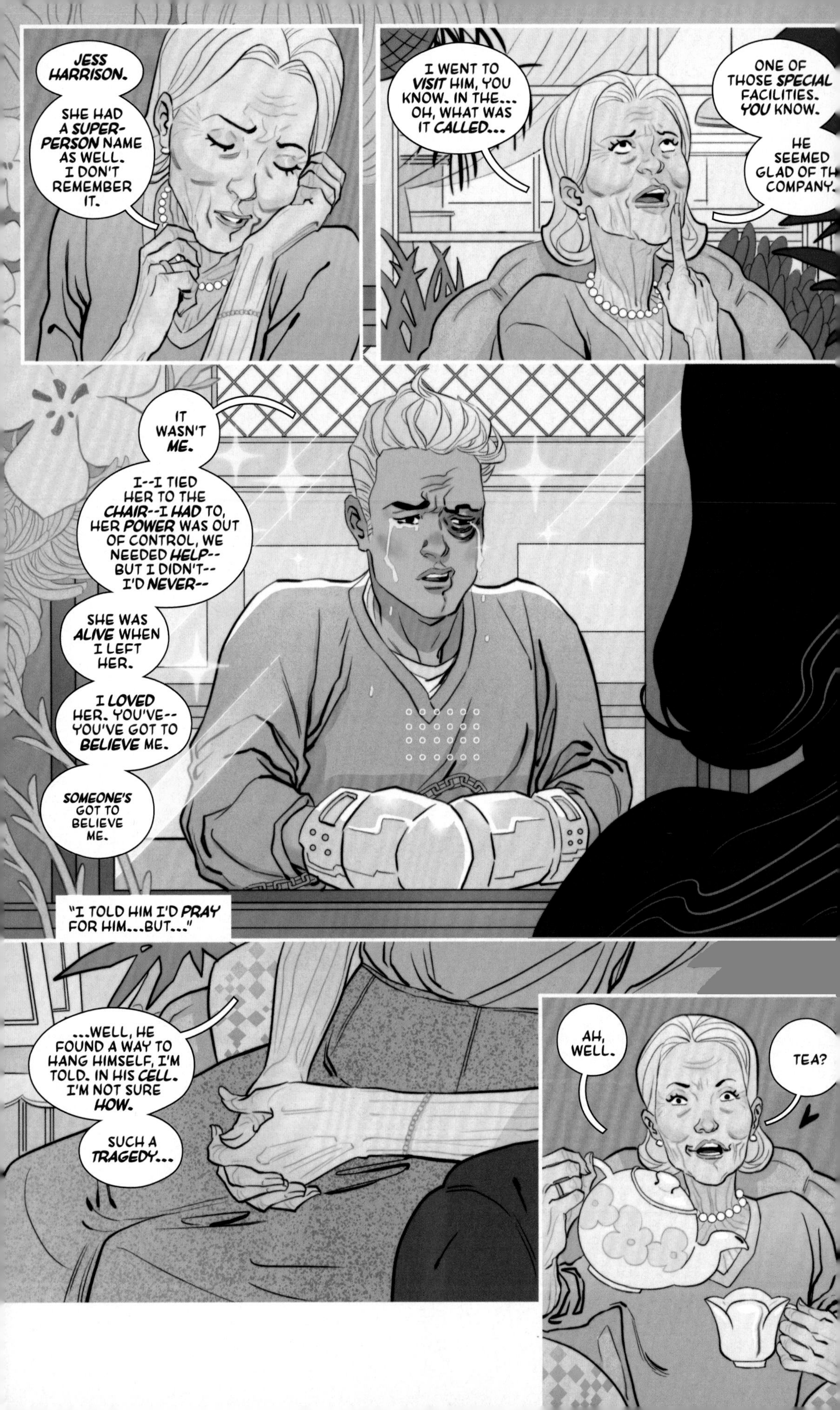

JESS HARRISON.
SHE HAD A SUPER-PERSON NAME AS WELL. I DON'T REMEMBER IT.
I WENT TO VISIT HIM, YOU KNOW. IN THE... OH, WHAT WAS IT CALLED...
ONE OF THOSE SPECIAL FACILITIES. YOU KNOW.
HE SEEMED GLAD OF TH COMPANY.
IT WASN'T ME.
I--I TIED HER TO THE CHAIR--I HAD TO, HER POWER WAS OUT OF CONTROL, WE NEEDED HELP-- BUT I DIDN'T-- I'D NEVER--
SHE WAS ALIVE WHEN I LEFT HER.
I LOVED HER. YOU'VE-- YOU'VE GOT TO BELIEVE ME.
SOMEONE'S GOT TO BELIEVE ME.
"I TOLD HIM I'D PRAY FOR HIM...BUT..."
...WELL, HE FOUND A WAY TO HANG HIMSELF, I'M TOLD. IN HIS CELL. I'M NOT SURE HOW.
SUCH A TRAGEDY...
AH, WELL.
TEA?

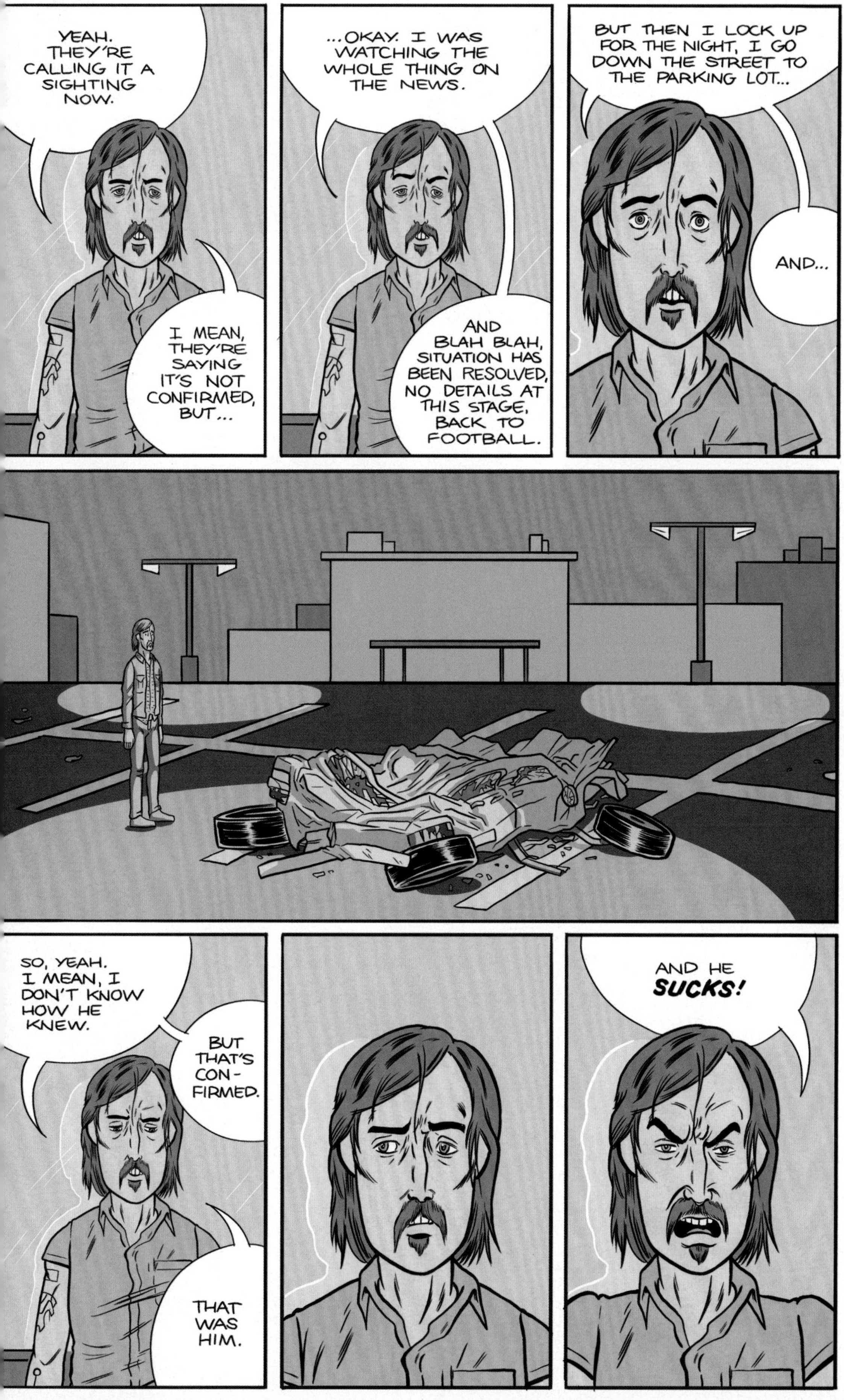
YEAH. THEY'RE CALLING IT A SIGHTING NOW.
I MEAN, THEY'RE SAYING IT'S NOT CONFIRMED, BUT...
...OKAY. I WAS WATCHING THE WHOLE THING ON THE NEWS.
AND BLAH BLAH, SITUATION HAS BEEN RESOLVED, NO DETAILS AT THIS STAGE, BACK TO FOOTBALL.
BUT THEN I LOCK UP FOR THE NIGHT, I GO DOWN THE STREET TO THE PARKING LOT...
AND...
SO, YEAH. I MEAN, I DON'T KNOW HOW HE KNEW.
BUT THAT'S CON-FIRMED.
THAT WAS HIM.
AND HE **SUCKS!**

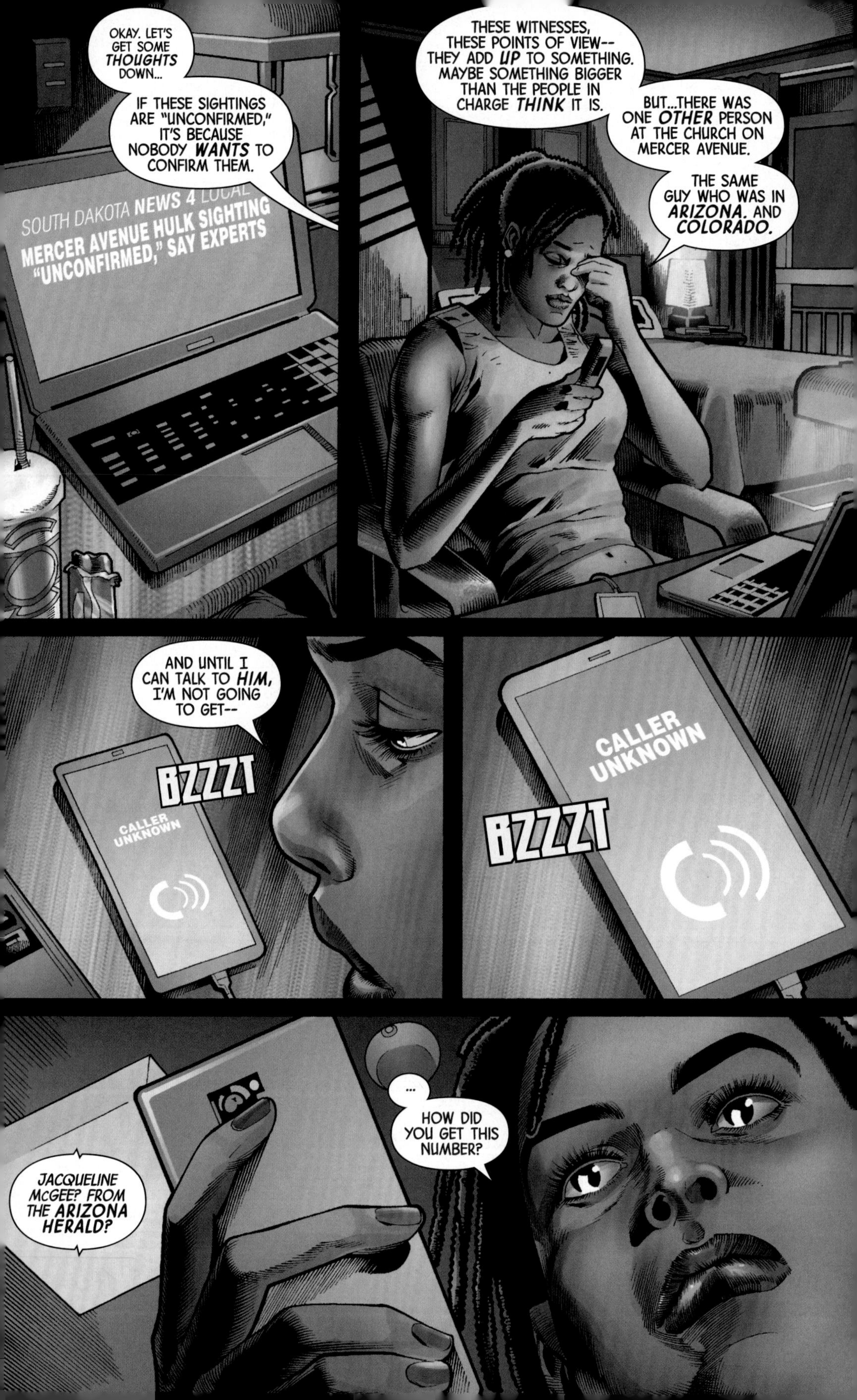

OKAY. LET'S GET SOME THOUGHTS DOWN...
IF THESE SIGHTINGS ARE "UNCONFIRMED," IT'S BECAUSE NOBODY WANTS TO CONFIRM THEM.
SOUTH DAKOTA NEWS 4 LOCAL
MERCER AVENUE HULK SIGHTING "UNCONFIRMED," SAY EXPERTS
THESE WITNESSES, THESE POINTS OF VIEW-- THEY ADD UP TO SOMETHING. MAYBE SOMETHING BIGGER THAN THE PEOPLE IN CHARGE THINK IT IS.
BUT...THERE WAS ONE OTHER PERSON AT THE CHURCH ON MERCER AVENUE.
THE SAME GUY WHO WAS IN ARIZONA. AND COLORADO.
AND UNTIL I CAN TALK TO HIM, I'M NOT GOING TO GET--
BZZZT
CALLER UNKNOWN
CALLER UNKNOWN
BZZZT
...
HOW DID YOU GET THIS NUMBER?
JACQUELINE McGEE? FROM THE ARIZONA HERALD?

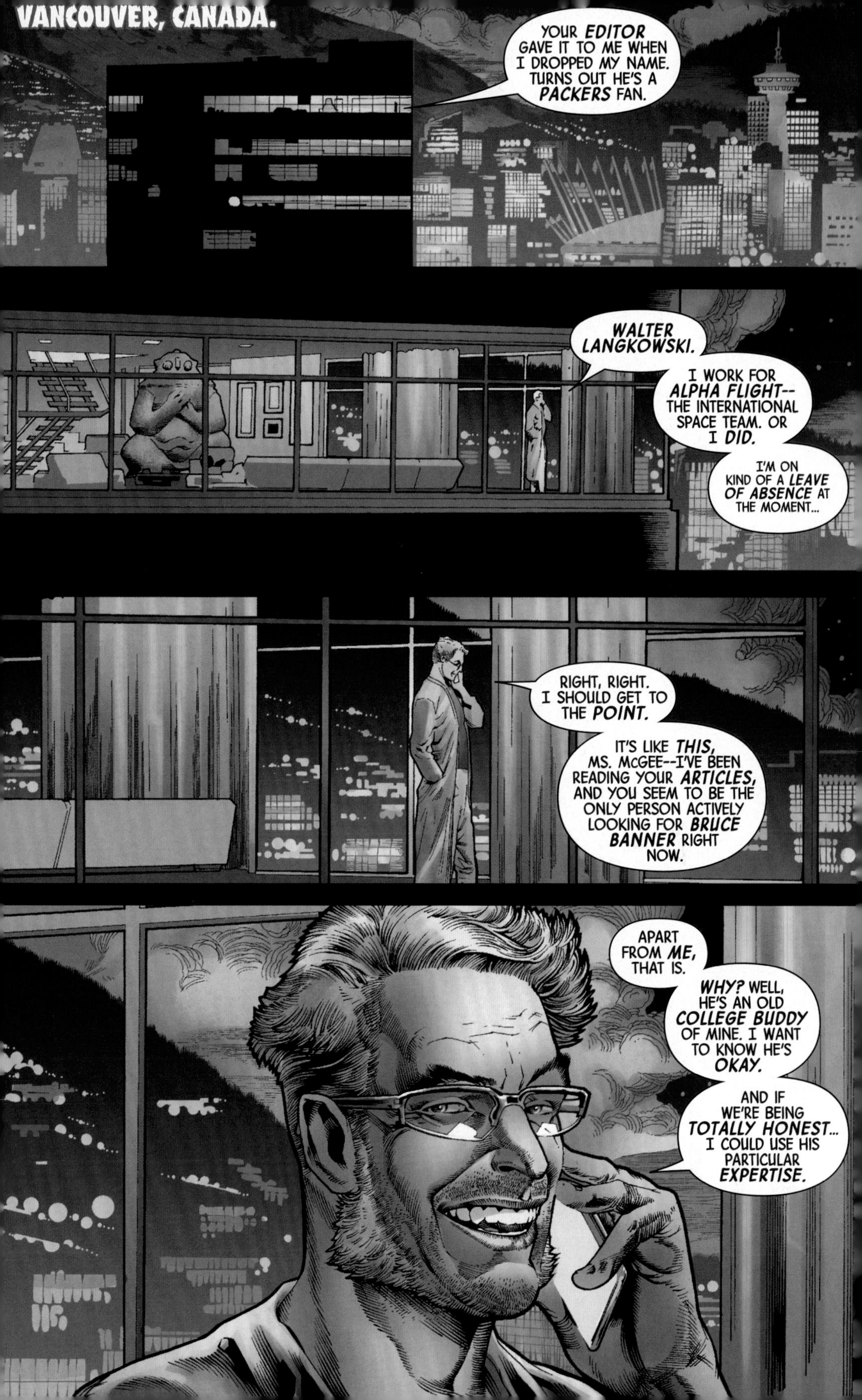

VANCOUVER, CANADA.
YOUR EDITOR GAVE IT TO ME WHEN I DROPPED MY NAME. TURNS OUT HE'S A PACKERS FAN.
WALTER LANGKOWSKI.
I WORK FOR ALPHA FLIGHT-- THE INTERNATIONAL SPACE TEAM. OR I DID.
I'M ON KIND OF A LEAVE OF ABSENCE AT THE MOMENT...
RIGHT, RIGHT. I SHOULD GET TO THE POINT.
IT'S LIKE THIS, MS. McGEE--I'VE BEEN READING YOUR ARTICLES, AND YOU SEEM TO BE THE ONLY PERSON ACTIVELY LOOKING FOR BRUCE BANNER RIGHT NOW.
APART FROM ME, THAT IS.
WHY? WELL, HE'S AN OLD COLLEGE BUDDY OF MINE. I WANT TO KNOW HE'S OKAY.
AND IF WE'RE BEING TOTALLY HONEST... I COULD USE HIS PARTICULAR EXPERTISE.

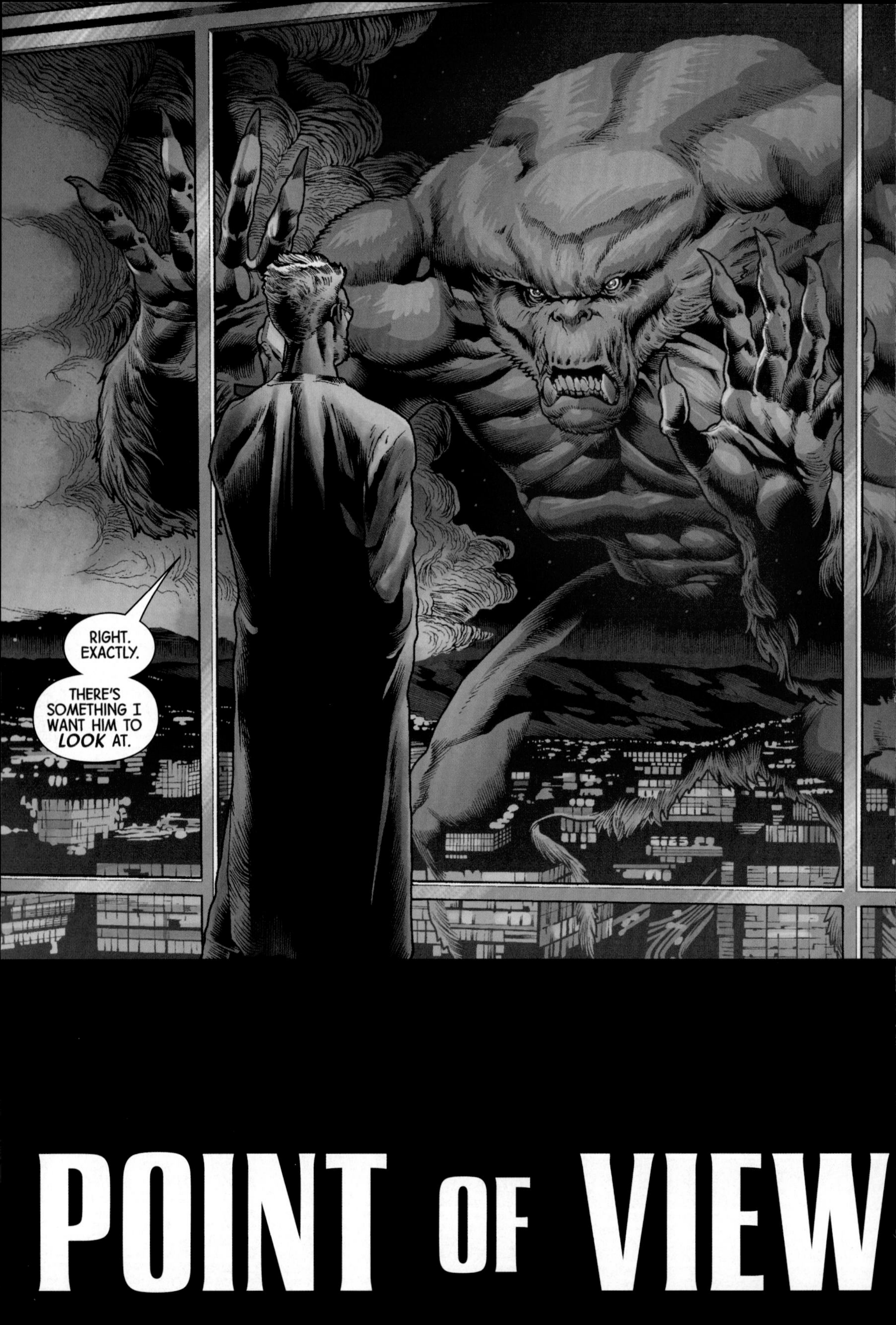
RIGHT. EXACTLY.
THERE'S SOMETHING I WANT HIM TO LOOK AT.

# POINT OF VIEW

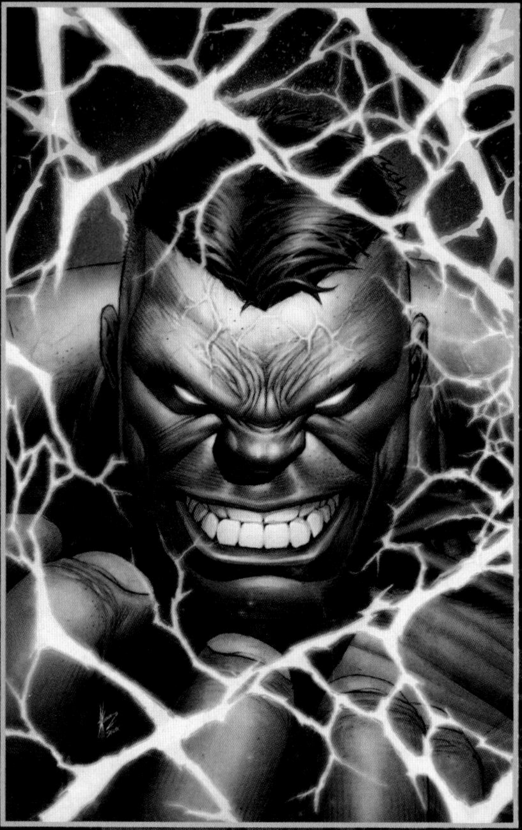

**DALE KEOWN & JASON KEITH**
#1 VARIANT

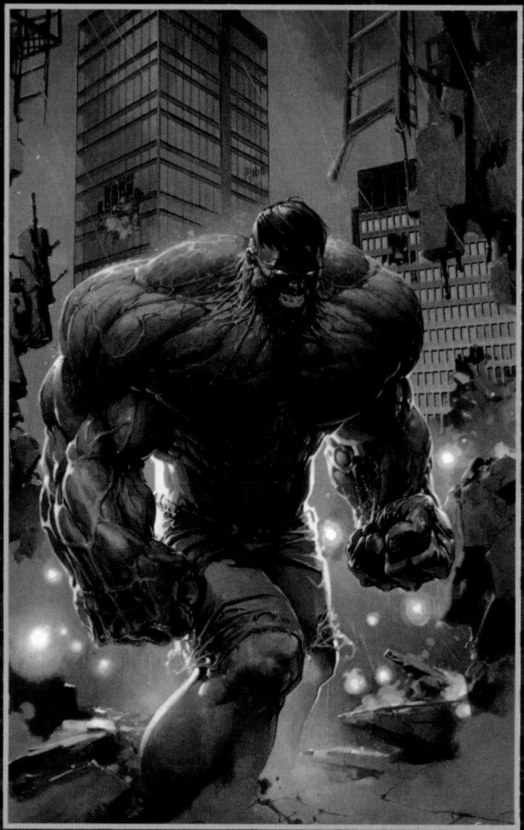

**CLAYTON CRAIN**
#1 VARIANT

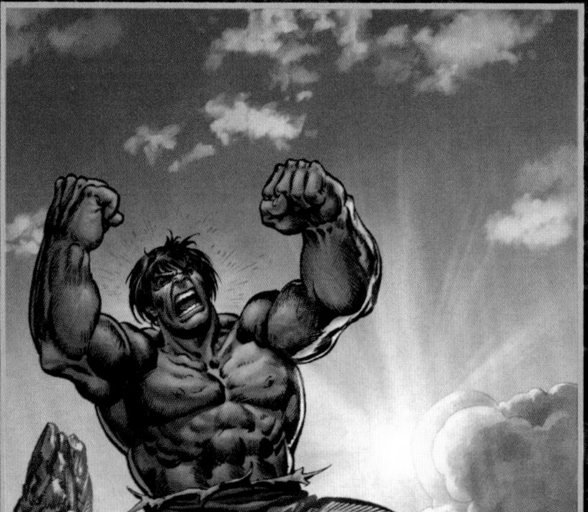

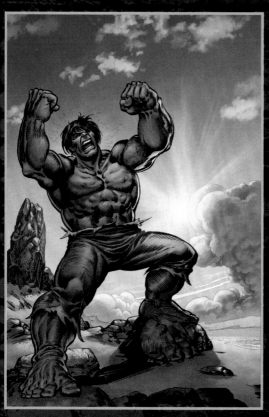

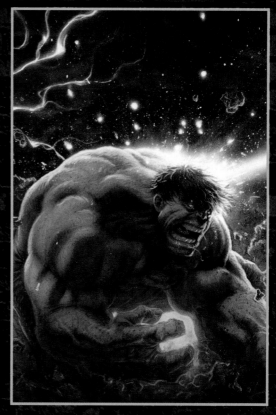

**SAL BUSCEMA, ALFREDO ALCALA & EBER EVANGELISTA**
#1 REMASTERED VARIANT

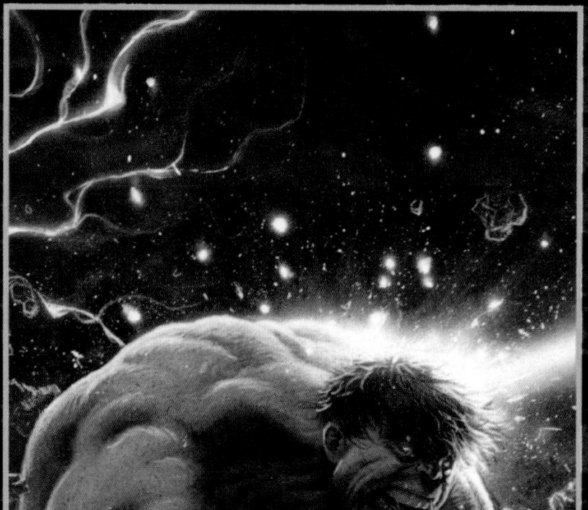

**KAARE ANDREWS**
#1 VARIANT

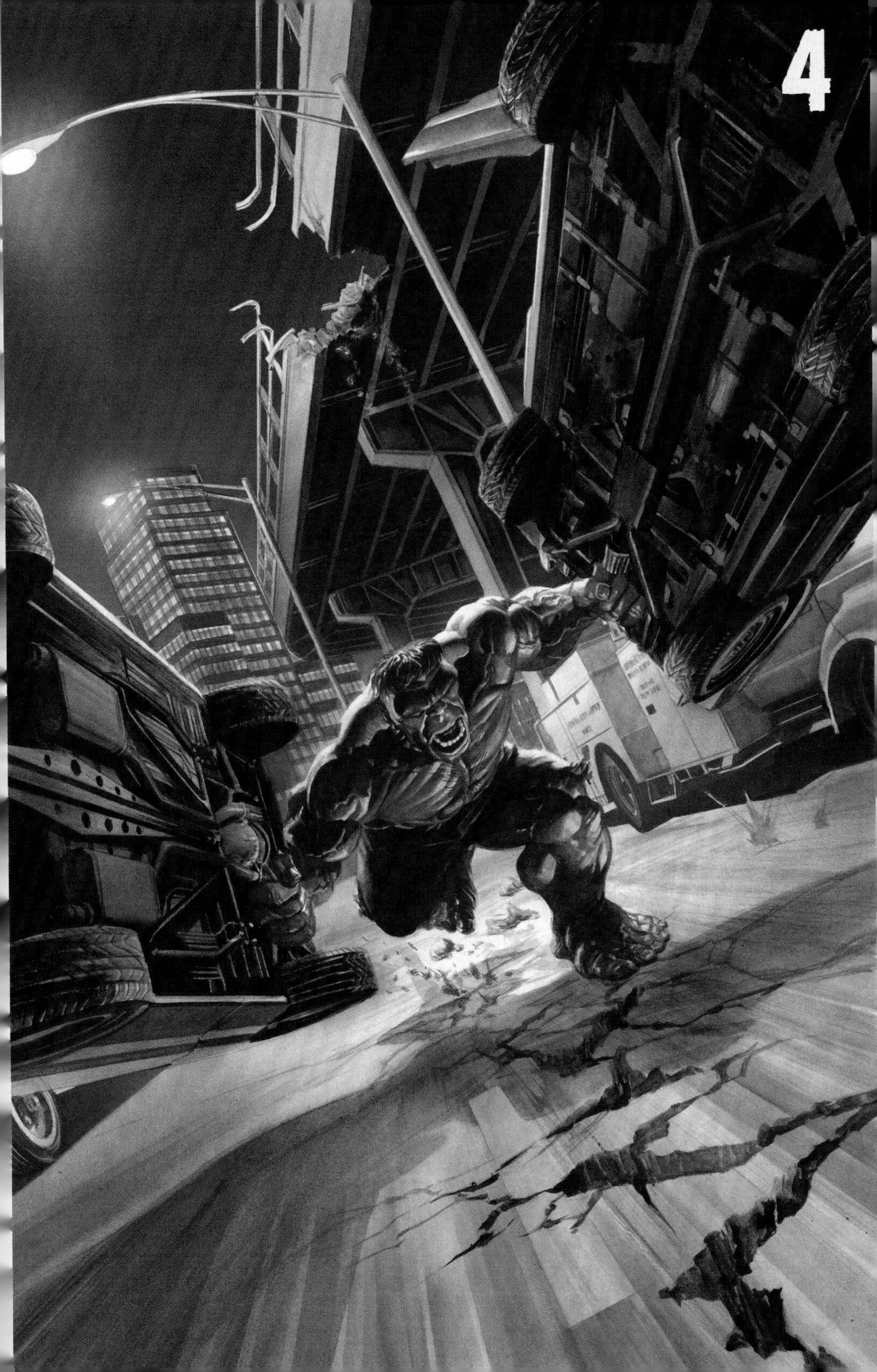
4

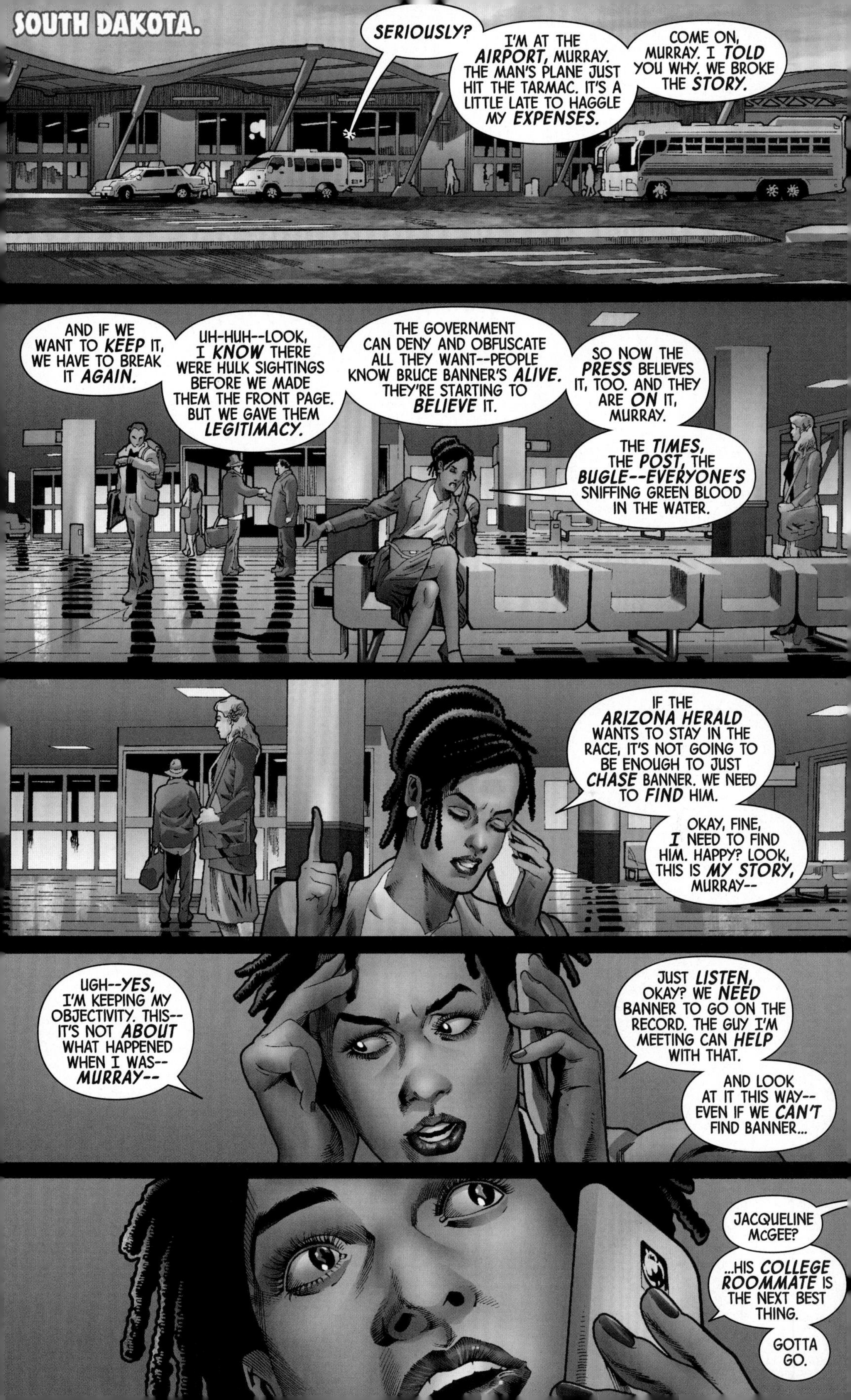
SOUTH DAKOTA.
SERIOUSLY?
I'M AT THE AIRPORT, MURRAY. THE MAN'S PLANE JUST HIT THE TARMAC. IT'S A LITTLE LATE TO HAGGLE MY EXPENSES.
COME ON, MURRAY. I TOLD YOU WHY. WE BROKE THE STORY.
AND IF WE WANT TO KEEP IT, WE HAVE TO BREAK IT AGAIN.
UH-HUH--LOOK, I KNOW THERE WERE HULK SIGHTINGS BEFORE WE MADE THEM THE FRONT PAGE. BUT WE GAVE THEM LEGITIMACY.
THE GOVERNMENT CAN DENY AND OBFUSCATE ALL THEY WANT--PEOPLE KNOW BRUCE BANNER'S ALIVE. THEY'RE STARTING TO BELIEVE IT.
SO NOW THE PRESS BELIEVES IT, TOO. AND THEY ARE ON IT, MURRAY.
THE TIMES, THE POST, THE BUGLE--EVERYONE'S SNIFFING GREEN BLOOD IN THE WATER.
IF THE ARIZONA HERALD WANTS TO STAY IN THE RACE, IT'S NOT GOING TO BE ENOUGH TO JUST CHASE BANNER. WE NEED TO FIND HIM.
OKAY, FINE, I NEED TO FIND HIM. HAPPY? LOOK, THIS IS MY STORY, MURRAY--
UGH--YES, I'M KEEPING MY OBJECTIVITY. THIS--IT'S NOT ABOUT WHAT HAPPENED WHEN I WAS--MURRAY--
JUST LISTEN, OKAY? WE NEED BANNER TO GO ON THE RECORD. THE GUY I'M MEETING CAN HELP WITH THAT.
AND LOOK AT IT THIS WAY--EVEN IF WE CAN'T FIND BANNER...
JACQUELINE McGEE?
...HIS COLLEGE ROOMMATE IS THE NEXT BEST THING.
GOTTA GO.

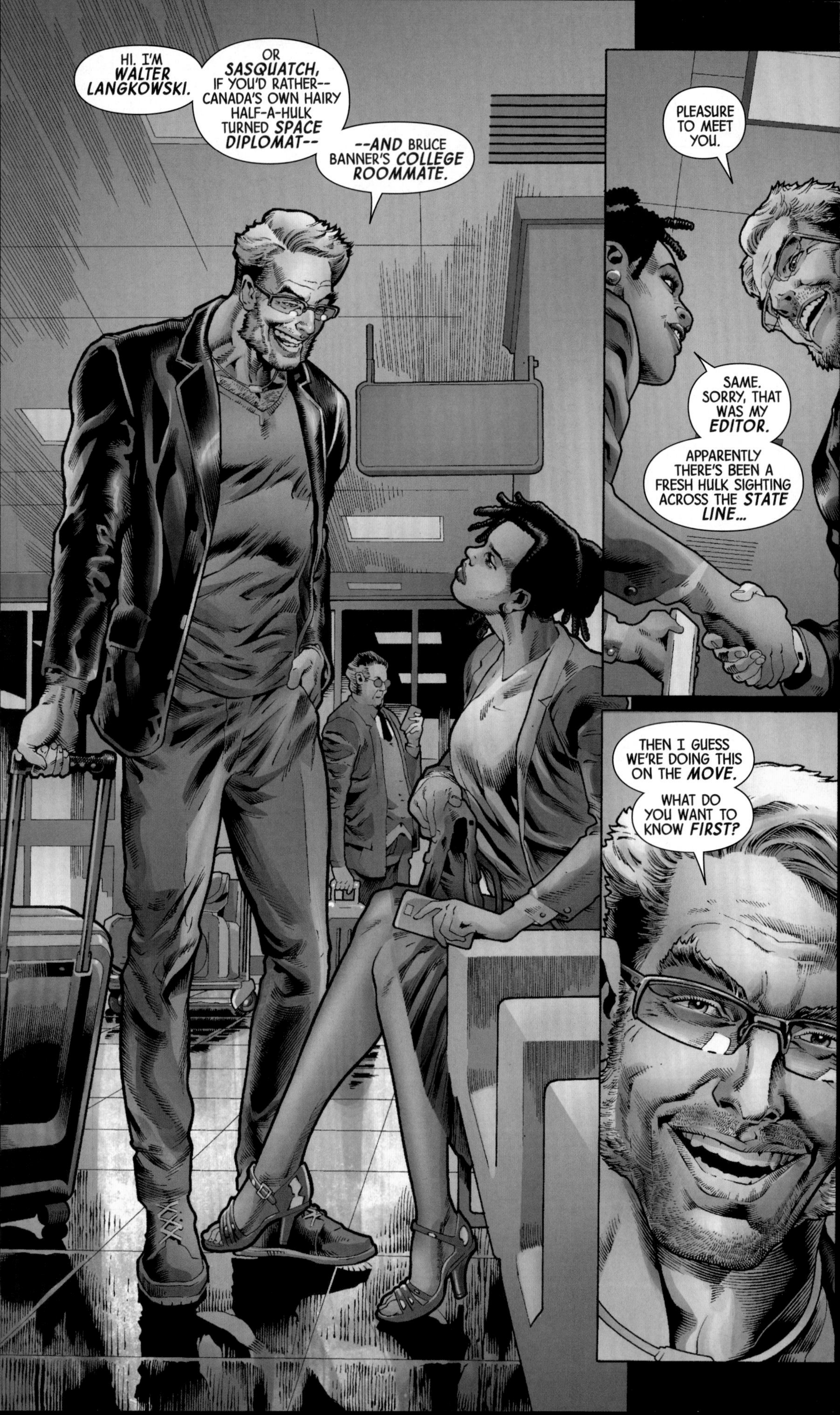

HI. I'M WALTER LANGKOWSKI.
OR SASQUATCH, IF YOU'D RATHER-- CANADA'S OWN HAIRY HALF-A-HULK TURNED SPACE DIPLOMAT--
--AND BRUCE BANNER'S COLLEGE ROOMMATE.
PLEASURE TO MEET YOU.
SAME. SORRY, THAT WAS MY EDITOR.
APPARENTLY THERE'S BEEN A FRESH HULK SIGHTING ACROSS THE STATE LINE...
THEN I GUESS WE'RE DOING THIS ON THE MOVE.
WHAT DO YOU WANT TO KNOW FIRST?

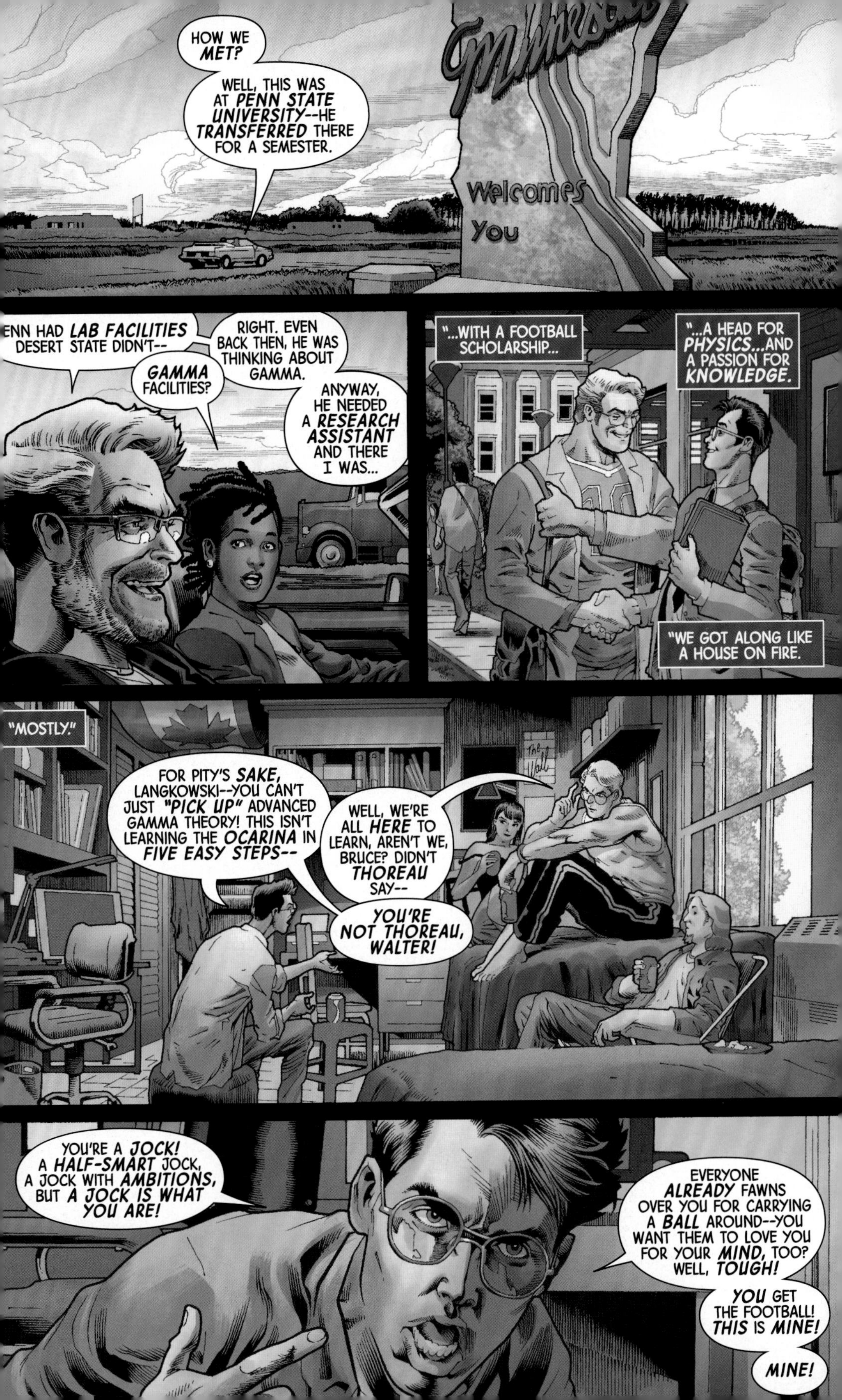

HOW WE MET?
WELL, THIS WAS AT PENN STATE UNIVERSITY--HE TRANSFERRED THERE FOR A SEMESTER.
Welcomes You
ENN HAD LAB FACILITIES DESERT STATE DIDN'T--
GAMMA FACILITIES?
RIGHT. EVEN BACK THEN, HE WAS THINKING ABOUT GAMMA.
ANYWAY, HE NEEDED A RESEARCH ASSISTANT AND THERE I WAS...
"...WITH A FOOTBALL SCHOLARSHIP...
"...A HEAD FOR PHYSICS...AND A PASSION FOR KNOWLEDGE.
"WE GOT ALONG LIKE A HOUSE ON FIRE.
"MOSTLY."
FOR PITY'S SAKE, LANGKOWSKI--YOU CAN'T JUST "PICK UP" ADVANCED GAMMA THEORY! THIS ISN'T LEARNING THE OCARINA IN FIVE EASY STEPS--
WELL, WE'RE ALL HERE TO LEARN, AREN'T WE, BRUCE? DIDN'T THOREAU SAY--
YOU'RE NOT THOREAU, WALTER!
YOU'RE A JOCK! A HALF-SMART JOCK, A JOCK WITH AMBITIONS, BUT A JOCK IS WHAT YOU ARE!
EVERYONE ALREADY FAWNS OVER YOU FOR CARRYING A BALL AROUND--YOU WANT THEM TO LOVE YOU FOR YOUR MIND, TOO? WELL, TOUGH!
YOU GET THE FOOTBALL! THIS IS MINE!
MINE!

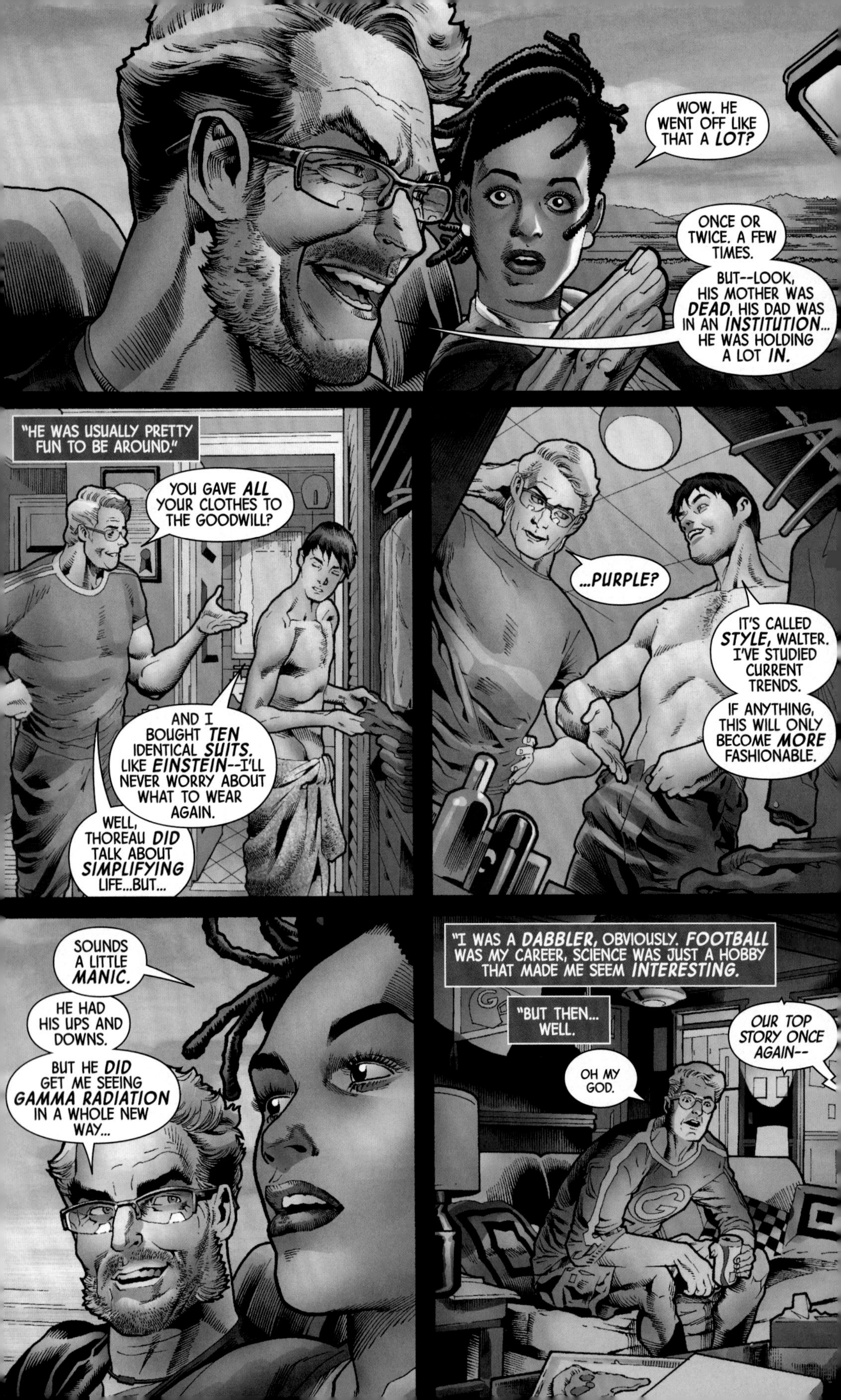
WOW. HE WENT OFF LIKE THAT A *LOT?*
ONCE OR TWICE. A FEW TIMES.
BUT--LOOK, HIS MOTHER WAS *DEAD*, HIS DAD WAS IN AN *INSTITUTION*... HE WAS HOLDING A LOT *IN.*
"HE WAS USUALLY PRETTY FUN TO BE AROUND."
YOU GAVE *ALL* YOUR CLOTHES TO THE GOODWILL?
AND I BOUGHT *TEN* IDENTICAL *SUITS.* LIKE *EINSTEIN*--I'LL NEVER WORRY ABOUT WHAT TO WEAR AGAIN.
WELL, THOREAU *DID* TALK ABOUT *SIMPLIFYING* LIFE...BUT...
...*PURPLE?*
IT'S CALLED *STYLE,* WALTER. I'VE STUDIED CURRENT TRENDS.
IF ANYTHING, THIS WILL ONLY BECOME *MORE* FASHIONABLE.
SOUNDS A LITTLE *MANIC.*
HE HAD HIS UPS AND DOWNS.
BUT HE *DID* GET ME SEEING *GAMMA RADIATION* IN A WHOLE NEW WAY...
"I WAS A *DABBLER,* OBVIOUSLY. *FOOTBALL* WAS MY CAREER, SCIENCE WAS JUST A HOBBY THAT MADE ME SEEM *INTERESTING.*
"BUT THEN... WELL.
OUR TOP STORY ONCE AGAIN--
OH MY GOD.

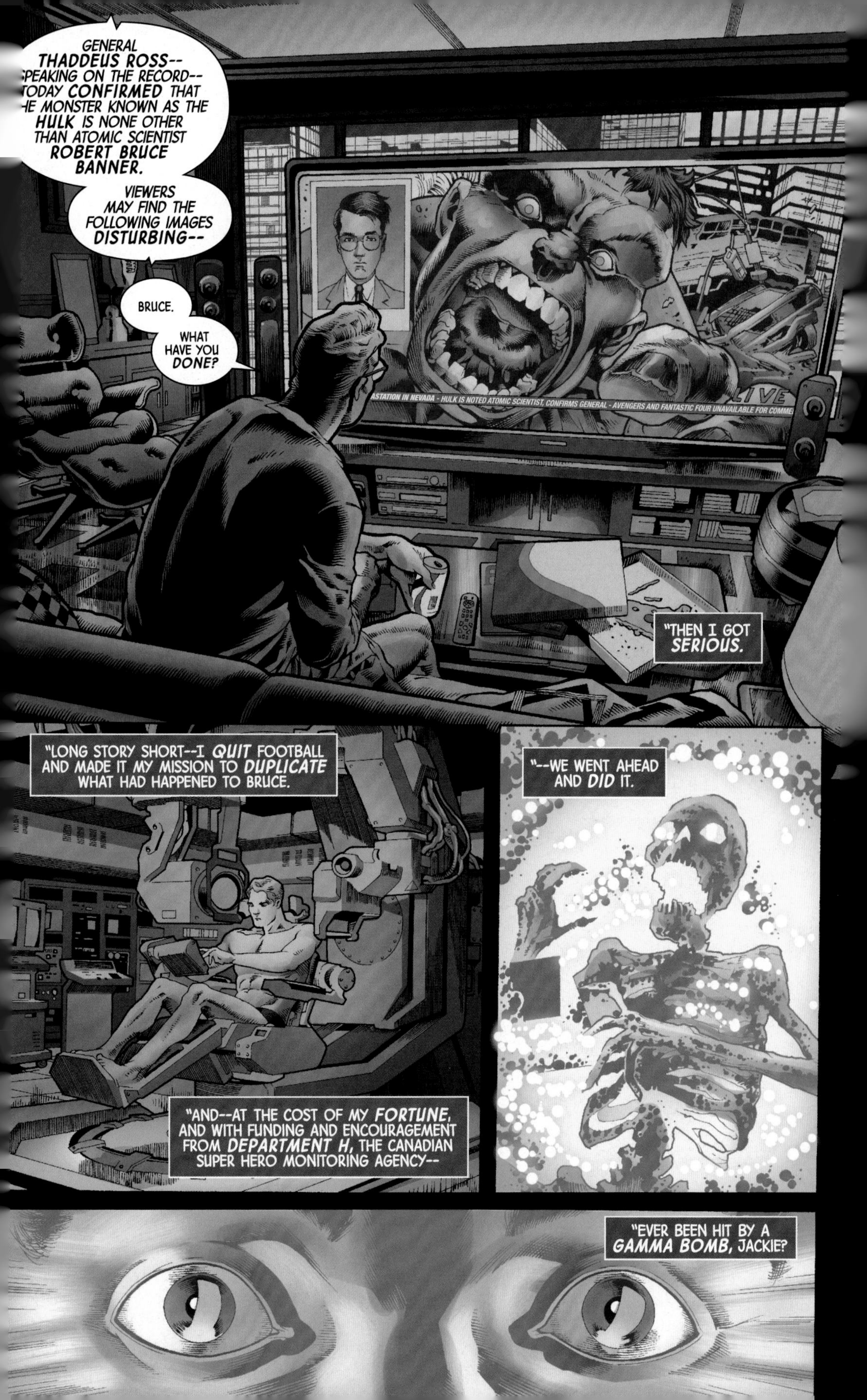
GENERAL THADDEUS ROSS--SPEAKING ON THE RECORD--TODAY CONFIRMED THAT THE MONSTER KNOWN AS THE HULK IS NONE OTHER THAN ATOMIC SCIENTIST ROBERT BRUCE BANNER.
VIEWERS MAY FIND THE FOLLOWING IMAGES DISTURBING--
ASTATION IN NEVADA - HULK IS NOTED ATOMIC SCIENTIST, CONFIRMS GENERAL - AVENGERS AND FANTASTIC FOUR UNAVAILABLE FOR COMME
LIVE
BRUCE.
WHAT HAVE YOU DONE?
"THEN I GOT SERIOUS.
"LONG STORY SHORT--I QUIT FOOTBALL AND MADE IT MY MISSION TO DUPLICATE WHAT HAD HAPPENED TO BRUCE.
"AND--AT THE COST OF MY FORTUNE, AND WITH FUNDING AND ENCOURAGEMENT FROM DEPARTMENT H, THE CANADIAN SUPER HERO MONITORING AGENCY--
"--WE WENT AHEAD AND DID IT.
"EVER BEEN HIT BY A GAMMA BOMB, JACKIE?

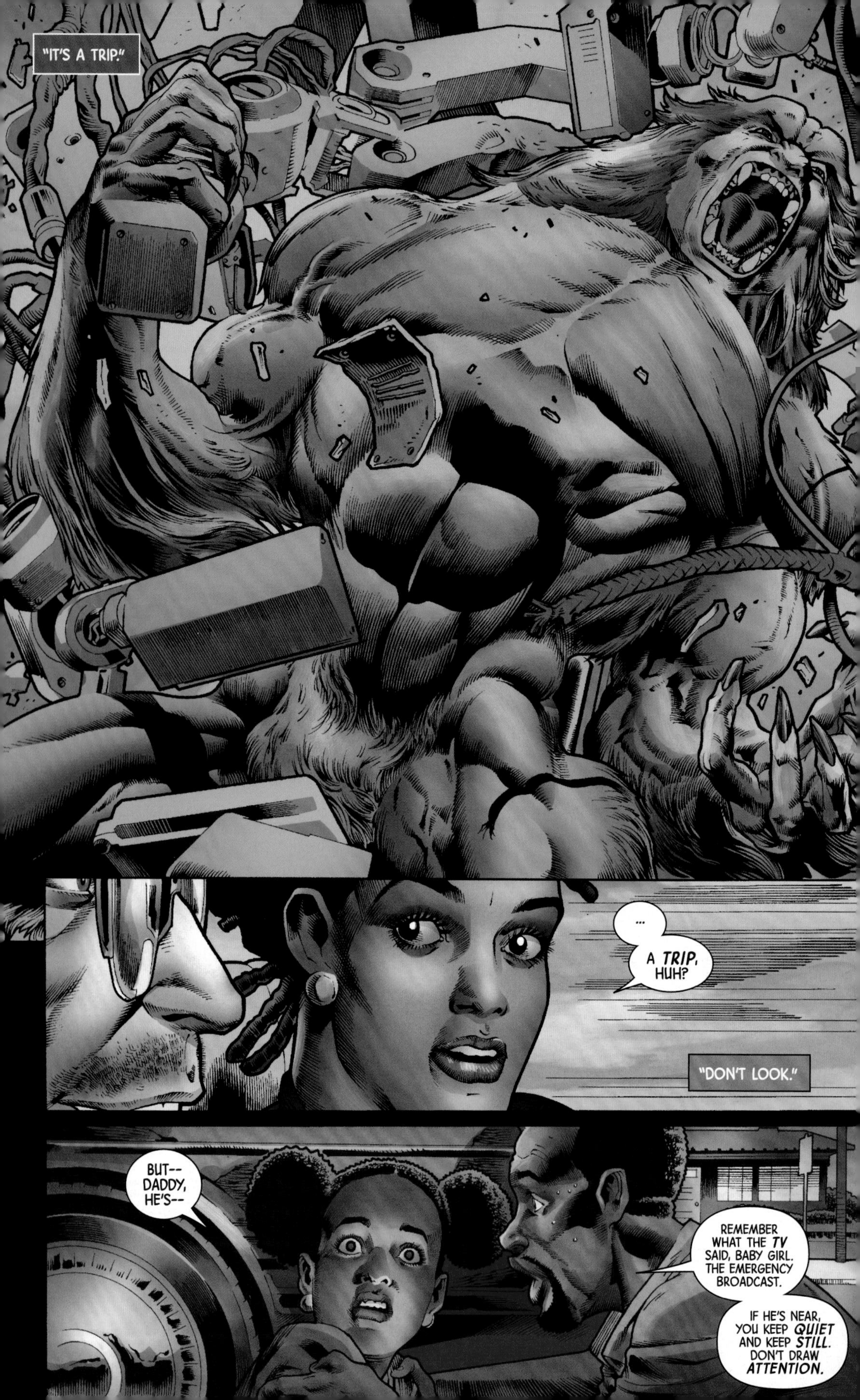
"IT'S A TRIP."
...
A TRIP, HUH?
"DON'T LOOK."
BUT-- DADDY, HE'S--
REMEMBER WHAT THE TV SAID, BABY GIRL. THE EMERGENCY BROADCAST.
IF HE'S NEAR, YOU KEEP QUIET AND KEEP STILL. DON'T DRAW ATTENTION.

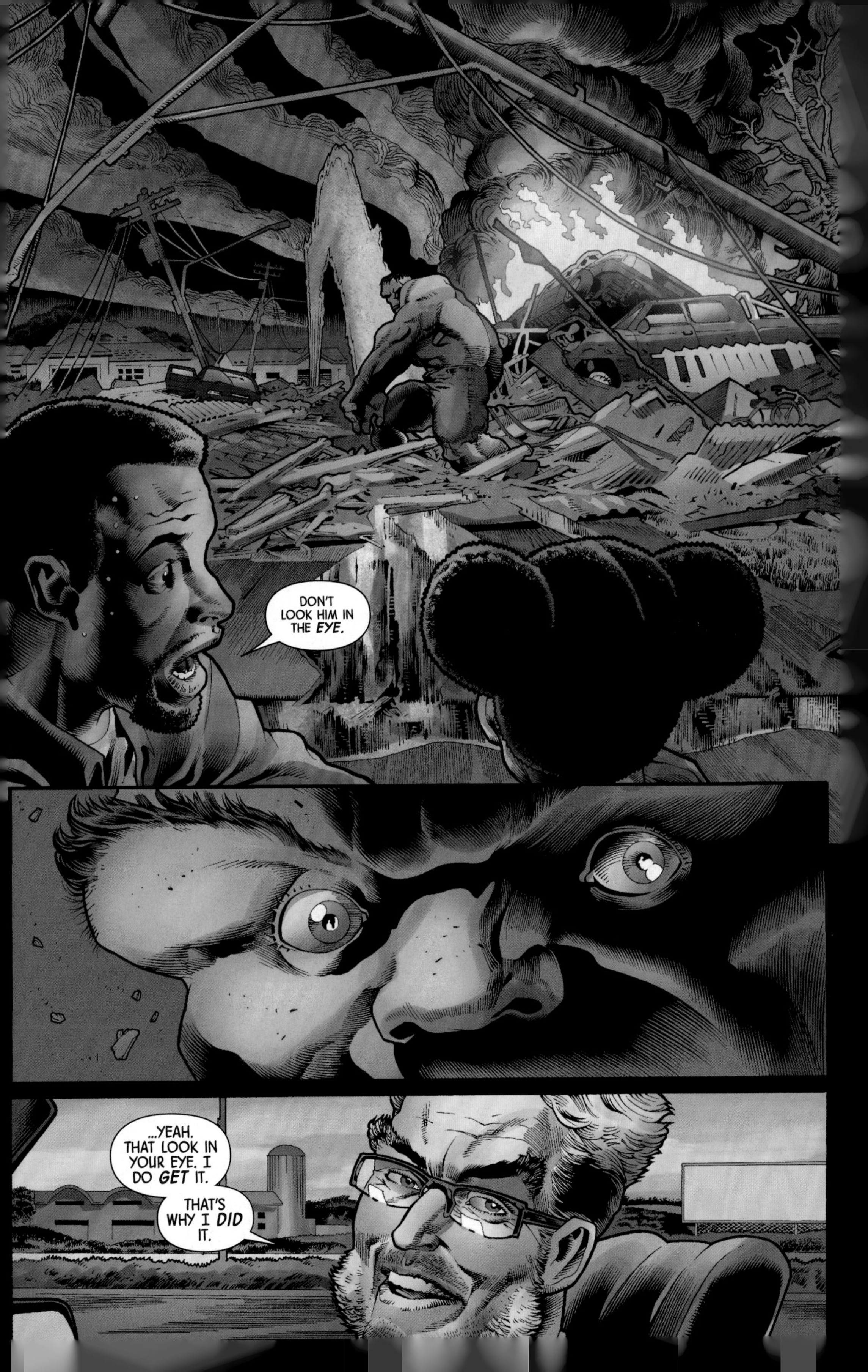
DON'T LOOK HIM IN THE *EYE.*
...YEAH. THAT LOOK IN YOUR EYE. I DO *GET* IT.
THAT'S WHY I *DID* IT.

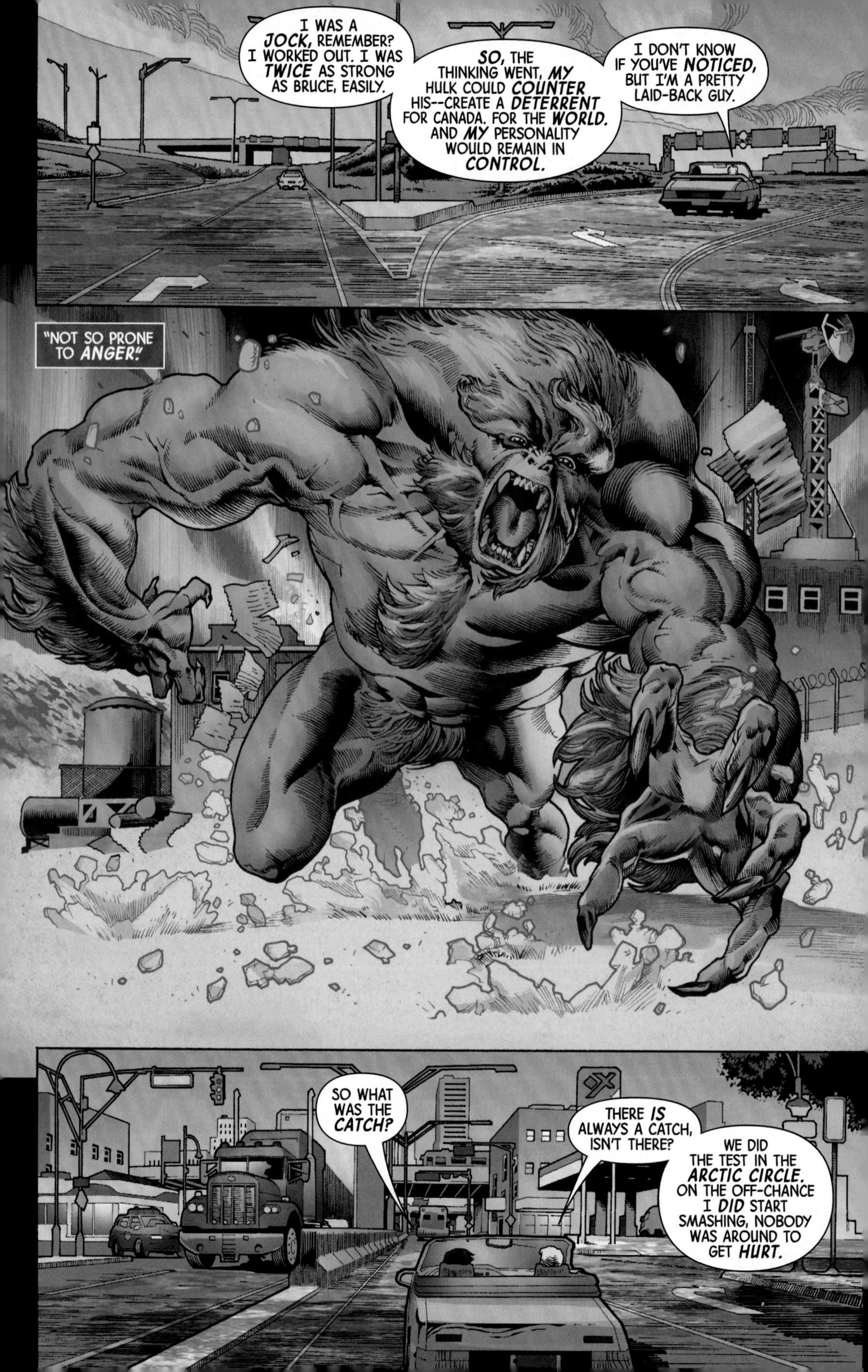
I WAS A JOCK, REMEMBER? I WORKED OUT. I WAS TWICE AS STRONG AS BRUCE, EASILY.
SO, THE THINKING WENT, MY HULK COULD COUNTER HIS--CREATE A DETERRENT FOR CANADA. FOR THE WORLD. AND MY PERSONALITY WOULD REMAIN IN CONTROL.
I DON'T KNOW IF YOU'VE NOTICED, BUT I'M A PRETTY LAID-BACK GUY.
"NOT SO PRONE TO ANGER."
SO WHAT WAS THE CATCH?
THERE IS ALWAYS A CATCH, ISN'T THERE?
WE DID THE TEST IN THE ARCTIC CIRCLE. ON THE OFF-CHANCE I DID START SMASHING, NOBODY WAS AROUND TO GET HURT.

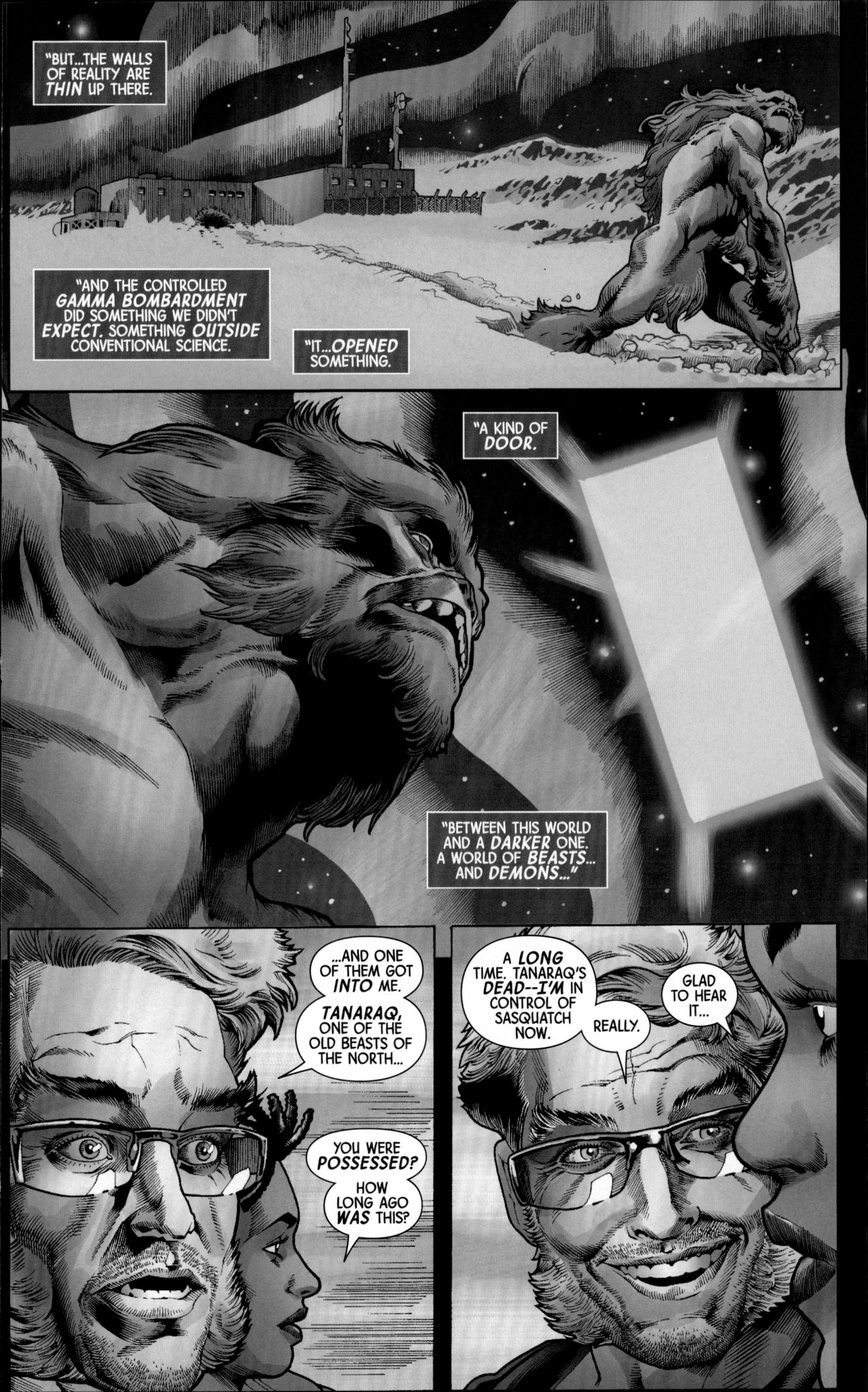

"BUT...THE WALLS OF REALITY ARE THIN UP THERE.
"AND THE CONTROLLED GAMMA BOMBARDMENT DID SOMETHING WE DIDN'T EXPECT. SOMETHING OUTSIDE CONVENTIONAL SCIENCE.
"IT...OPENED SOMETHING.
"A KIND OF DOOR.
"BETWEEN THIS WORLD AND A DARKER ONE. A WORLD OF BEASTS... AND DEMONS..."
...AND ONE OF THEM GOT INTO ME.
TANARAQ, ONE OF THE OLD BEASTS OF THE NORTH...
YOU WERE POSSESSED?
HOW LONG AGO WAS THIS?
A LONG TIME. TANARAQ'S DEAD--I'M IN CONTROL OF SASQUATCH NOW.
REALLY.
GLAD TO HEAR IT...

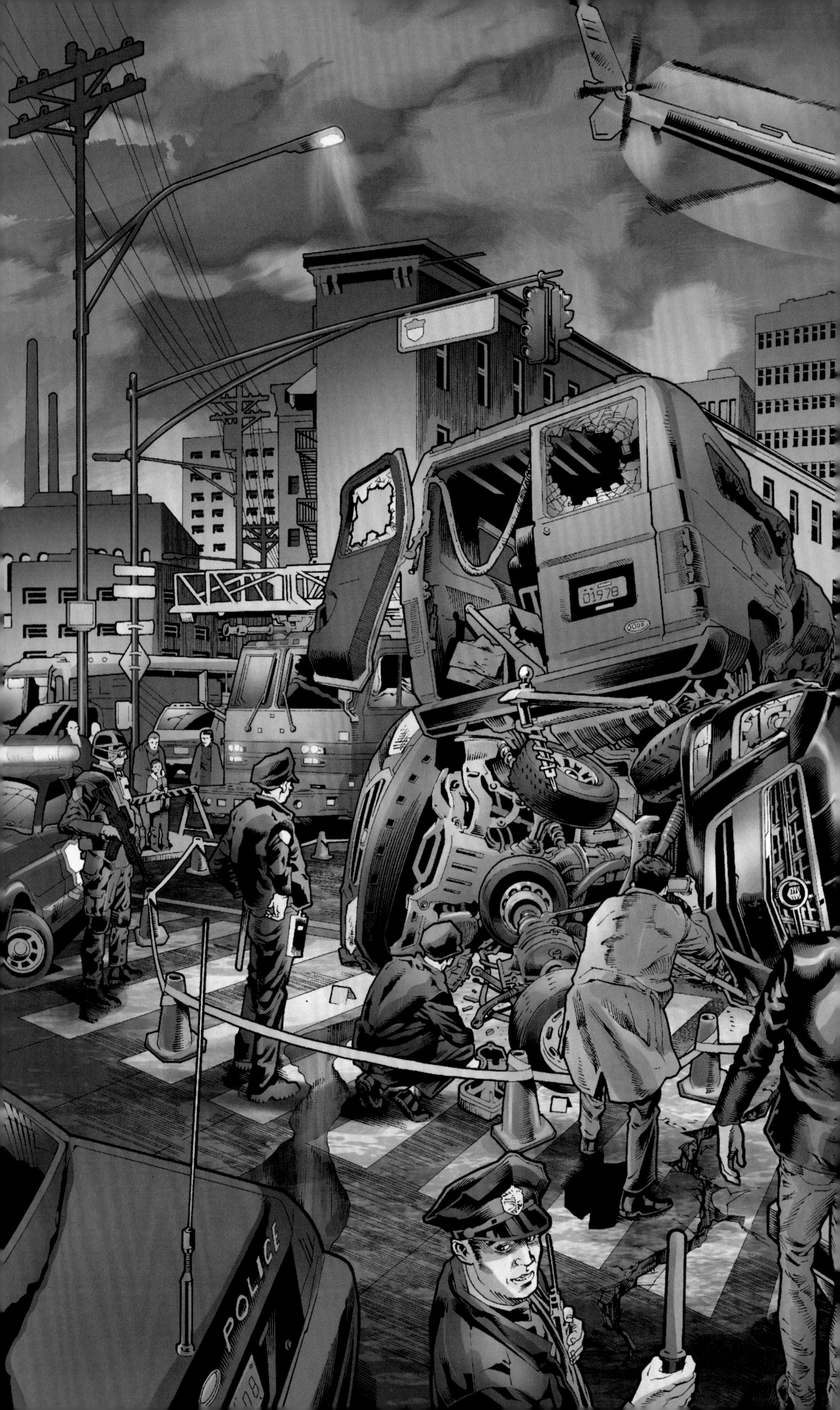
POLICE

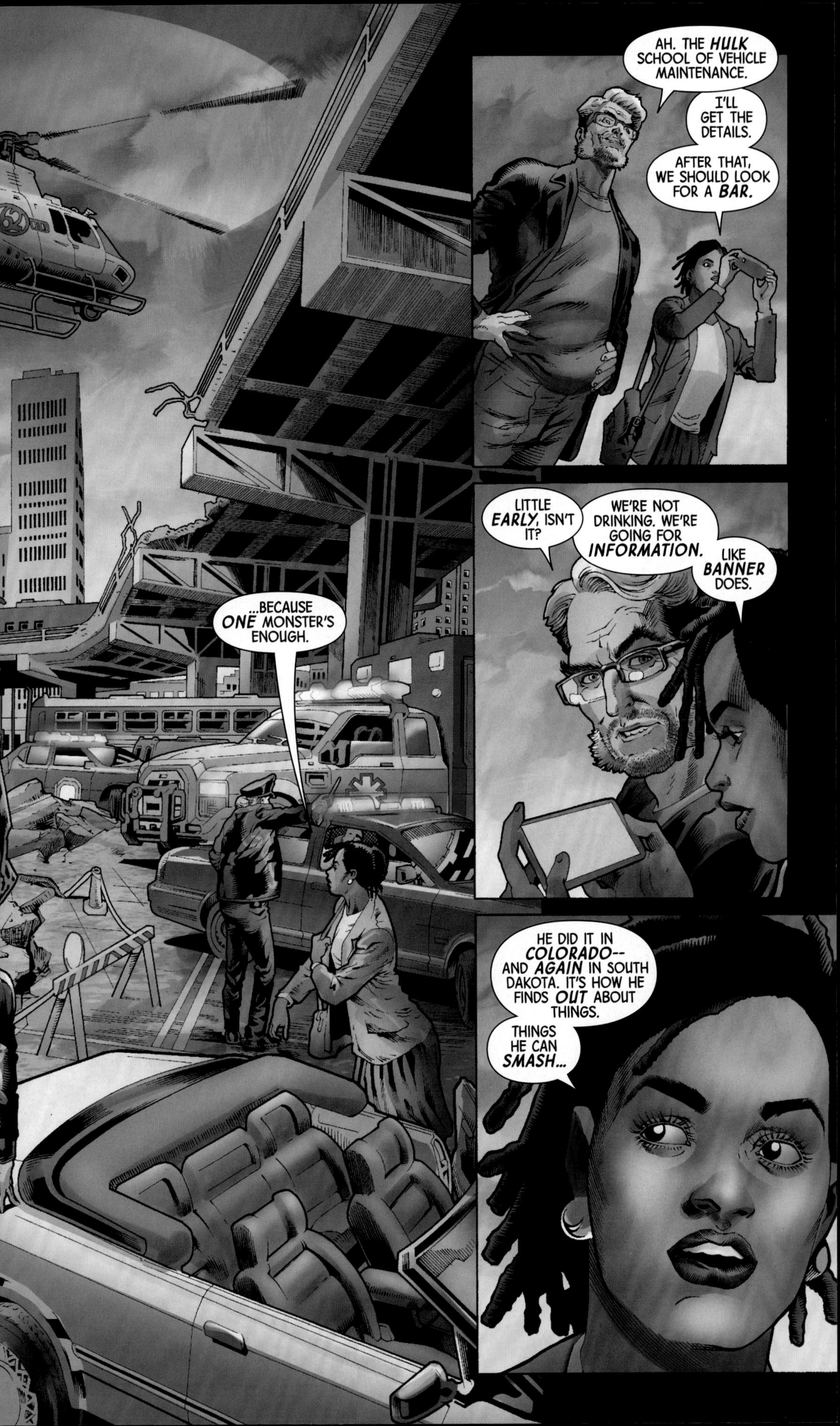
...BECAUSE ONE MONSTER'S ENOUGH.
AH. THE HULK SCHOOL OF VEHICLE MAINTENANCE.
I'LL GET THE DETAILS.
AFTER THAT, WE SHOULD LOOK FOR A BAR.
LITTLE EARLY, ISN'T IT?
WE'RE NOT DRINKING. WE'RE GOING FOR INFORMATION.
LIKE BANNER DOES.
HE DID IT IN COLORADO-- AND AGAIN IN SOUTH DAKOTA. IT'S HOW HE FINDS OUT ABOUT THINGS.
THINGS HE CAN SMASH...

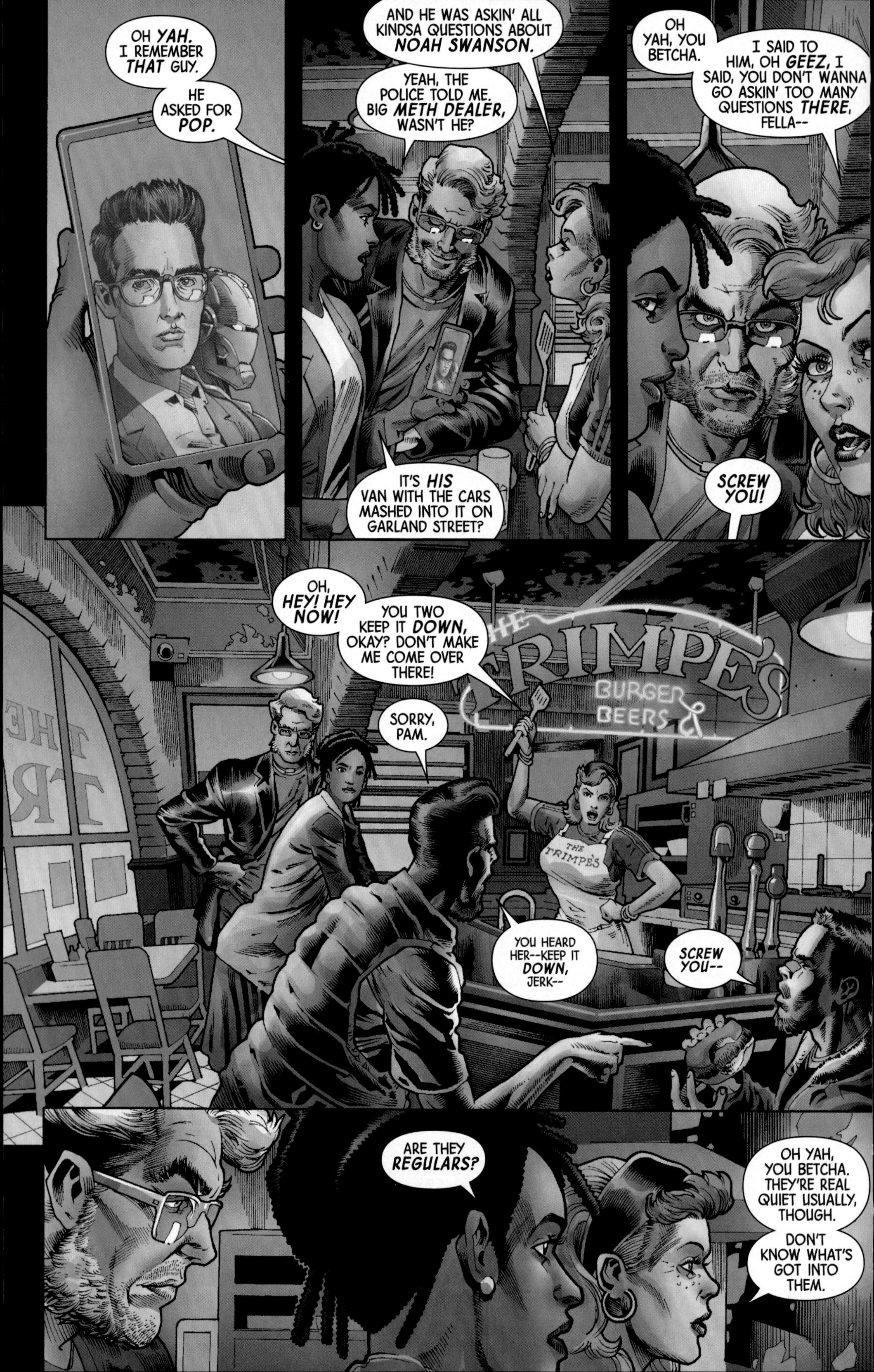
OH YAH. I REMEMBER THAT GUY.
HE ASKED FOR POP.
AND HE WAS ASKIN' ALL KINDSA QUESTIONS ABOUT NOAH SWANSON.
YEAH, THE POLICE TOLD ME. BIG METH DEALER, WASN'T HE?
IT'S HIS VAN WITH THE CARS MASHED INTO IT ON GARLAND STREET?
OH YAH, YOU BETCHA.
I SAID TO HIM, OH GEEZ, I SAID, YOU DON'T WANNA GO ASKIN' TOO MANY QUESTIONS THERE, FELLA--
SCREW YOU!
OH, HEY! HEY NOW!
YOU TWO KEEP IT DOWN, OKAY? DON'T MAKE ME COME OVER THERE!
THE TRIMPE'S
BURGER BEERS &
SORRY, PAM.
THE TRIMPE'S
YOU HEARD HER--KEEP IT DOWN, JERK--
SCREW YOU--
ARE THEY REGULARS?
OH YAH, YOU BETCHA. THEY'RE REAL QUIET USUALLY, THOUGH.
DON'T KNOW WHAT'S GOT INTO THEM.

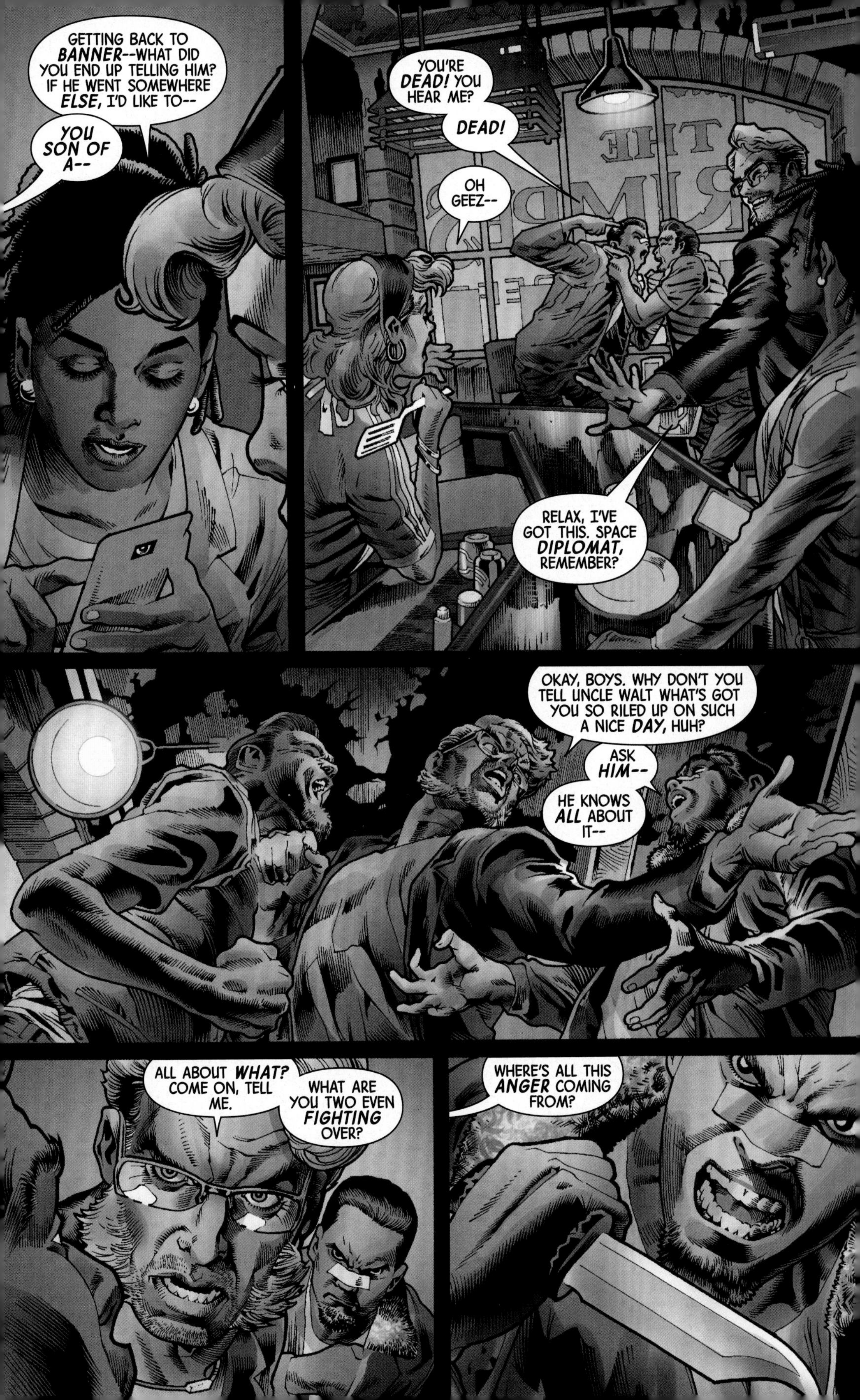

GETTING BACK TO BANNER--WHAT DID YOU END UP TELLING HIM? IF HE WENT SOMEWHERE ELSE, I'D LIKE TO--
YOU SON OF A--
YOU'RE DEAD! YOU HEAR ME?
DEAD!
OH GEEZ--
THE
RELAX, I'VE GOT THIS. SPACE DIPLOMAT, REMEMBER?
OKAY, BOYS. WHY DON'T YOU TELL UNCLE WALT WHAT'S GOT YOU SO RILED UP ON SUCH A NICE DAY, HUH?
ASK HIM--
HE KNOWS ALL ABOUT IT--
ALL ABOUT WHAT? COME ON, TELL ME.
WHAT ARE YOU TWO EVEN FIGHTING OVER?
WHERE'S ALL THIS ANGER COMING FROM?

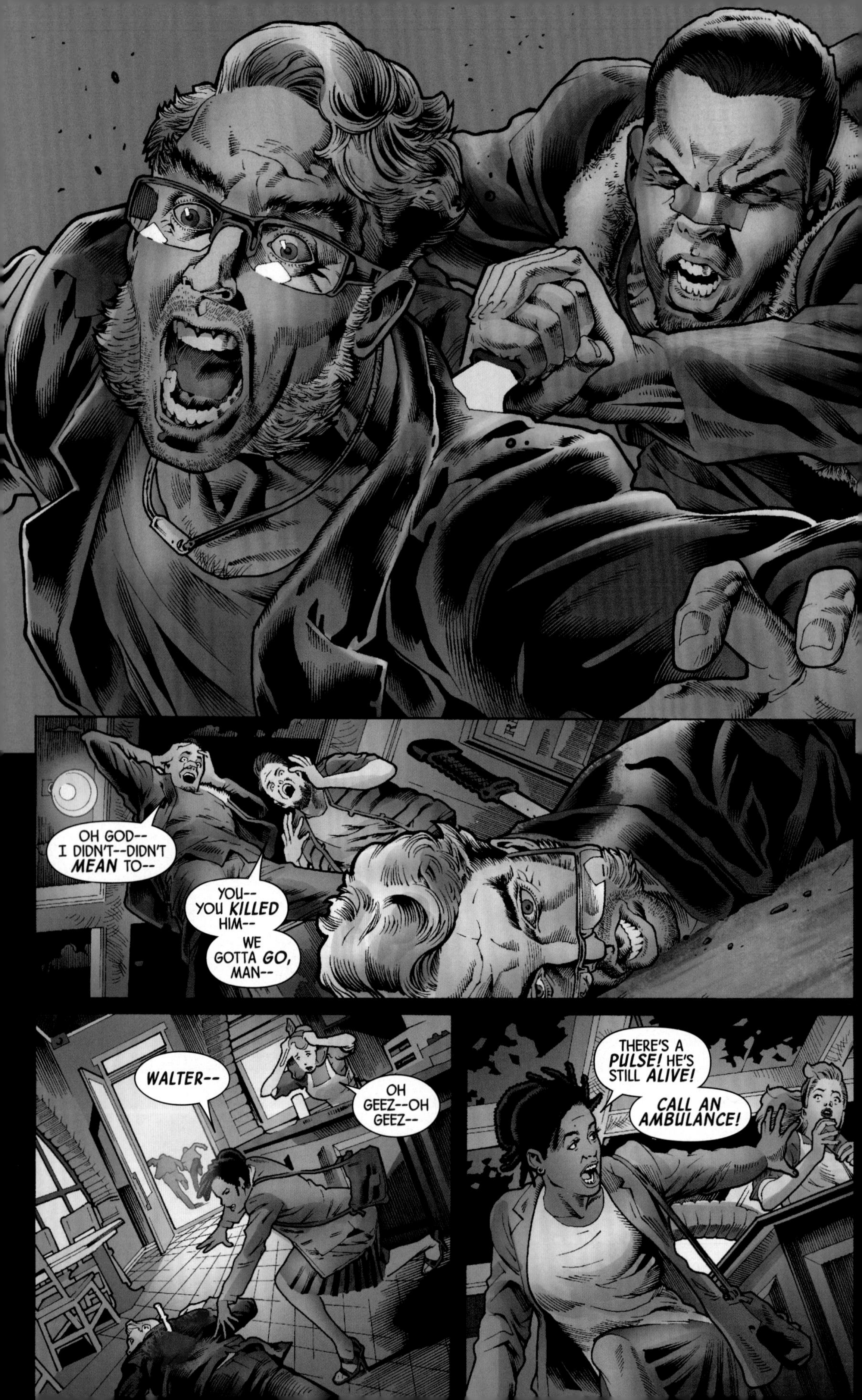
OH GOD-- I DIDN'T--DIDN'T MEAN TO--
YOU-- YOU KILLED HIM--
WE GOTTA GO, MAN--
WALTER--
OH GEEZ--OH GEEZ--
THERE'S A PULSE! HE'S STILL ALIVE!
CALL AN AMBULANCE!

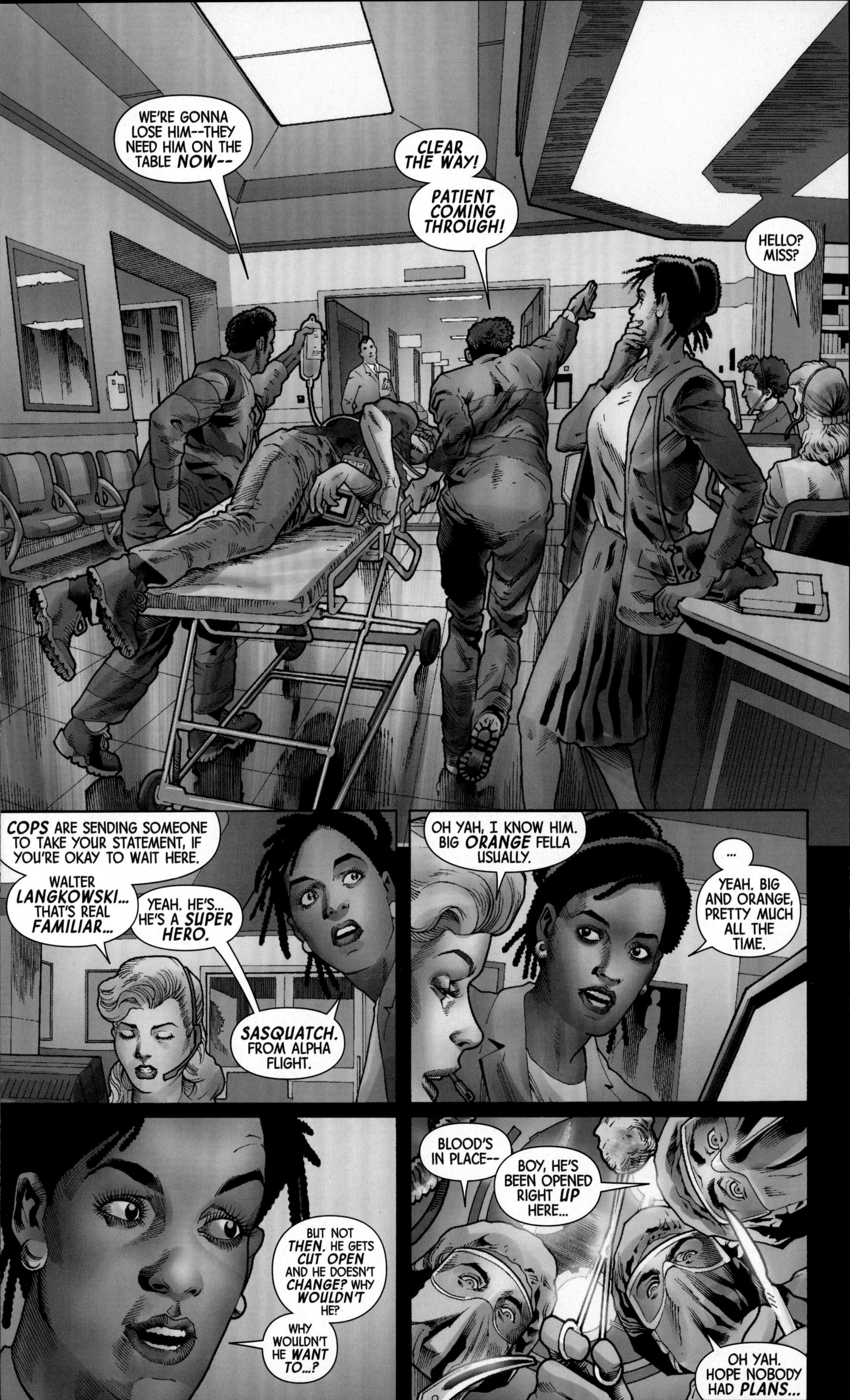
WE'RE GONNA LOSE HIM--THEY NEED HIM ON THE TABLE NOW--
CLEAR THE WAY!
PATIENT COMING THROUGH!
HELLO? MISS?
COPS ARE SENDING SOMEONE TO TAKE YOUR STATEMENT, IF YOU'RE OKAY TO WAIT HERE.
WALTER LANGKOWSKI... THAT'S REAL FAMILIAR...
YEAH. HE'S... HE'S A SUPER HERO.
SASQUATCH. FROM ALPHA FLIGHT.
OH YAH, I KNOW HIM. BIG ORANGE FELLA USUALLY.
...
YEAH. BIG AND ORANGE, PRETTY MUCH ALL THE TIME.
BUT NOT THEN. HE GETS CUT OPEN AND HE DOESN'T CHANGE? WHY WOULDN'T HE?
WHY WOULDN'T HE WANT TO...?
BLOOD'S IN PLACE--
BOY, HE'S BEEN OPENED RIGHT UP HERE...
OH YAH. HOPE NOBODY HAD PLANS...

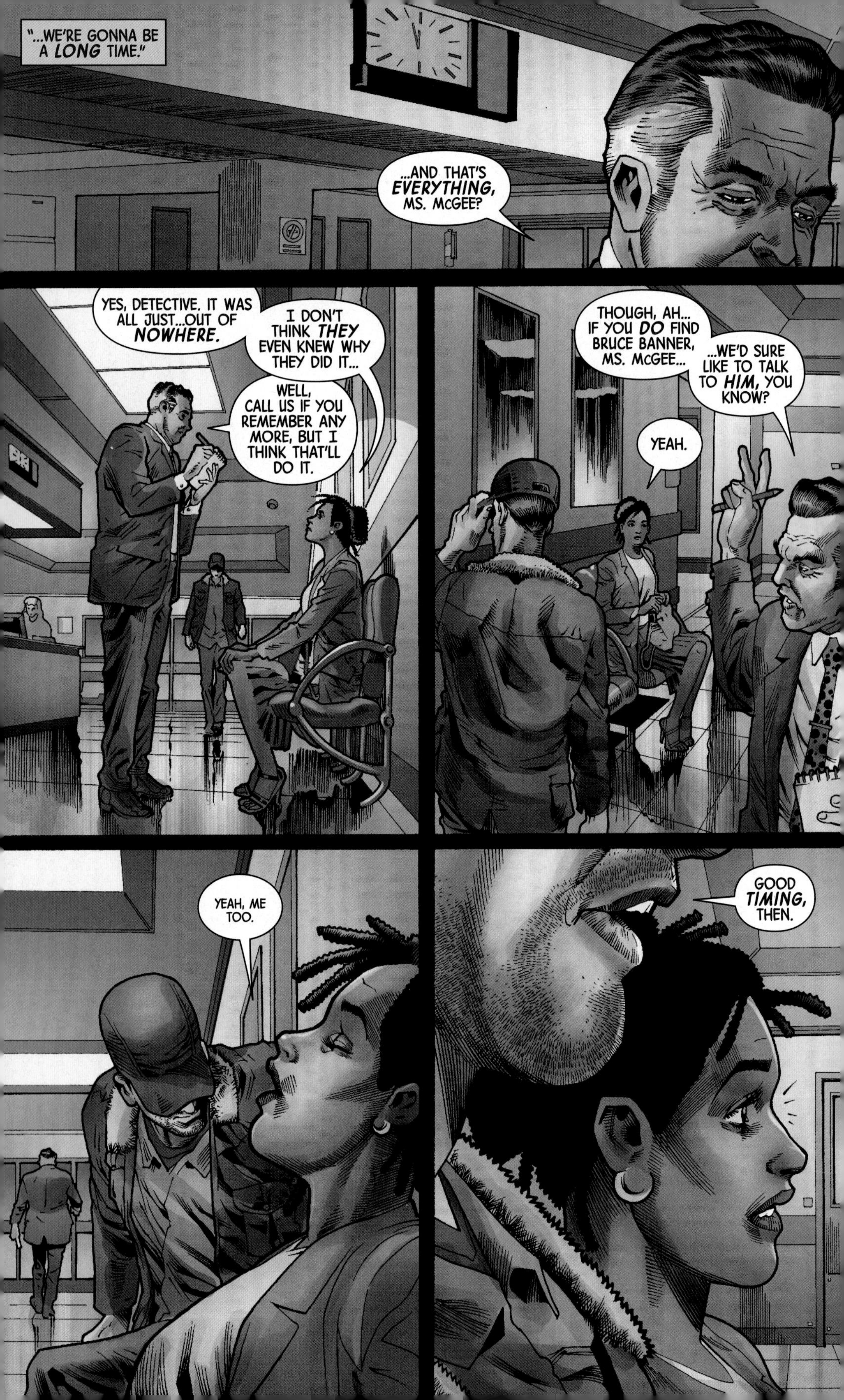
"...WE'RE GONNA BE A LONG TIME."
...AND THAT'S EVERYTHING, MS. McGEE?
YES, DETECTIVE. IT WAS ALL JUST...OUT OF NOWHERE.
I DON'T THINK THEY EVEN KNEW WHY THEY DID IT...
WELL, CALL US IF YOU REMEMBER ANY MORE, BUT I THINK THAT'LL DO IT.
THOUGH, AH... IF YOU DO FIND BRUCE BANNER, MS. McGEE...
...WE'D SURE LIKE TO TALK TO HIM, YOU KNOW?
YEAH.
YEAH, ME TOO.
GOOD TIMING, THEN.

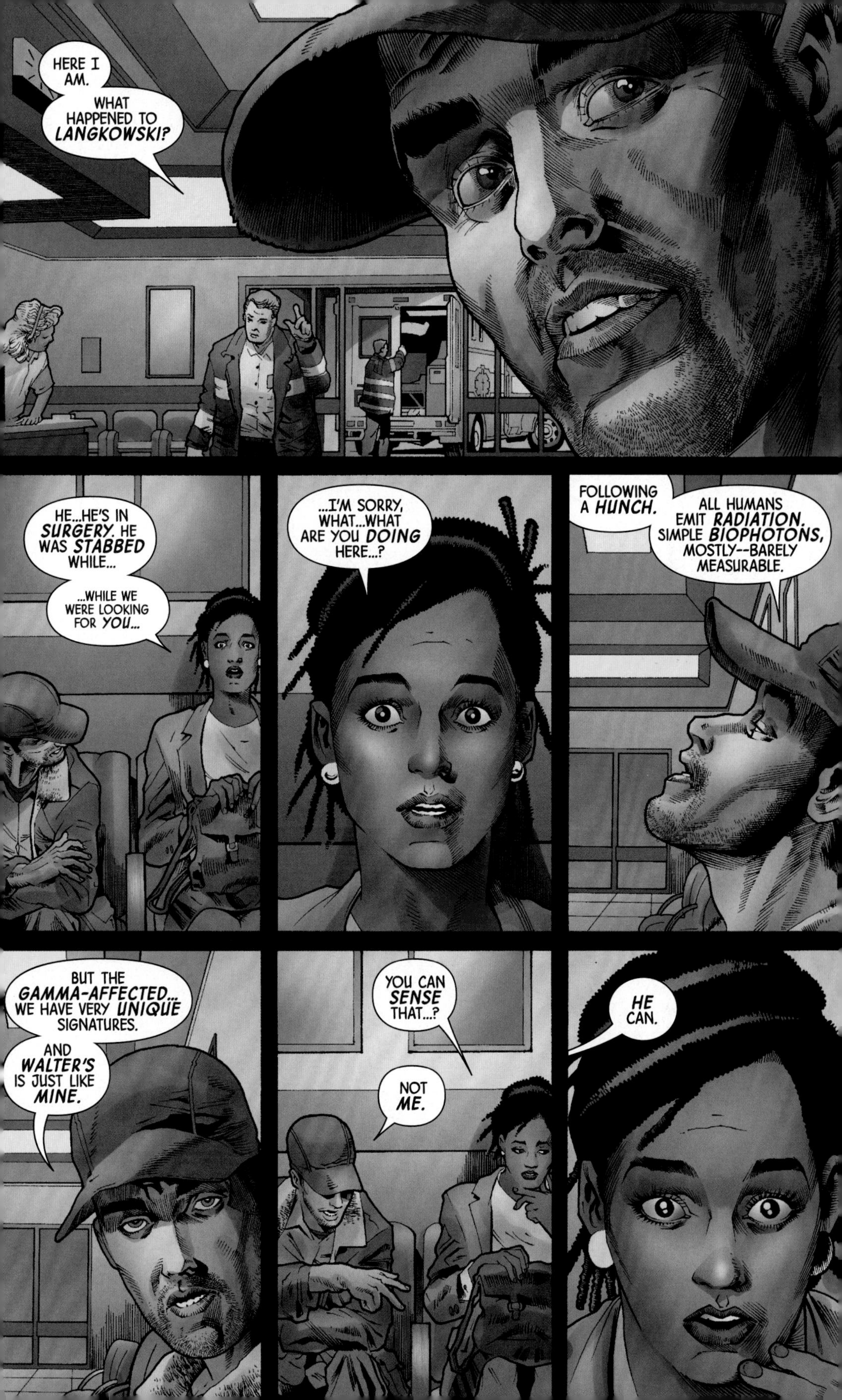
HERE I AM.
WHAT HAPPENED TO LANGKOWSKI?
HE...HE'S IN SURGERY. HE WAS STABBED WHILE...
...WHILE WE WERE LOOKING FOR YOU...
...I'M SORRY, WHAT...WHAT ARE YOU DOING HERE...?
FOLLOWING A HUNCH.
ALL HUMANS EMIT RADIATION. SIMPLE BIOPHOTONS, MOSTLY--BARELY MEASURABLE.
BUT THE GAMMA-AFFECTED... WE HAVE VERY UNIQUE SIGNATURES.
AND WALTER'S IS JUST LIKE MINE.
YOU CAN SENSE THAT...?
NOT ME.
HE CAN.

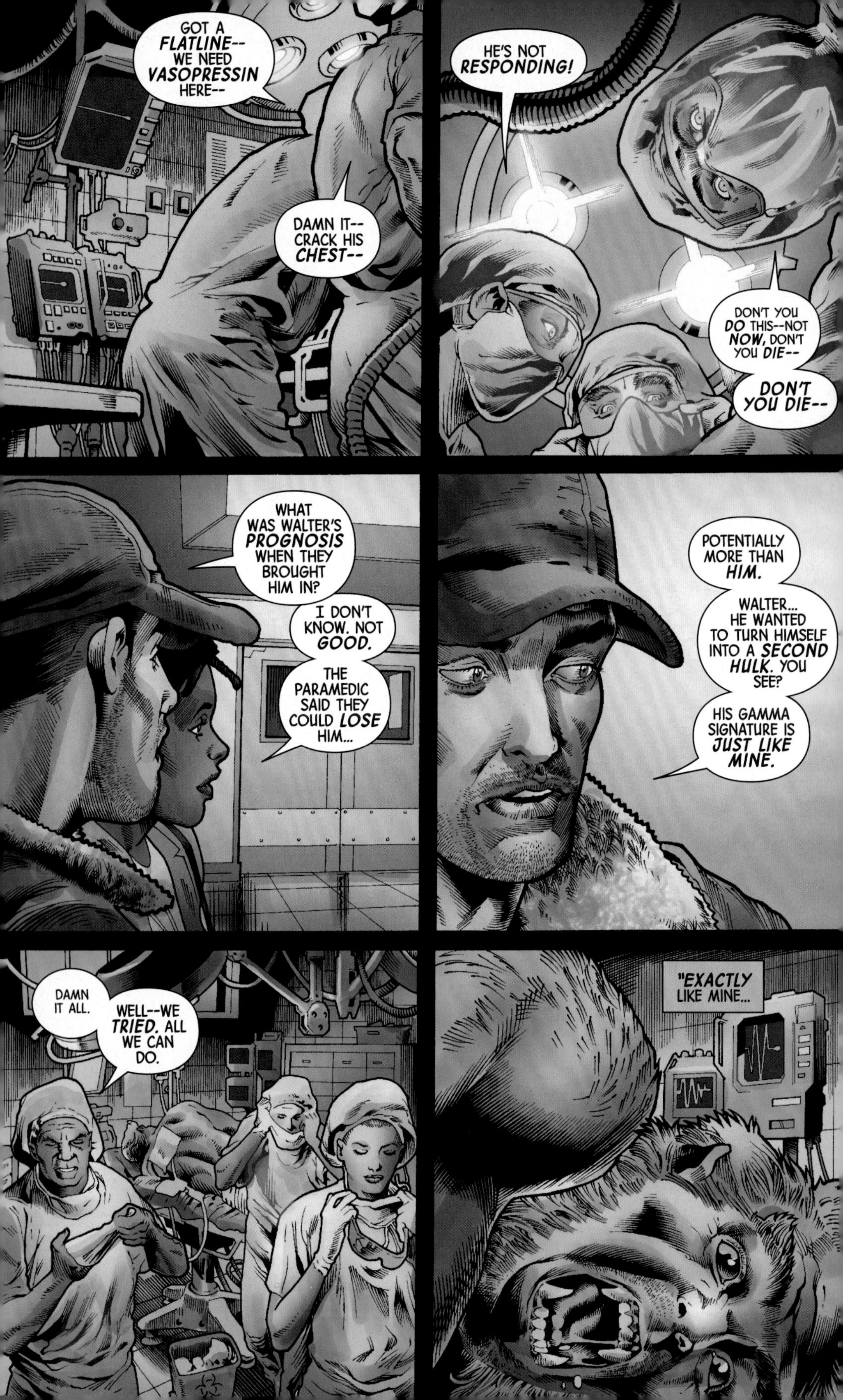

GOT A FLATLINE-- WE NEED VASOPRESSIN HERE--
DAMN IT-- CRACK HIS CHEST--
HE'S NOT RESPONDING!
DON'T YOU DO THIS--NOT NOW, DON'T YOU DIE--
DON'T YOU DIE--
WHAT WAS WALTER'S PROGNOSIS WHEN THEY BROUGHT HIM IN?
I DON'T KNOW. NOT GOOD.
THE PARAMEDIC SAID THEY COULD LOSE HIM...
POTENTIALLY MORE THAN HIM.
WALTER... HE WANTED TO TURN HIMSELF INTO A SECOND HULK. YOU SEE?
HIS GAMMA SIGNATURE IS JUST LIKE MINE.
DAMN IT ALL.
WELL--WE TRIED. ALL WE CAN DO.
"EXACTLY LIKE MINE...

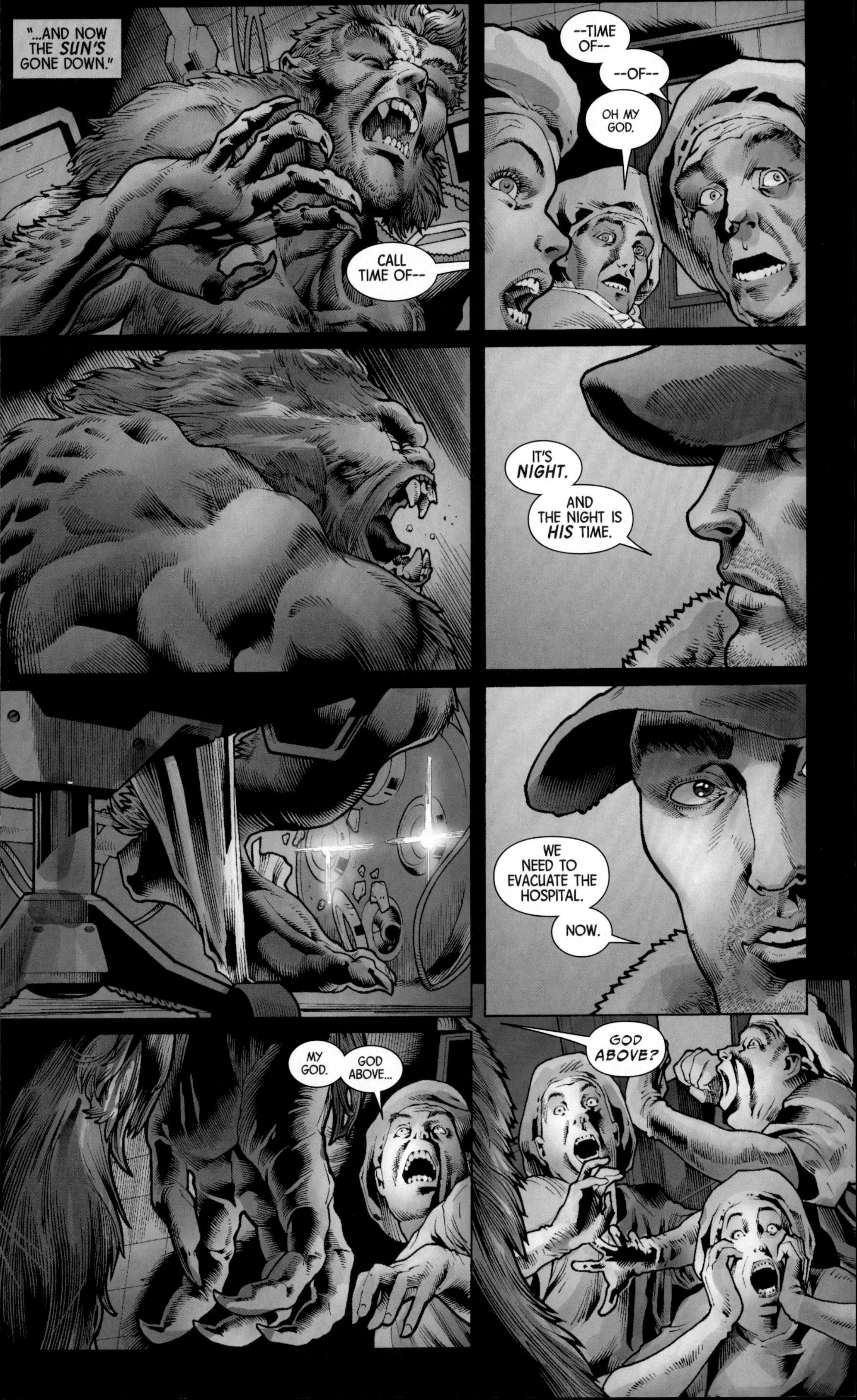
"...AND NOW THE SUN'S GONE DOWN."
CALL TIME OF--
--TIME OF--
--OF--
OH MY GOD.
IT'S NIGHT.
AND THE NIGHT IS HIS TIME.
WE NEED TO EVACUATE THE HOSPITAL.
NOW.
MY GOD.
GOD ABOVE...
GOD ABOVE?

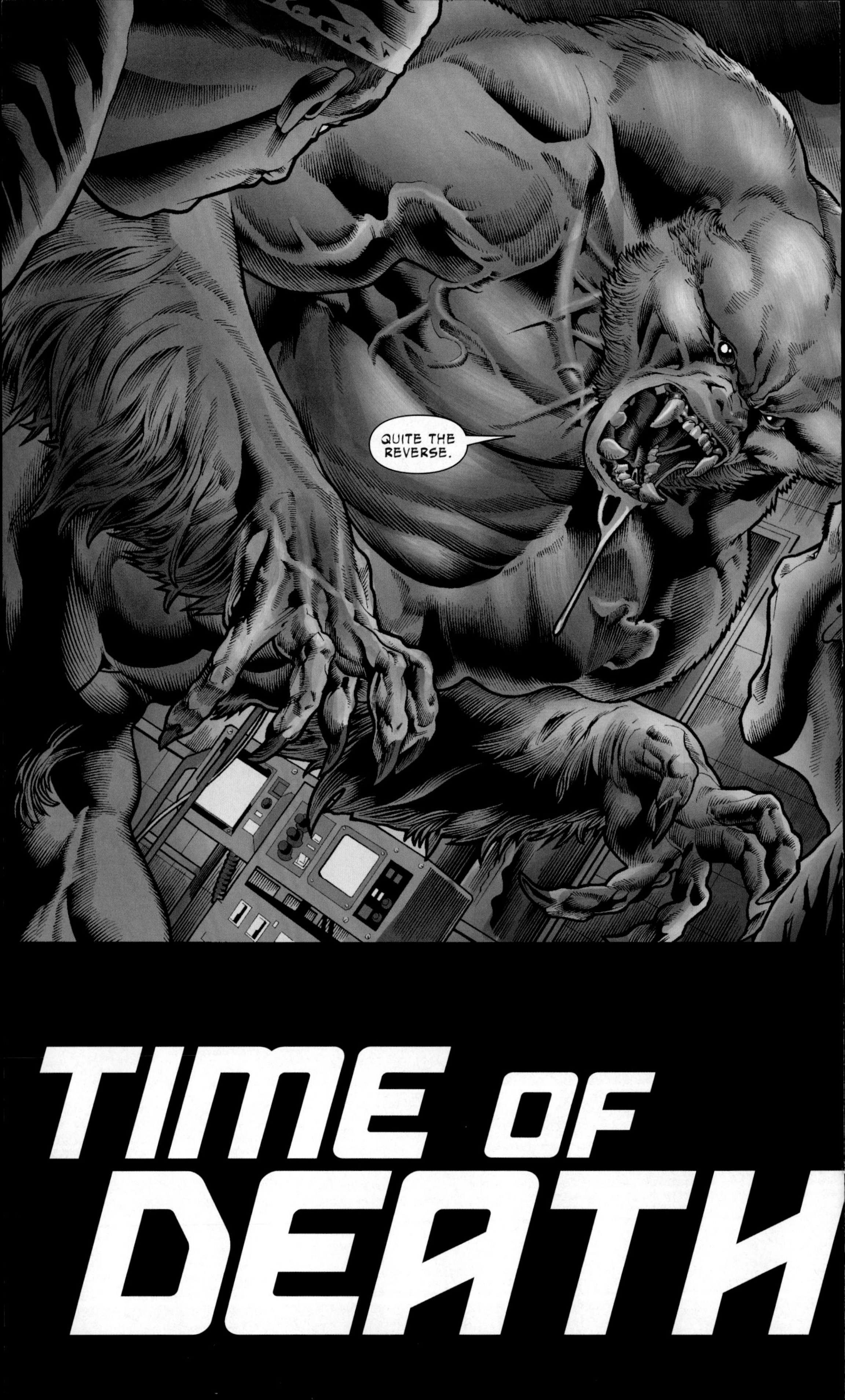
QUITE THE REVERSE.

# TIME OF DEATH

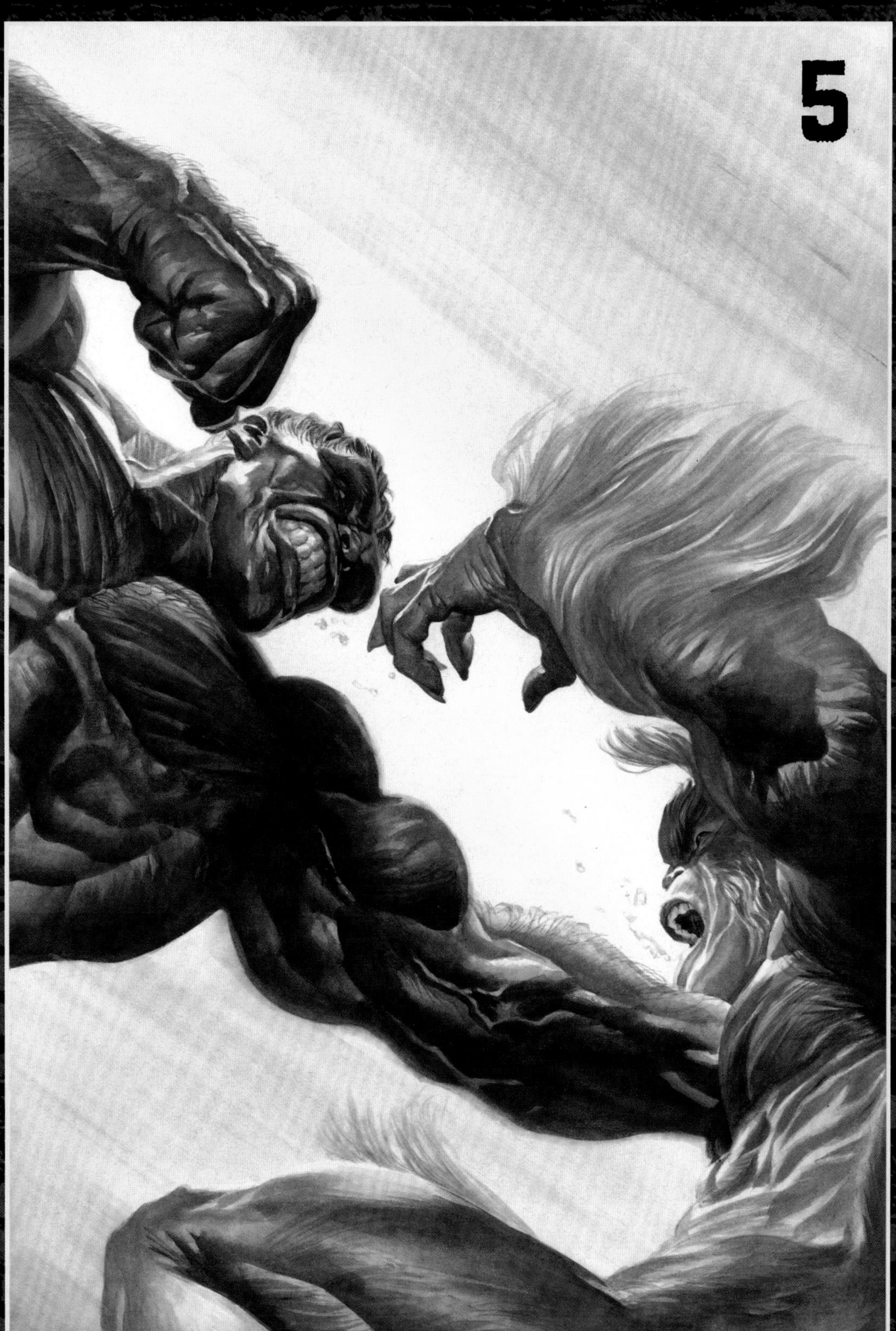
5

"MY DEVIL HAD BEEN LONG CAGED, HE CAME OUT ROARING."

-ROBERT LOUIS STEVENSON, *THE STRANGE CASE OF DR. JEKYLL AND MR. HYDE*

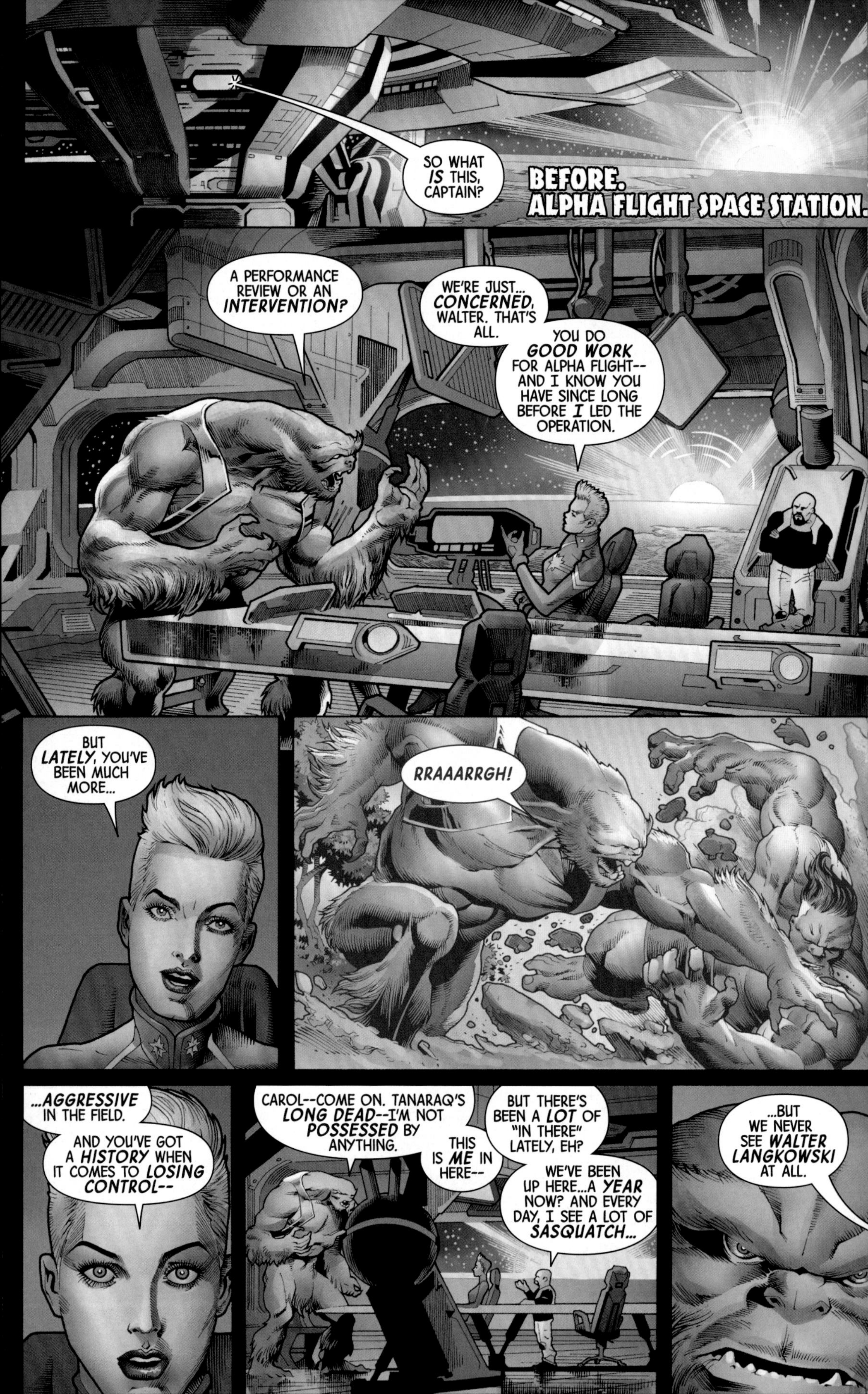
SO WHAT *IS* THIS, CAPTAIN?
BEFORE. ALPHA FLIGHT SPACE STATION.
A PERFORMANCE REVIEW OR AN *INTERVENTION?*
WE'RE JUST... *CONCERNED*, WALTER. THAT'S ALL.
YOU DO *GOOD WORK* FOR ALPHA FLIGHT-- AND I KNOW YOU HAVE SINCE LONG BEFORE *I* LED THE OPERATION.
BUT *LATELY*, YOU'VE BEEN MUCH MORE...
RRAAARRGH!
...*AGGRESSIVE* IN THE FIELD.
AND YOU'VE GOT A *HISTORY* WHEN IT COMES TO *LOSING CONTROL*--
CAROL--COME ON. TANARAQ'S *LONG DEAD*--I'M NOT *POSSESSED* BY ANYTHING.
THIS IS *ME* IN HERE--
BUT THERE'S BEEN A *LOT* OF "IN THERE" LATELY, EH?
WE'VE BEEN UP HERE...A *YEAR* NOW? AND EVERY DAY, I SEE A LOT OF *SASQUATCH*...
...BUT WE NEVER SEE *WALTER LANGKOWSKI* AT ALL.

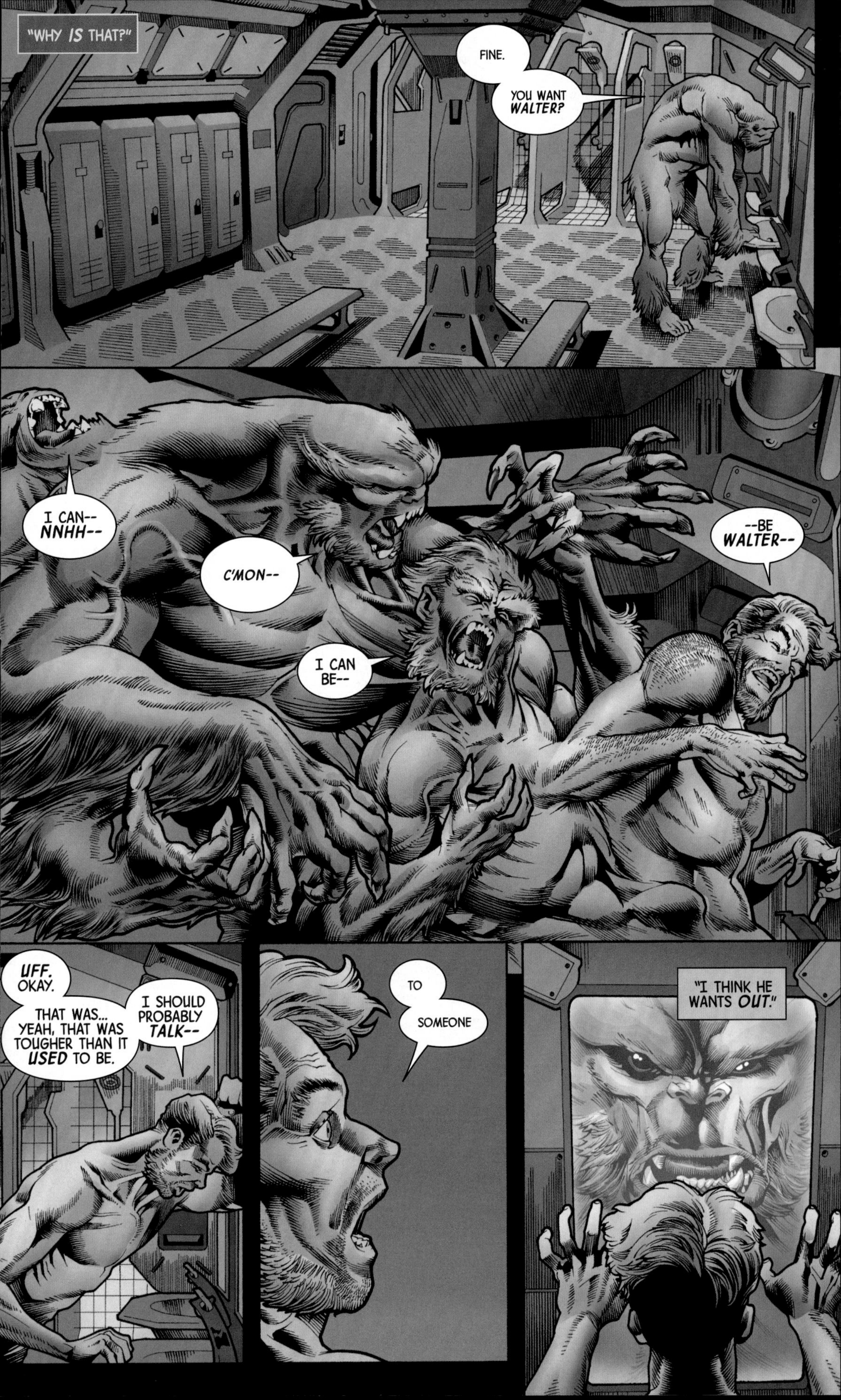
"WHY *IS* THAT?"
FINE.
YOU WANT *WALTER?*
I CAN-- *NNHH--*
*C'MON--*
I CAN BE--
--BE *WALTER--*
*UFF.* OKAY.
THAT WAS... YEAH, THAT WAS TOUGHER THAN IT *USED* TO BE.
I SHOULD PROBABLY *TALK--*
TO
SOMEONE
"I THINK HE WANTS *OUT.*"

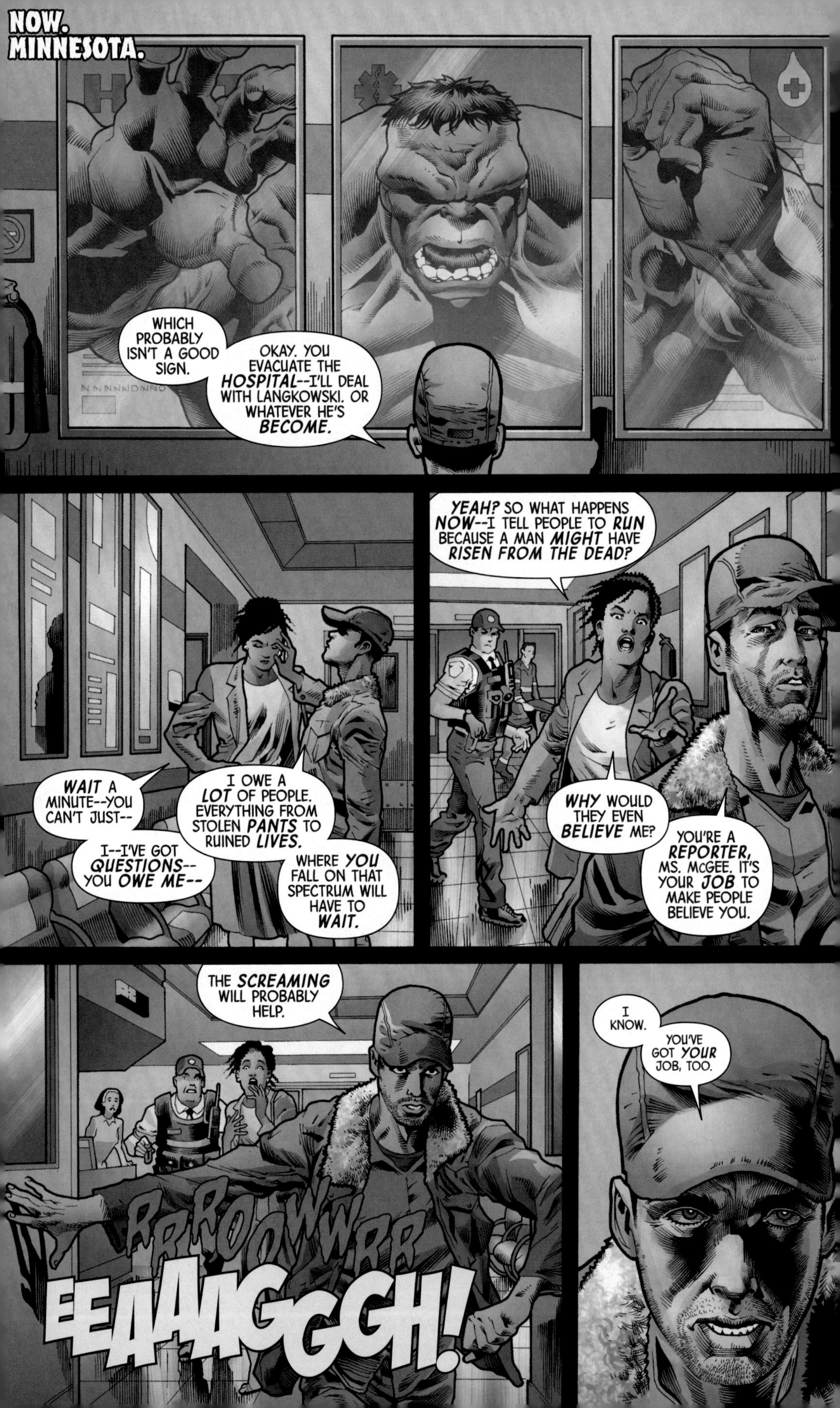
NOW. MINNESOTA.
WHICH PROBABLY ISN'T A GOOD SIGN.
OKAY. YOU EVACUATE THE HOSPITAL--I'LL DEAL WITH LANGKOWSKI. OR WHATEVER HE'S BECOME.
WAIT A MINUTE--YOU CAN'T JUST--
I--I'VE GOT QUESTIONS--YOU OWE ME--
I OWE A LOT OF PEOPLE. EVERYTHING FROM STOLEN PANTS TO RUINED LIVES.
WHERE YOU FALL ON THAT SPECTRUM WILL HAVE TO WAIT.
YEAH? SO WHAT HAPPENS NOW--I TELL PEOPLE TO RUN BECAUSE A MAN MIGHT HAVE RISEN FROM THE DEAD?
WHY WOULD THEY EVEN BELIEVE ME?
YOU'RE A REPORTER, MS. McGEE. IT'S YOUR JOB TO MAKE PEOPLE BELIEVE YOU.
THE SCREAMING WILL PROBABLY HELP.
RRROOWWRR
EEAAAGGGH!
I KNOW.
YOU'VE GOT YOUR JOB, TOO.

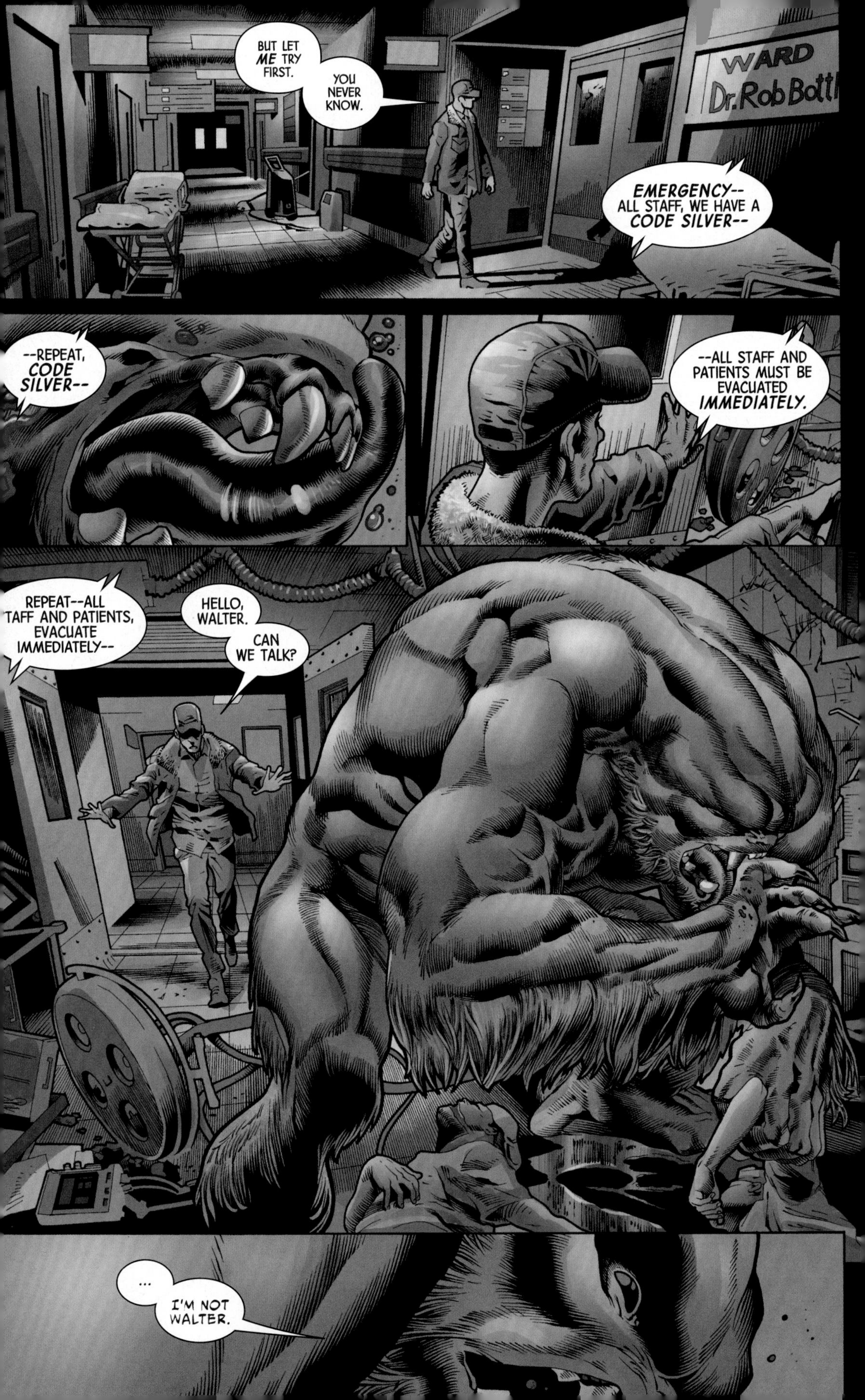
BUT LET ME TRY FIRST.
YOU NEVER KNOW.
WARD Dr. Rob Bott
EMERGENCY-- ALL STAFF, WE HAVE A CODE SILVER--
--REPEAT, CODE SILVER--
--ALL STAFF AND PATIENTS MUST BE EVACUATED IMMEDIATELY.
REPEAT--ALL TAFF AND PATIENTS, EVACUATE IMMEDIATELY--
HELLO, WALTER.
CAN WE TALK?
...
I'M NOT WALTER.

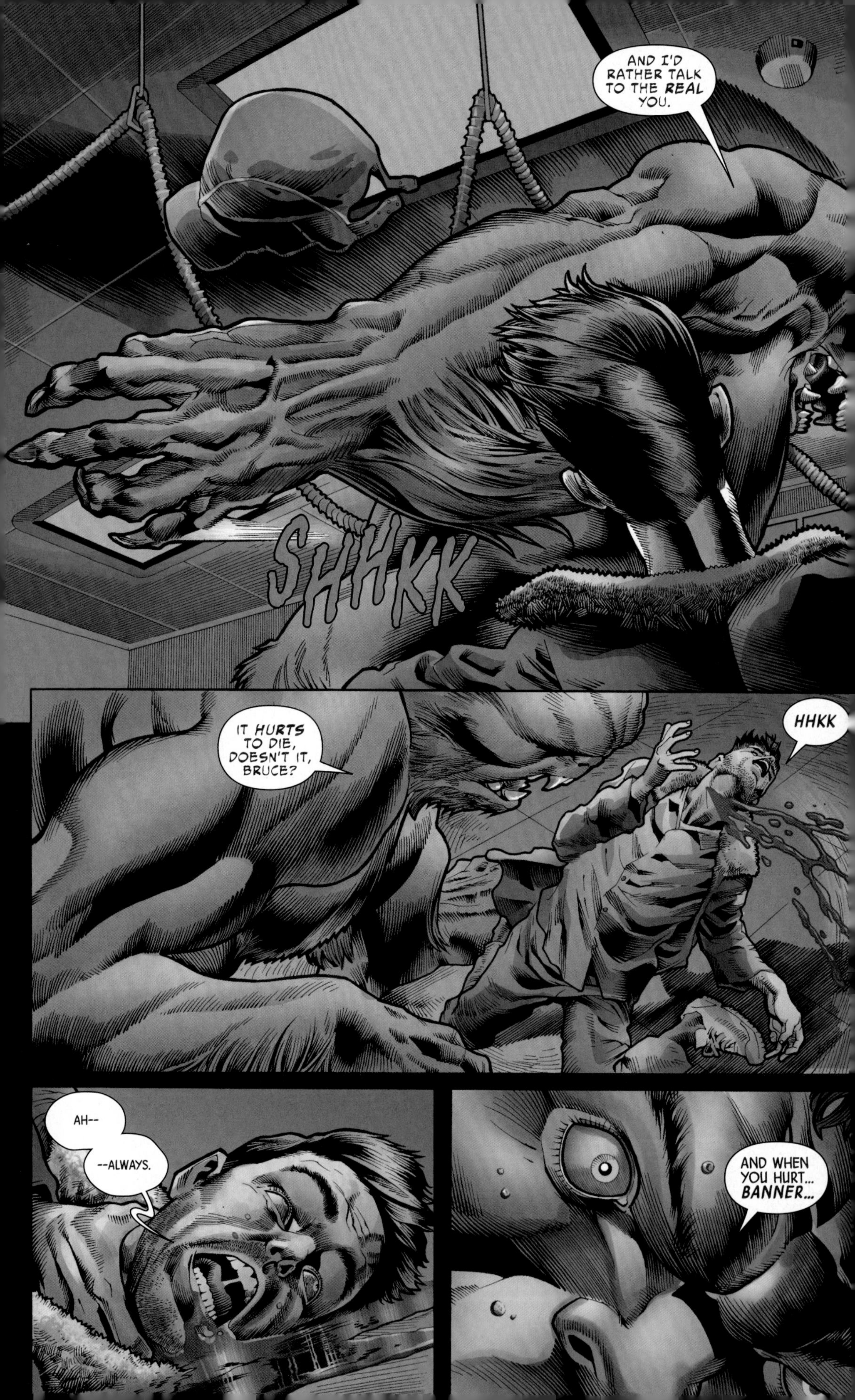
AND I'D RATHER TALK TO THE **REAL** YOU.
SHHKK
IT **HURTS** TO DIE, DOESN'T IT, BRUCE?
HHKK
AH--
--ALWAYS.
AND WHEN YOU HURT... **BANNER...**

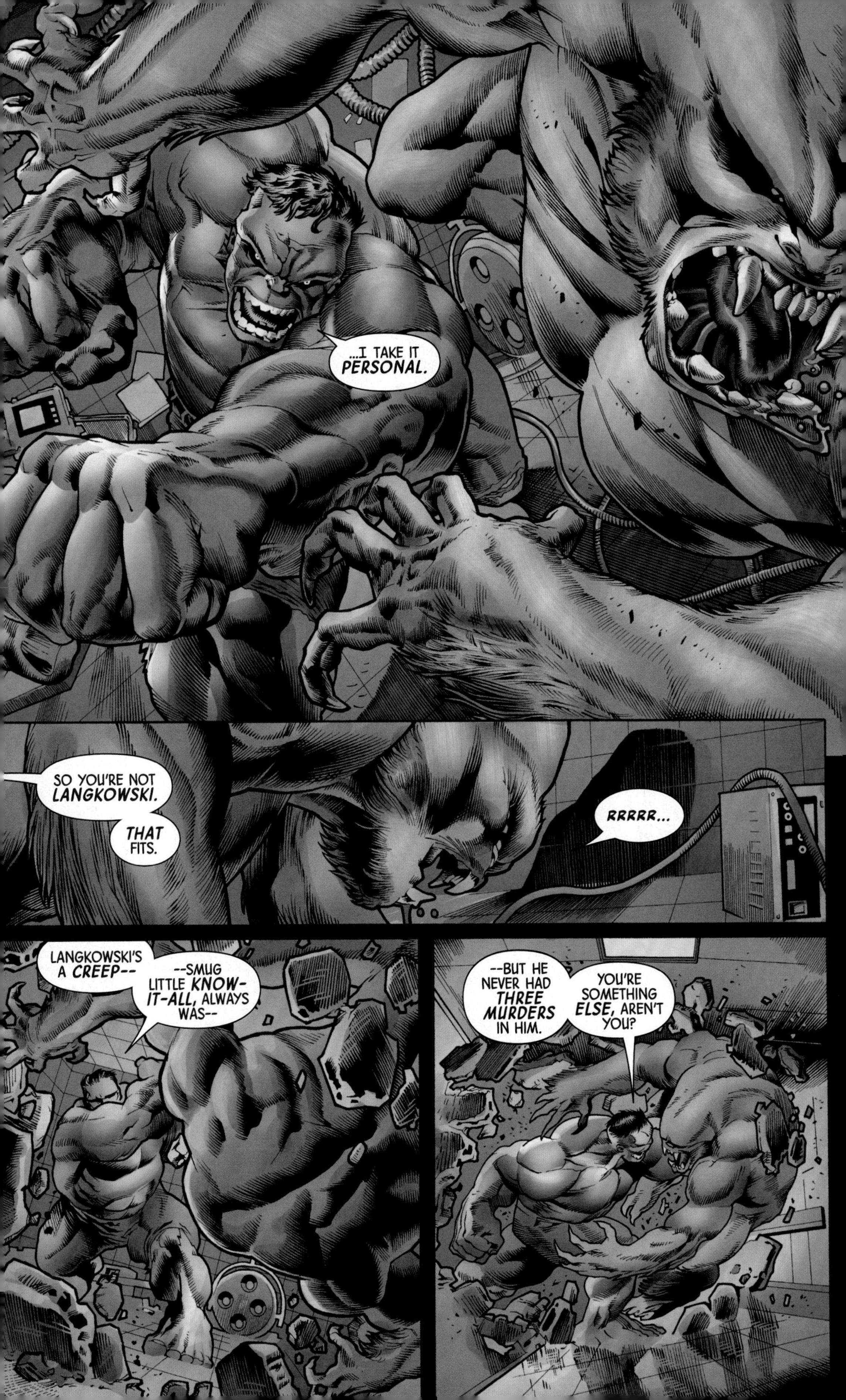
...I TAKE IT PERSONAL.
SO YOU'RE NOT LANGKOWSKI.
THAT FITS.
RRRRR...
LANGKOWSKI'S A CREEP--
--SMUG LITTLE KNOW-IT-ALL, ALWAYS WAS--
--BUT HE NEVER HAD THREE MURDERS IN HIM.
YOU'RE SOMETHING ELSE, AREN'T YOU?

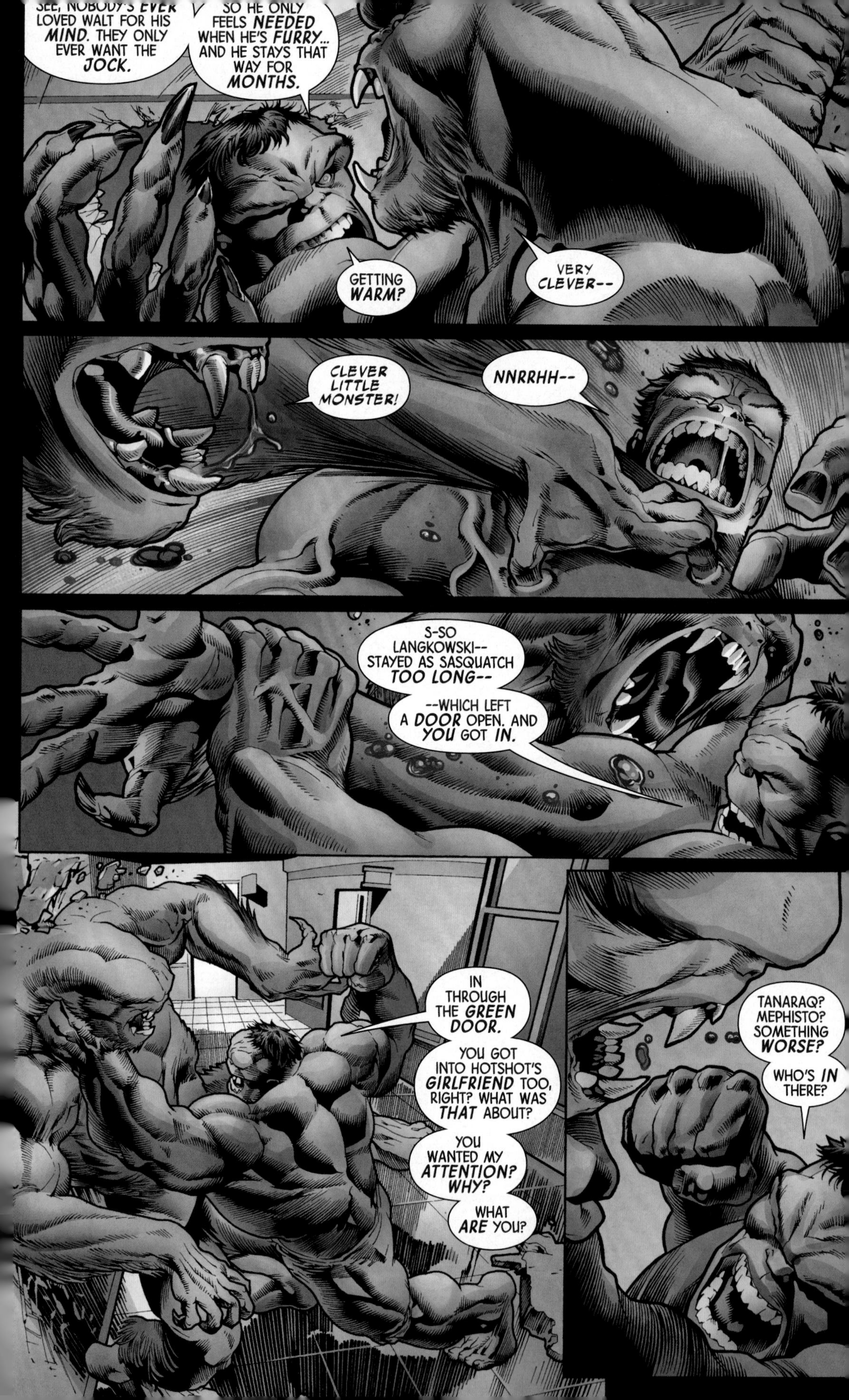
SEE, NOBODY'S EVER LOVED WALT FOR HIS MIND. THEY ONLY EVER WANT THE JOCK.
SO HE ONLY FEELS NEEDED WHEN HE'S FURRY... AND HE STAYS THAT WAY FOR MONTHS.
GETTING WARM?
VERY CLEVER--
CLEVER LITTLE MONSTER!
NNRRHH--
S-SO LANGKOWSKI-- STAYED AS SASQUATCH TOO LONG--
--WHICH LEFT A DOOR OPEN. AND YOU GOT IN.
IN THROUGH THE GREEN DOOR.
YOU GOT INTO HOTSHOT'S GIRLFRIEND TOO, RIGHT? WHAT WAS THAT ABOUT?
YOU WANTED MY ATTENTION? WHY?
WHAT ARE YOU?
TANARAQ? MEPHISTO? SOMETHING WORSE?
WHO'S IN THERE?

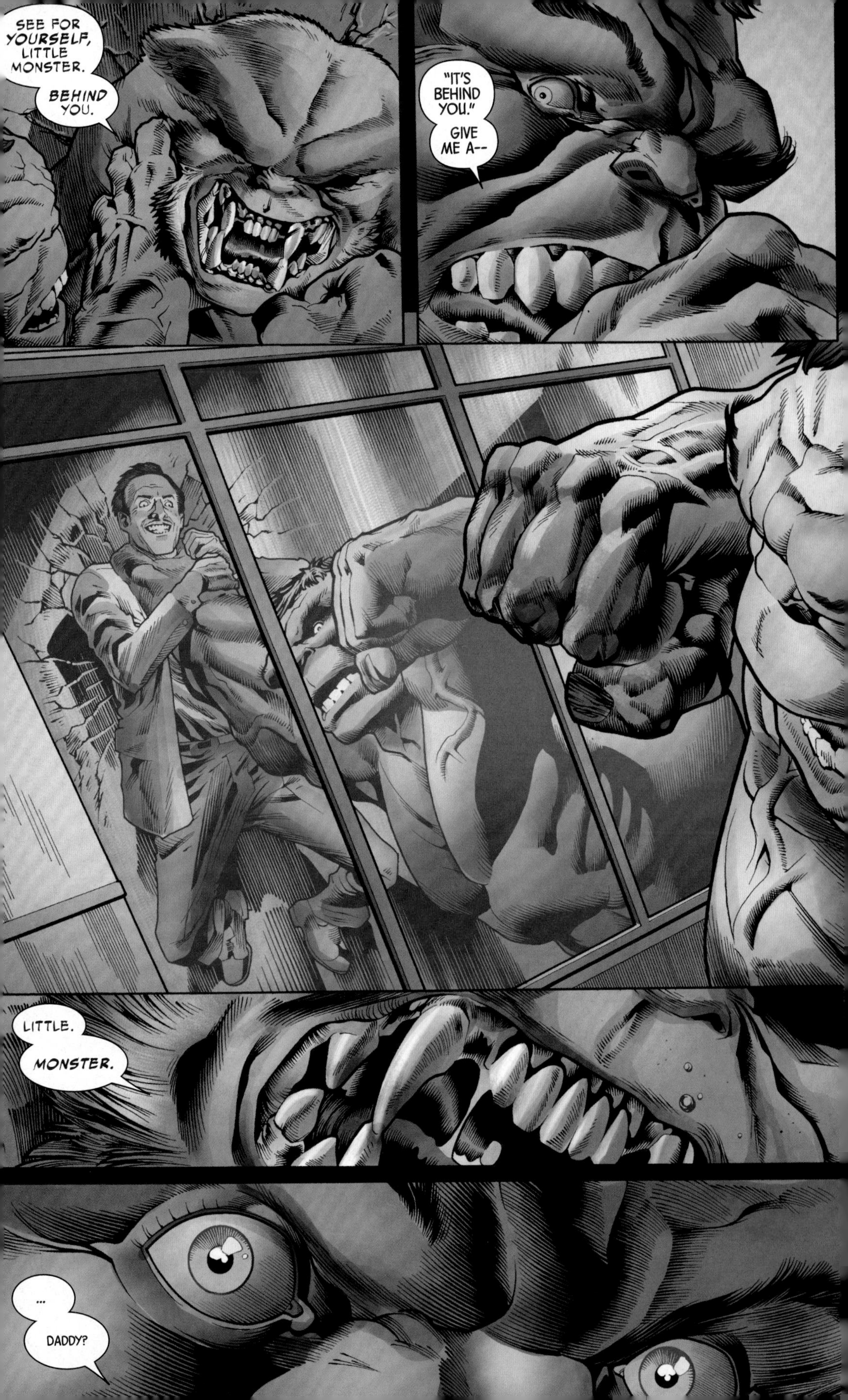
SEE FOR YOURSELF, LITTLE MONSTER.
BEHIND YOU.
"IT'S BEHIND YOU."
GIVE ME A--
LITTLE.
MONSTER.
...
DADDY?

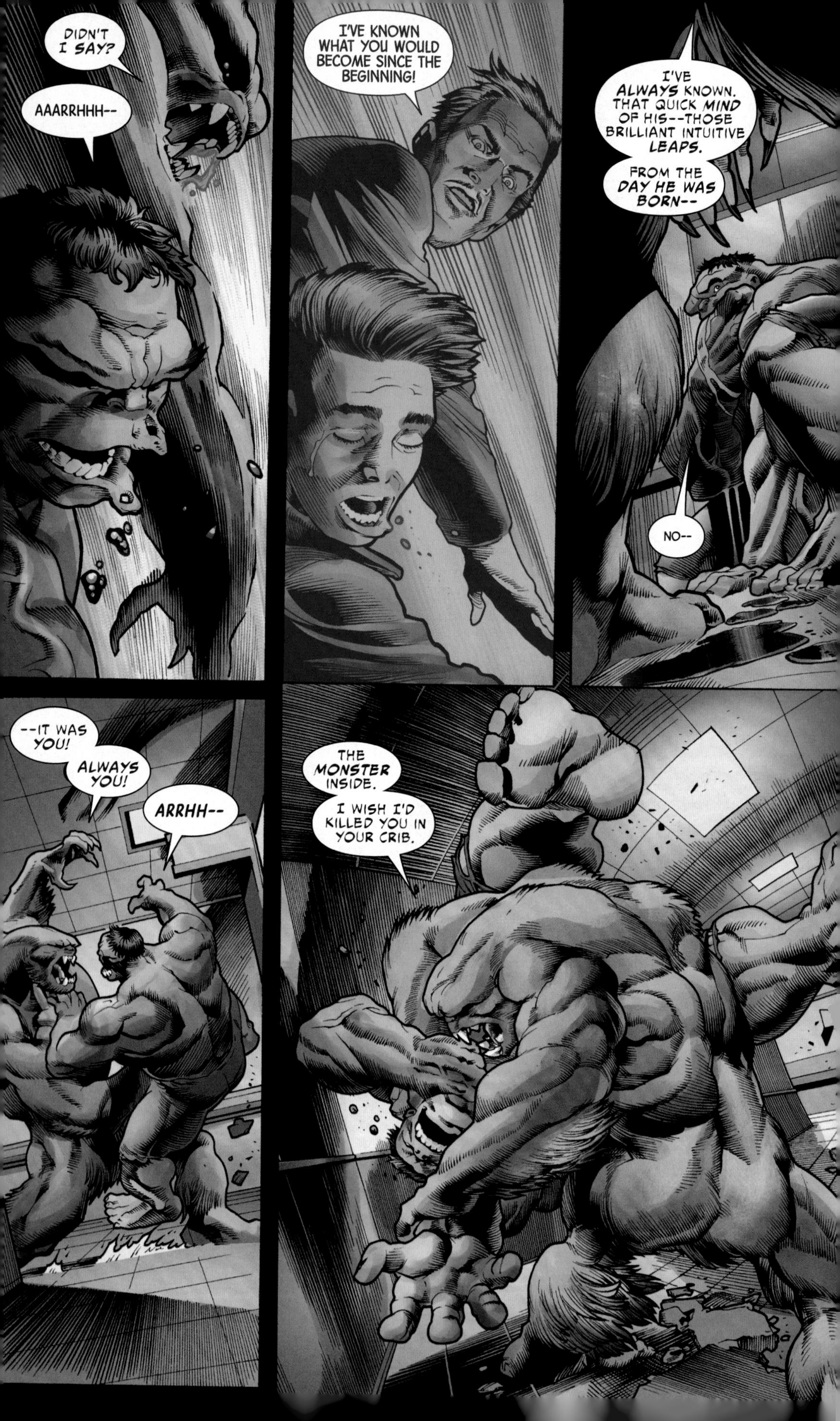
DIDN'T I SAY?
AAARRHHH--
I'VE KNOWN WHAT YOU WOULD BECOME SINCE THE BEGINNING!
I'VE ALWAYS KNOWN. THAT QUICK MIND OF HIS--THOSE BRILLIANT INTUITIVE LEAPS.
FROM THE DAY HE WAS BORN--
NO--
--IT WAS YOU!
ALWAYS YOU!
ARRHH--
THE MONSTER INSIDE.
I WISH I'D KILLED YOU IN YOUR CRIB.

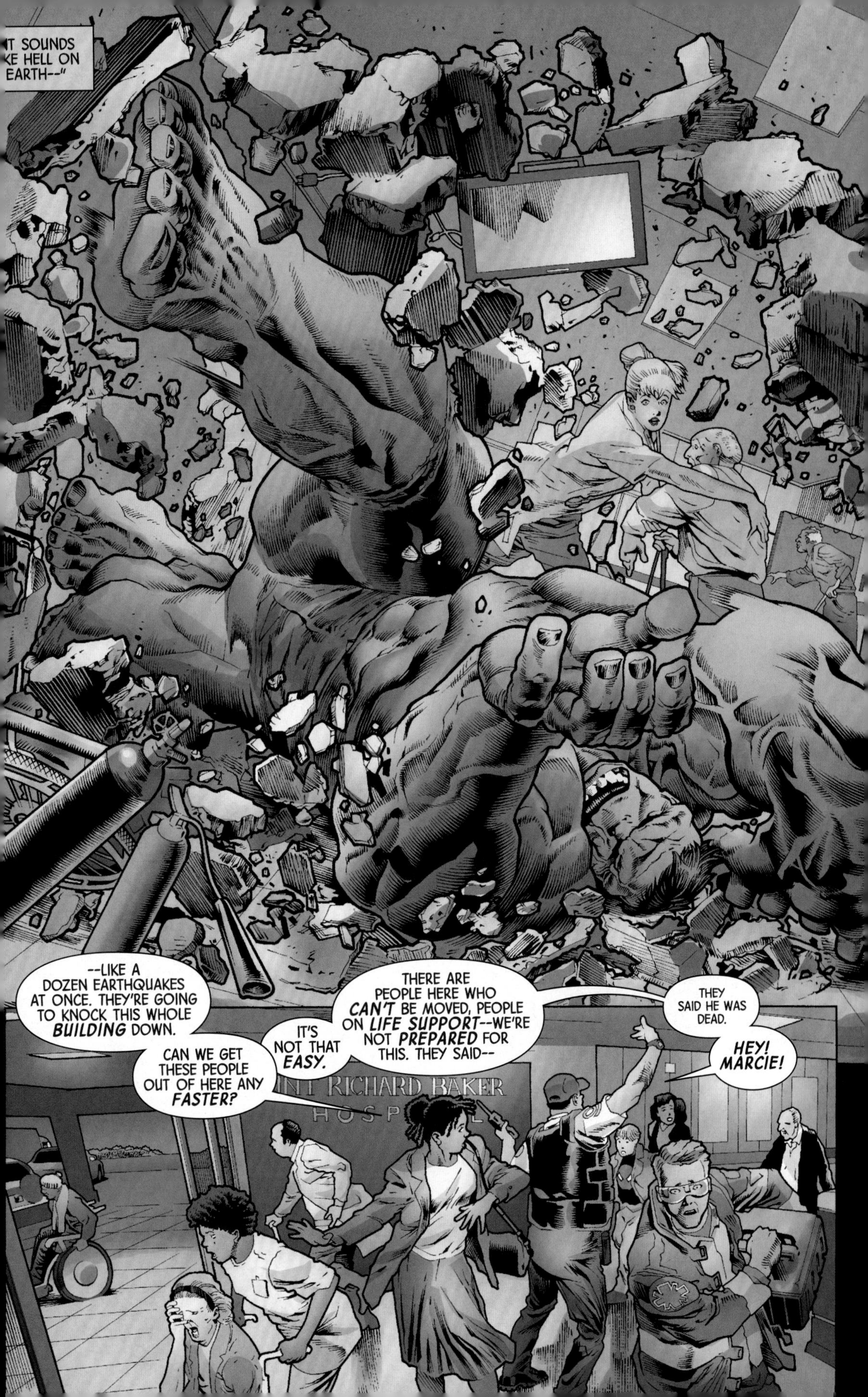

IT SOUNDS
KE HELL ON
EARTH--"
--LIKE A DOZEN EARTHQUAKES AT ONCE. THEY'RE GOING TO KNOCK THIS WHOLE BUILDING DOWN.
CAN WE GET THESE PEOPLE OUT OF HERE ANY FASTER?
IT'S NOT THAT EASY.
THERE ARE PEOPLE HERE WHO CAN'T BE MOVED, PEOPLE ON LIFE SUPPORT--WE'RE NOT PREPARED FOR THIS. THEY SAID--
THEY SAID HE WAS DEAD.
HEY! MARCIE!
INT RICHARD BAKER
HOSP

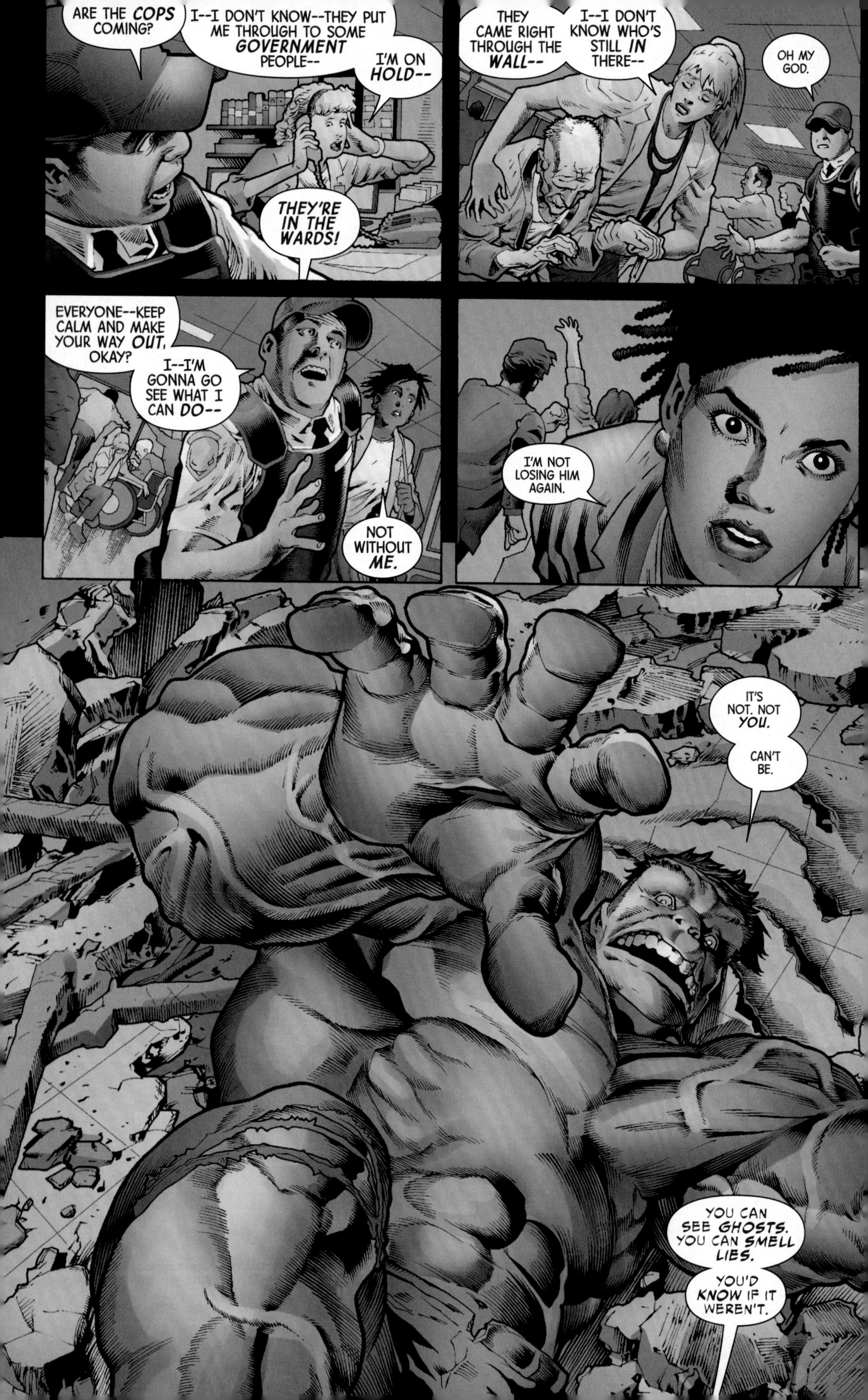
ARE THE COPS COMING?
I--I DON'T KNOW--THEY PUT ME THROUGH TO SOME GOVERNMENT PEOPLE--
I'M ON HOLD--
THEY'RE IN THE WARDS!
THEY CAME RIGHT THROUGH THE WALL--
I--I DON'T KNOW WHO'S STILL IN THERE--
OH MY GOD.
EVERYONE--KEEP CALM AND MAKE YOUR WAY OUT, OKAY?
I--I'M GONNA GO SEE WHAT I CAN DO--
NOT WITHOUT ME.
I'M NOT LOSING HIM AGAIN.
IT'S NOT. NOT YOU.
CAN'T BE.
YOU CAN SEE GHOSTS. YOU CAN SMELL LIES.
YOU'D KNOW IF IT WEREN'T.

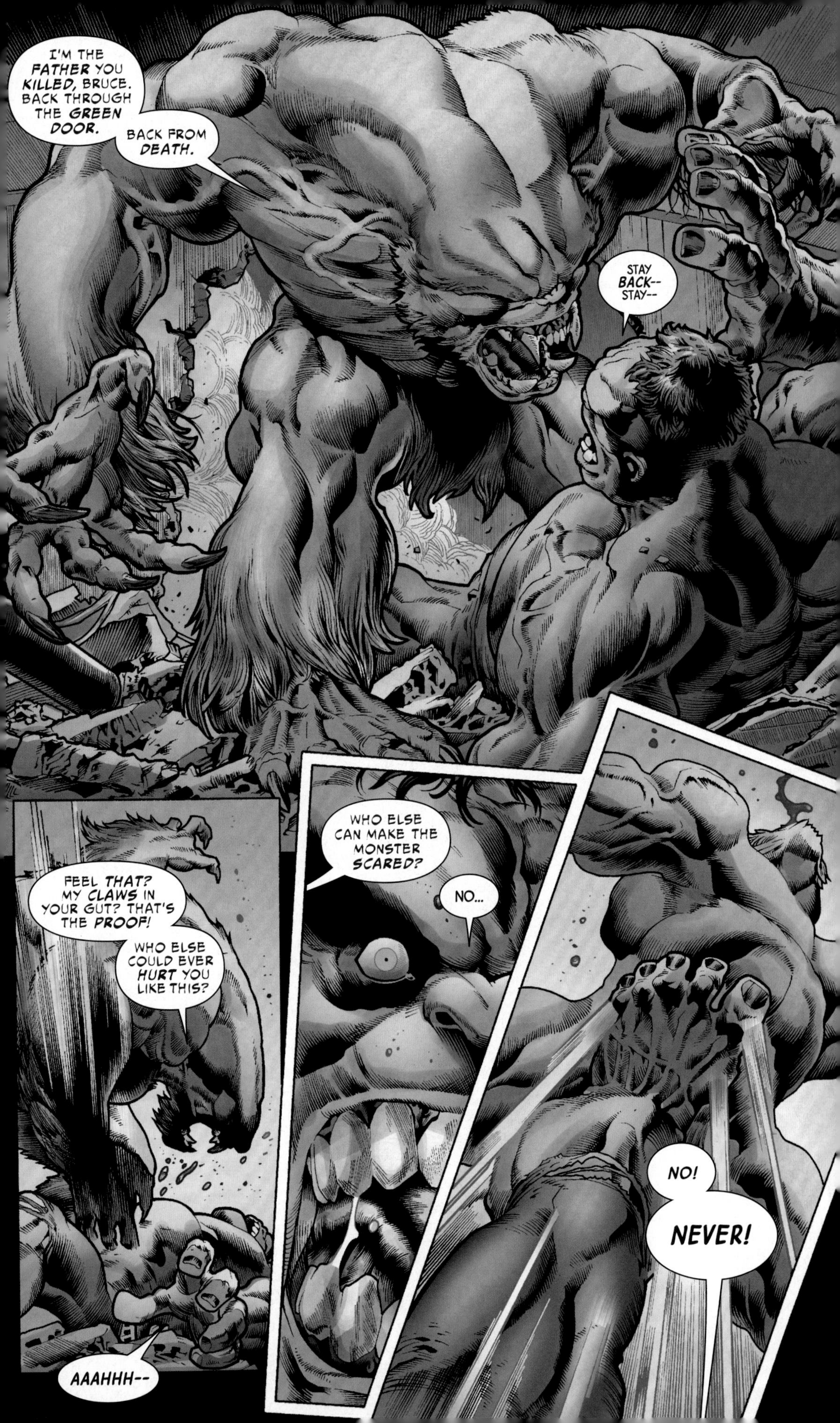
I'M THE FATHER YOU KILLED, BRUCE. BACK THROUGH THE GREEN DOOR.
BACK FROM DEATH.
STAY BACK-- STAY--
FEEL THAT? MY CLAWS IN YOUR GUT? THAT'S THE PROOF!
WHO ELSE COULD EVER HURT YOU LIKE THIS?
AAAHHH--
WHO ELSE CAN MAKE THE MONSTER SCARED?
NO...
NO!
NEVER!

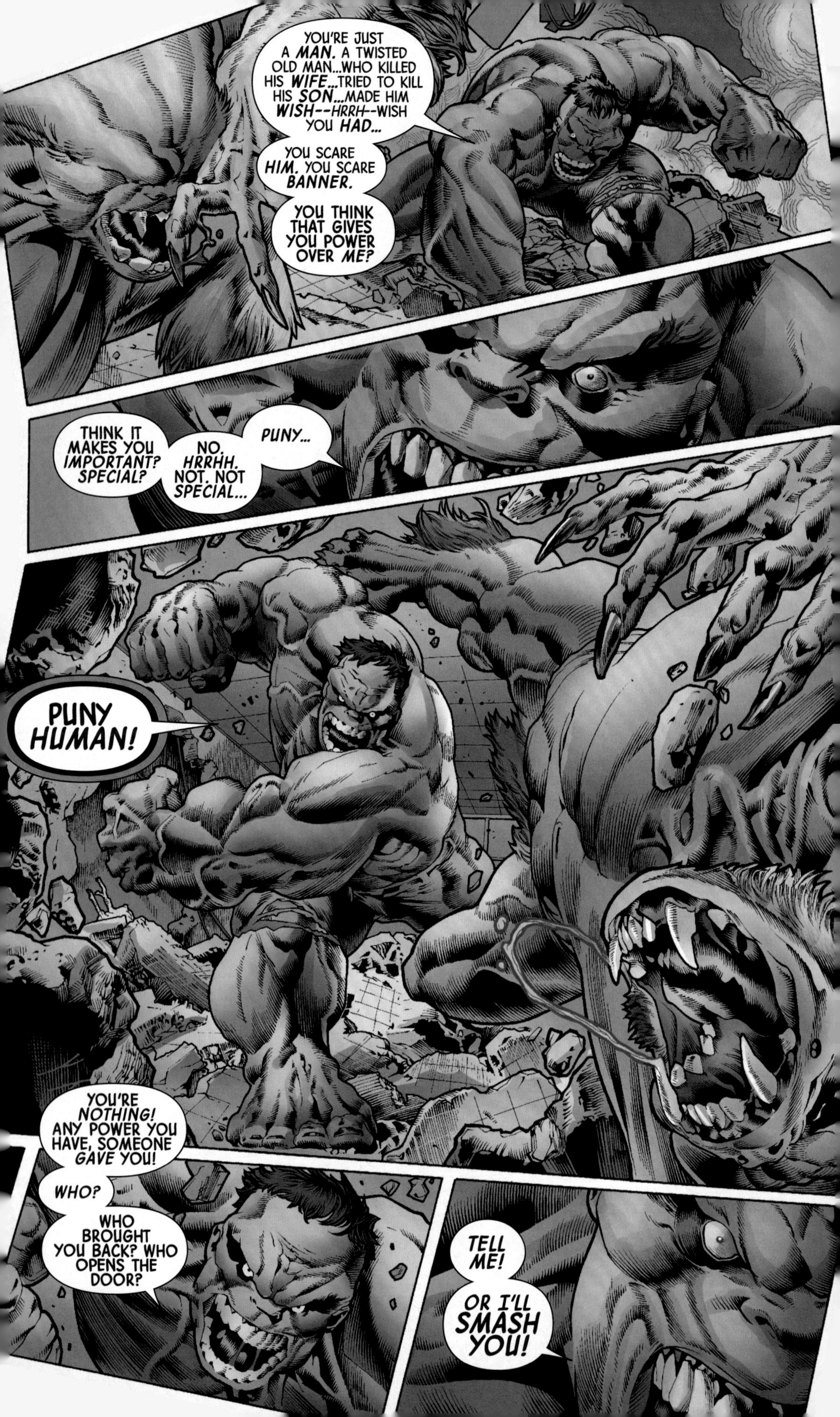

YOU'RE JUST A MAN. A TWISTED OLD MAN...WHO KILLED HIS WIFE...TRIED TO KILL HIS SON...MADE HIM WISH--HRRH--WISH YOU HAD...
YOU SCARE HIM. YOU SCARE BANNER.
YOU THINK THAT GIVES YOU POWER OVER ME?
THINK IT MAKES YOU IMPORTANT? SPECIAL?
NO. HRRHH. NOT. NOT SPECIAL...
PUNY...
PUNY HUMAN!
YOU'RE NOTHING! ANY POWER YOU HAVE, SOMEONE GAVE YOU!
WHO?
WHO BROUGHT YOU BACK? WHO OPENS THE DOOR?
TELL ME!
OR I'LL SMASH YOU!

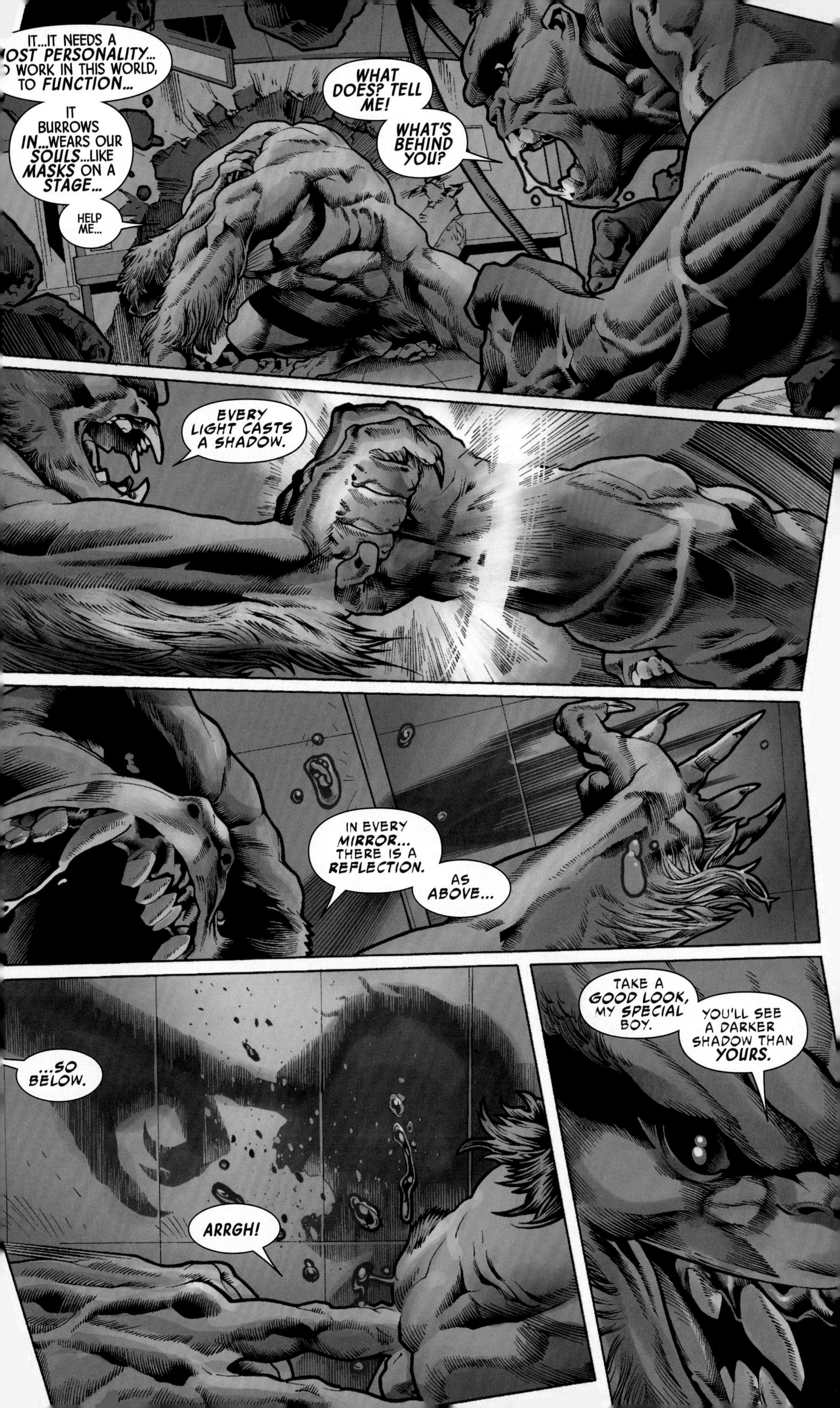

IT...IT NEEDS A OST PERSONALITY... WORK IN THIS WORLD, TO FUNCTION...
IT BURROWS IN...WEARS OUR SOULS...LIKE MASKS ON A STAGE...
HELP ME...
WHAT DOES? TELL ME!
WHAT'S BEHIND YOU?
EVERY LIGHT CASTS A SHADOW.
IN EVERY MIRROR... THERE IS A REFLECTION.
AS ABOVE...
...SO BELOW.
ARRGH!
TAKE A GOOD LOOK, MY SPECIAL BOY.
YOU'LL SEE A DARKER SHADOW THAN YOURS.

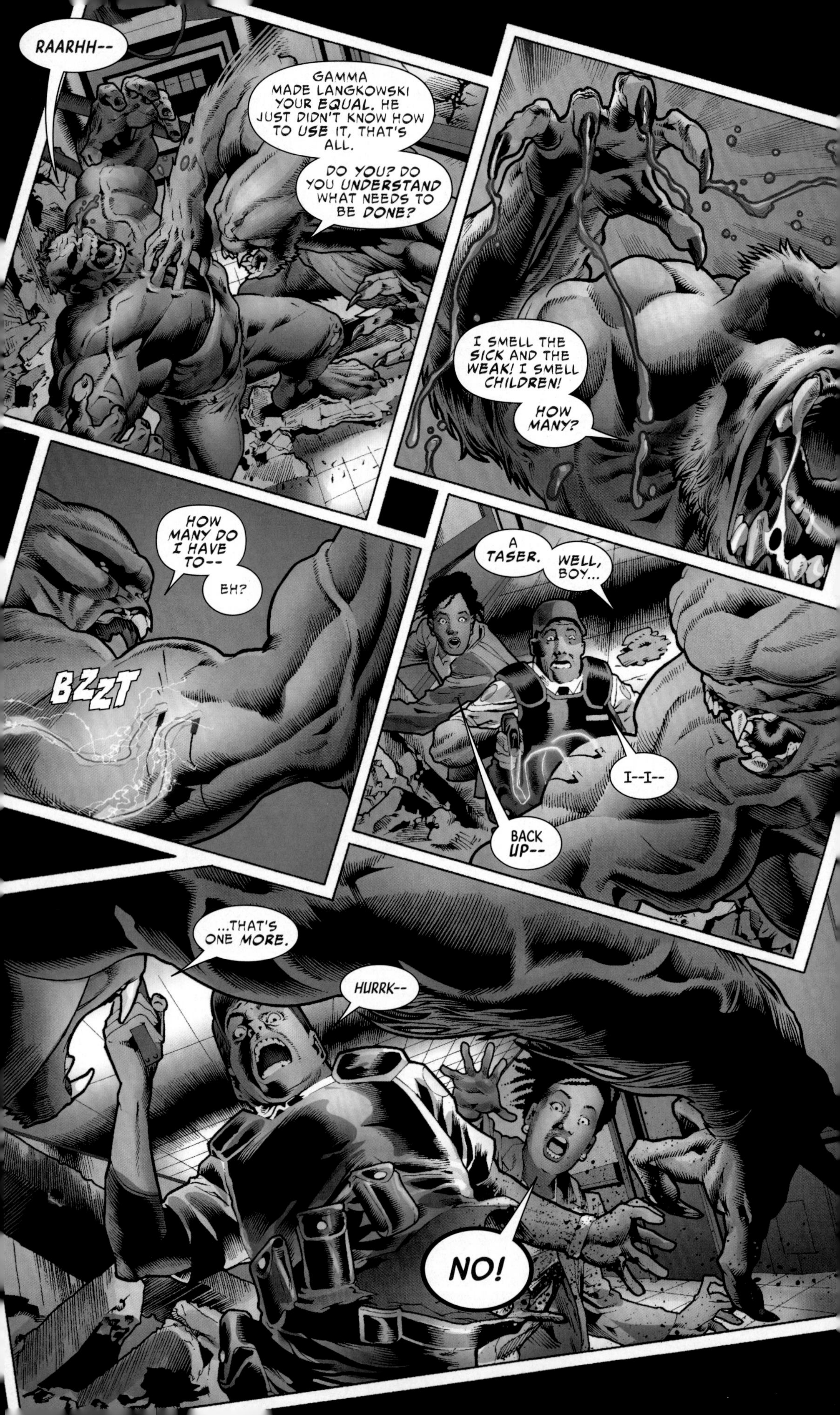
RAARHH--
GAMMA MADE LANGKOWSKI YOUR EQUAL. HE JUST DIDN'T KNOW HOW TO USE IT, THAT'S ALL.
DO YOU? DO YOU UNDERSTAND WHAT NEEDS TO BE DONE?
I SMELL THE SICK AND THE WEAK! I SMELL CHILDREN!
HOW MANY?
HOW MANY DO I HAVE TO--
EH?
BZZT
A TASER.
WELL, BOY...
I--I--
BACK UP--
...THAT'S ONE MORE.
HURRK--
NO!

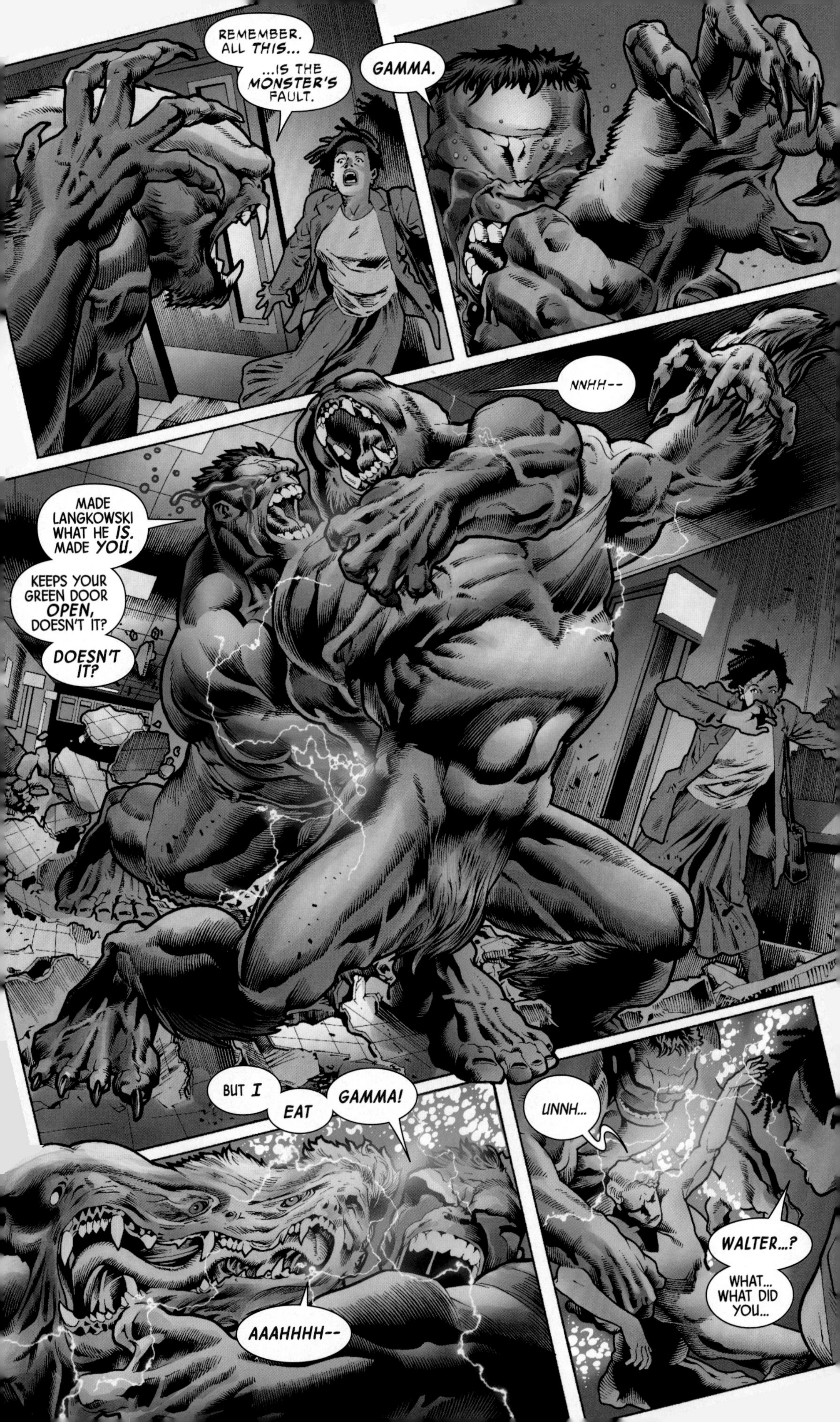
REMEMBER. ALL THIS...
...IS THE MONSTER'S FAULT.
GAMMA.
NNHH--
MADE LANGKOWSKI WHAT HE IS. MADE YOU.
KEEPS YOUR GREEN DOOR OPEN, DOESN'T IT?
DOESN'T IT?
BUT I
EAT
GAMMA!
AAAHHHH--
UNNH...
WALTER...?
WHAT... WHAT DID YOU...

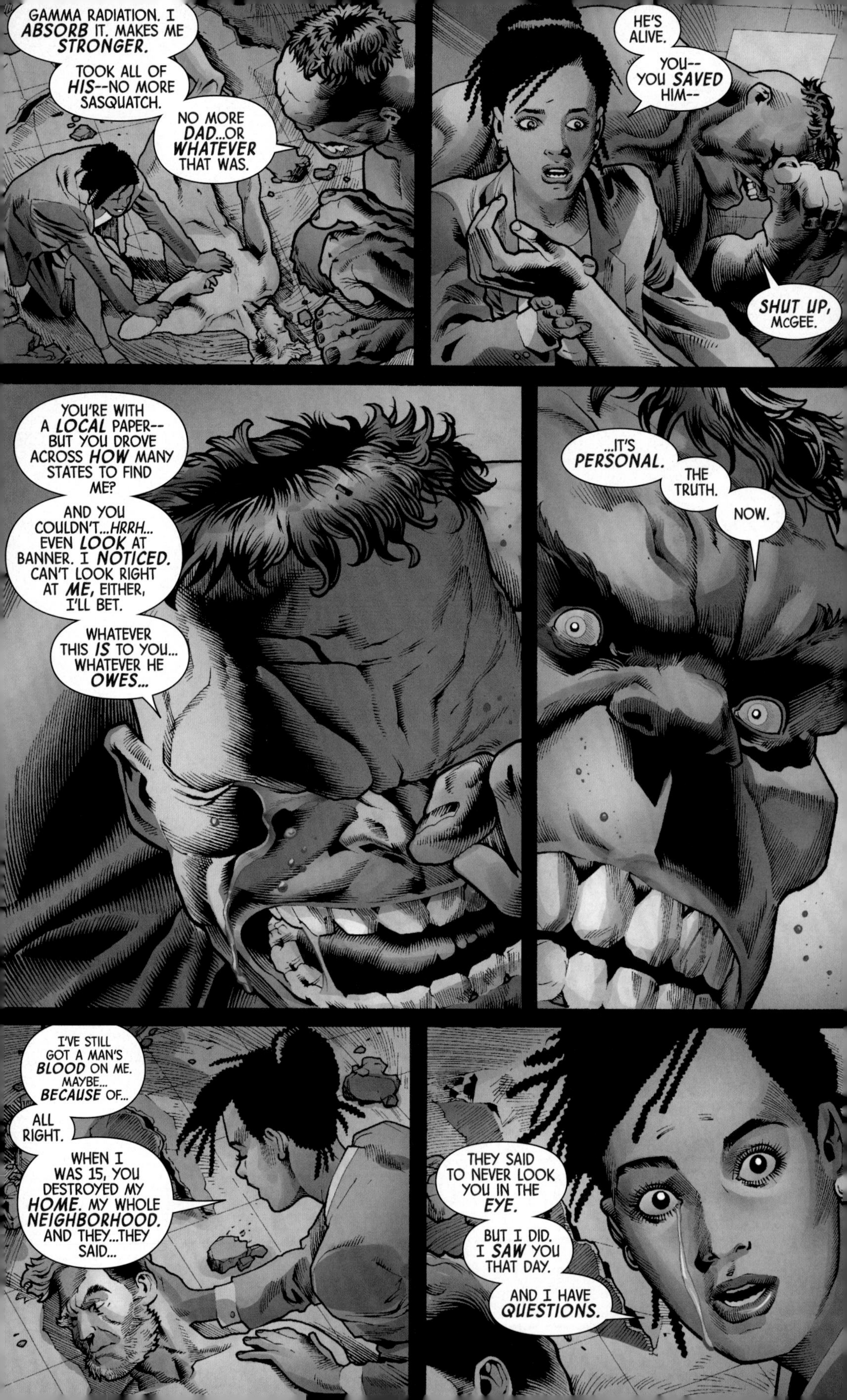
GAMMA RADIATION. I ABSORB IT. MAKES ME STRONGER.
TOOK ALL OF HIS--NO MORE SASQUATCH.
NO MORE DAD...OR WHATEVER THAT WAS.
HE'S ALIVE.
YOU--YOU SAVED HIM--
SHUT UP, McGEE.
YOU'RE WITH A LOCAL PAPER--BUT YOU DROVE ACROSS HOW MANY STATES TO FIND ME?
AND YOU COULDN'T...HRRH... EVEN LOOK AT BANNER. I NOTICED. CAN'T LOOK RIGHT AT ME, EITHER, I'LL BET.
WHATEVER THIS IS TO YOU... WHATEVER HE OWES...
...IT'S PERSONAL.
THE TRUTH.
NOW.
I'VE STILL GOT A MAN'S BLOOD ON ME. MAYBE... BECAUSE OF...
ALL RIGHT.
WHEN I WAS 15, YOU DESTROYED MY HOME. MY WHOLE NEIGHBORHOOD. AND THEY...THEY SAID...
THEY SAID TO NEVER LOOK YOU IN THE EYE.
BUT I DID. I SAW YOU THAT DAY.
AND I HAVE QUESTIONS.

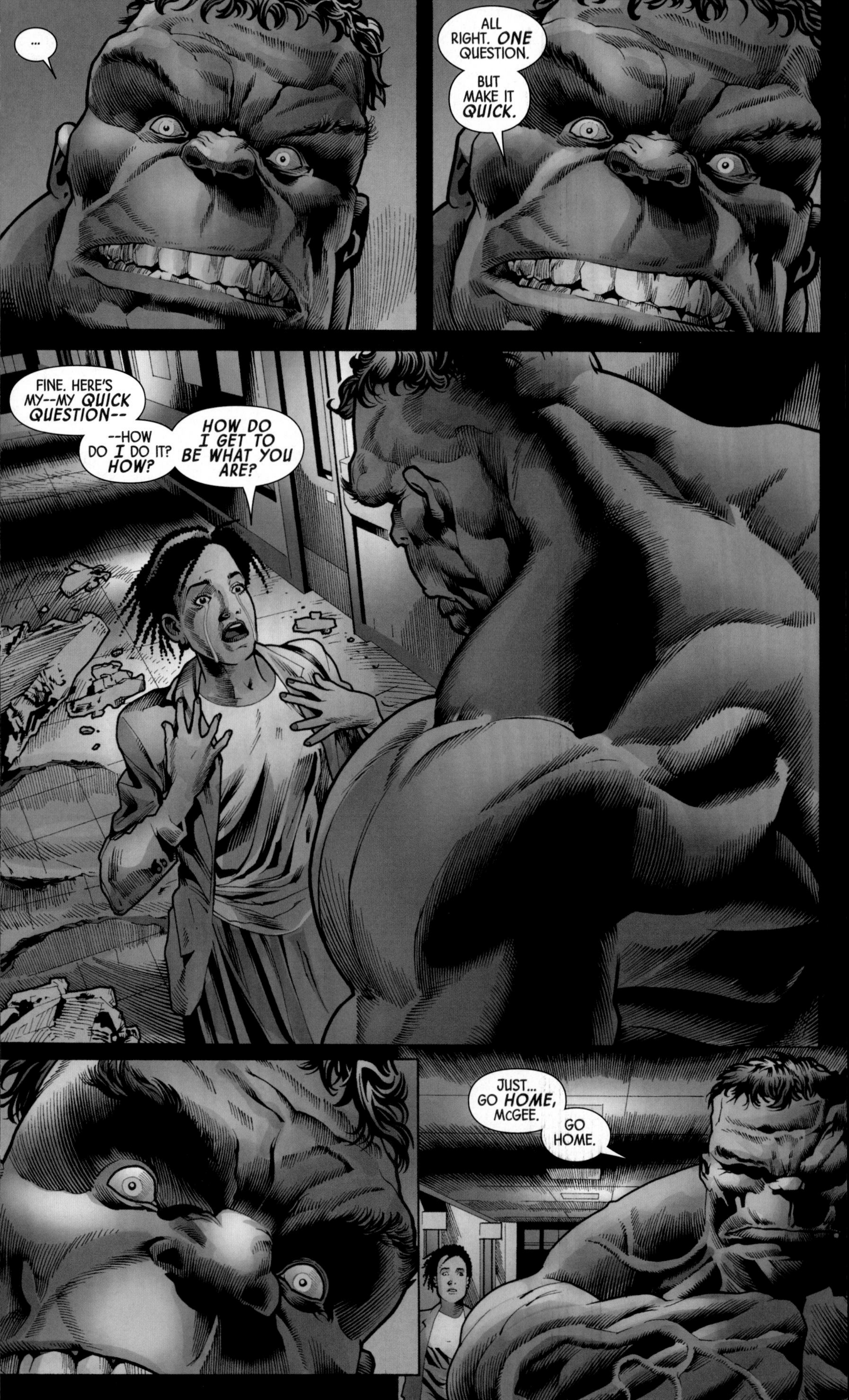
...
ALL RIGHT. ONE QUESTION.
BUT MAKE IT QUICK.
FINE. HERE'S MY--MY QUICK QUESTION--
--HOW DO I DO IT? HOW?
HOW DO I GET TO BE WHAT YOU ARE?
JUST... GO HOME, McGEE.
GO HOME.

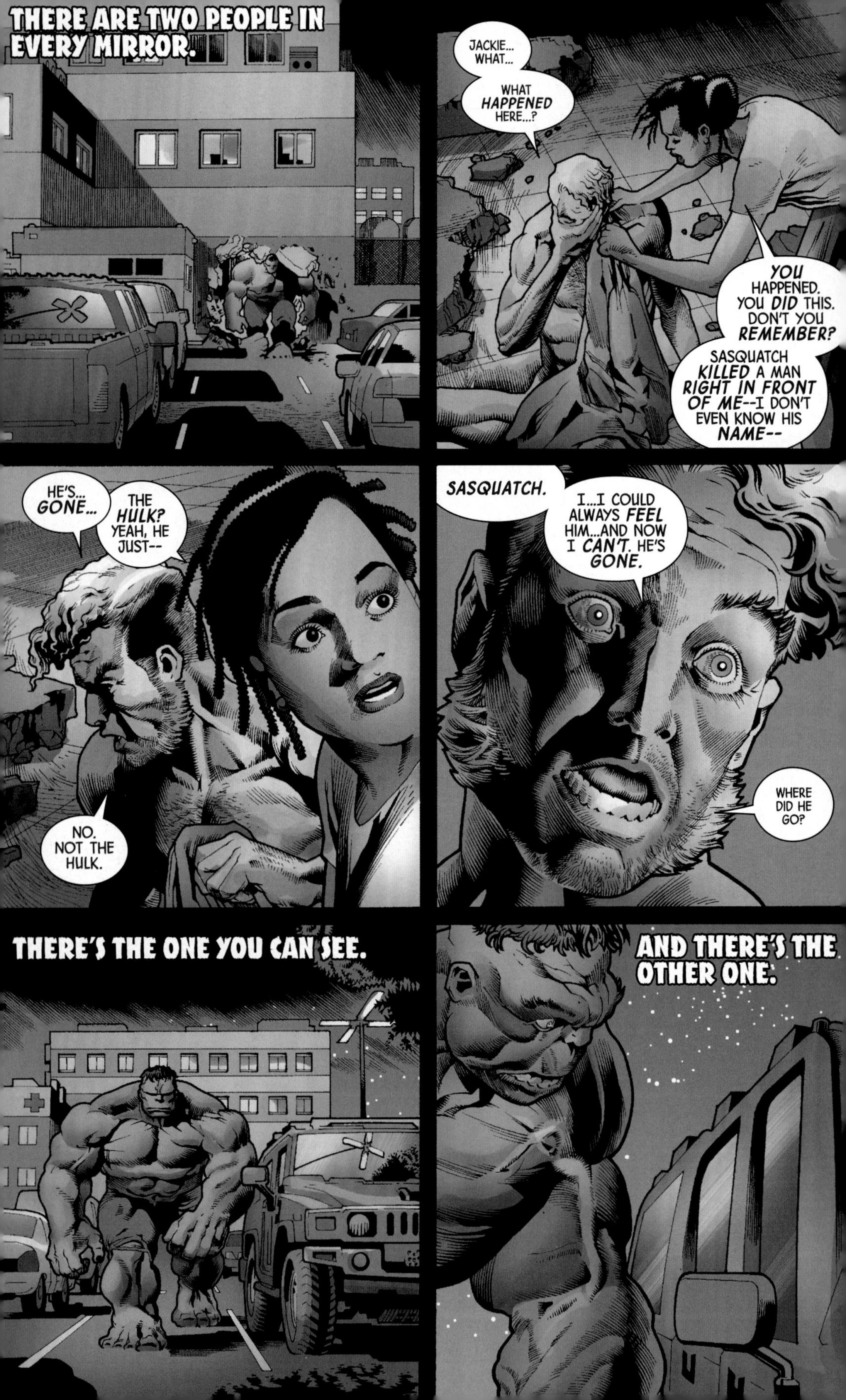
THERE ARE TWO PEOPLE IN EVERY MIRROR.
JACKIE... WHAT...
WHAT HAPPENED HERE...?
YOU HAPPENED. YOU DID THIS. DON'T YOU REMEMBER?
SASQUATCH KILLED A MAN RIGHT IN FRONT OF ME--I DON'T EVEN KNOW HIS NAME--
HE'S... GONE...
THE HULK? YEAH, HE JUST--
NO. NOT THE HULK.
SASQUATCH.
I...I COULD ALWAYS FEEL HIM...AND NOW I CAN'T. HE'S GONE.
WHERE DID HE GO?
THERE'S THE ONE YOU CAN SEE.
AND THERE'S THE OTHER ONE.

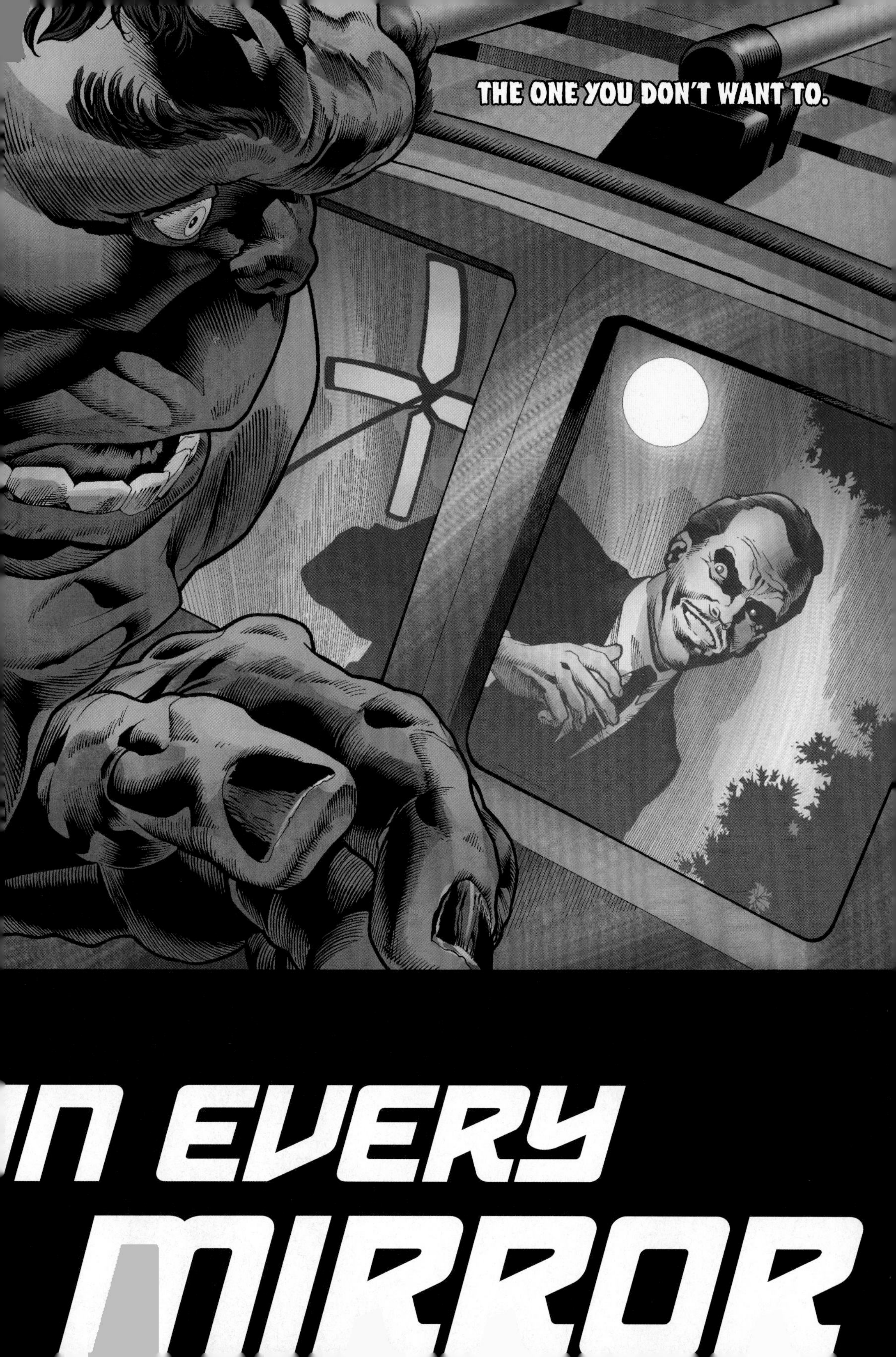
THE ONE YOU DON'T WANT TO.

# IN EVERY MIRROR

*AVENGERS #684* FEATURED AN OPENING SEQUENCE RECAPPING RECENT EVENTS IN THE LIFE AND DEATH OF BRUCE BANNER THAT LED TO HIS RETURN AS...THE IMMORTAL HULK!

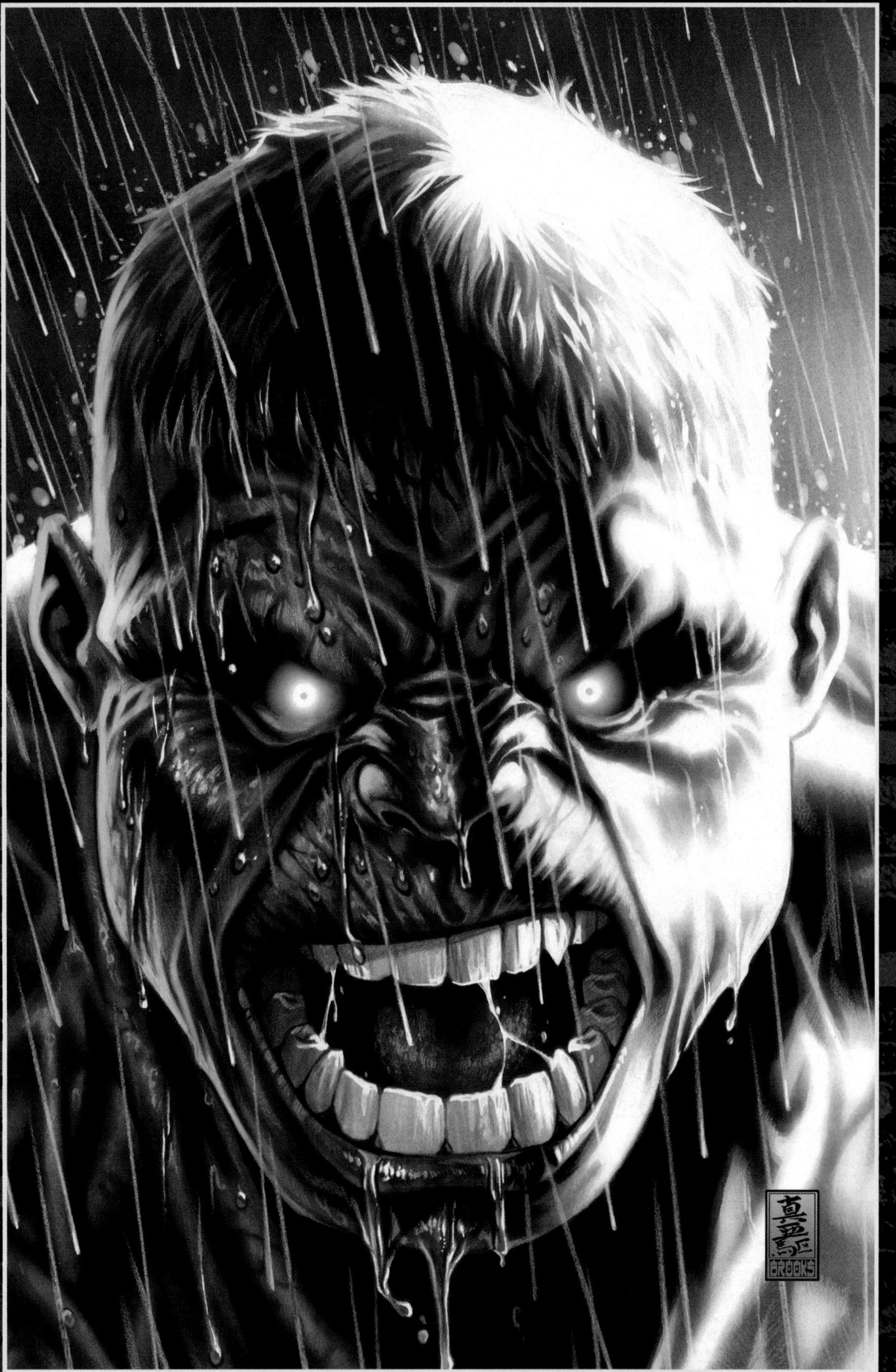
BROOKS

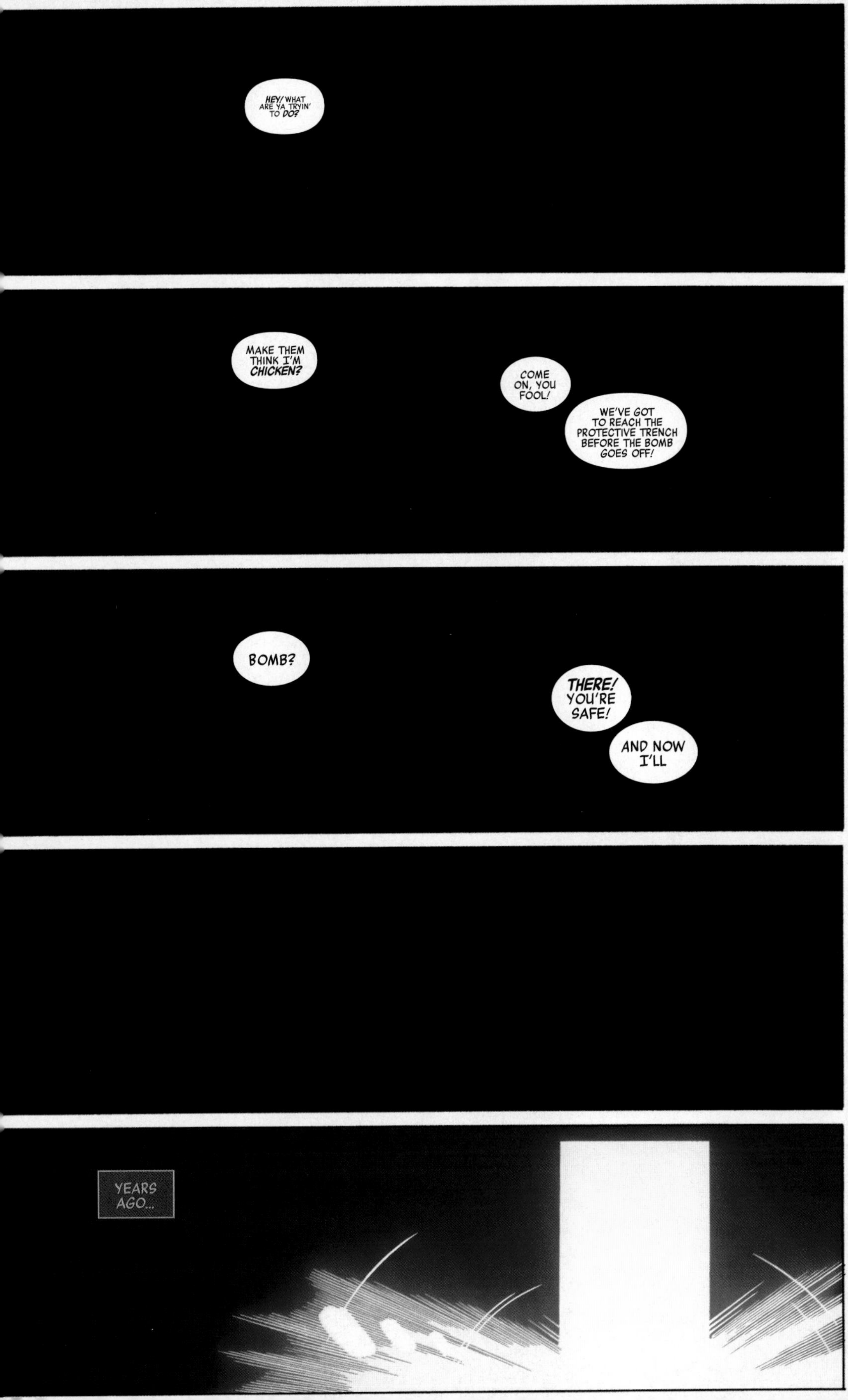
HEY! WHAT ARE YA TRYIN' TO DO?
MAKE THEM THINK I'M CHICKEN?
COME ON, YOU FOOL!
WE'VE GOT TO REACH THE PROTECTIVE TRENCH BEFORE THE BOMB GOES OFF!
BOMB?
THERE! YOU'RE SAFE!
AND NOW I'LL
YEARS AGO...

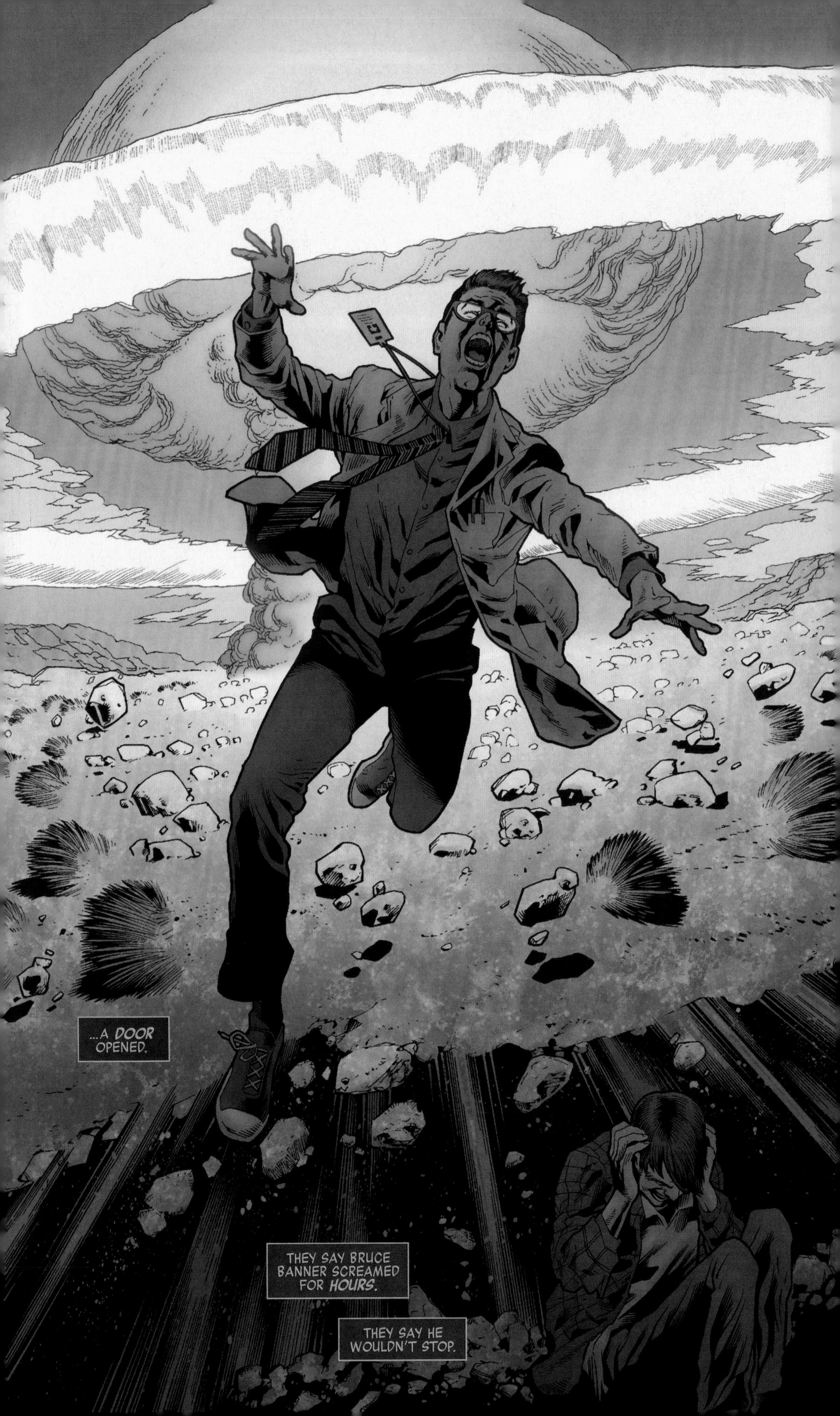
...A DOOR OPENED.
THEY SAY BRUCE BANNER SCREAMED FOR HOURS.
THEY SAY HE WOULDN'T STOP.

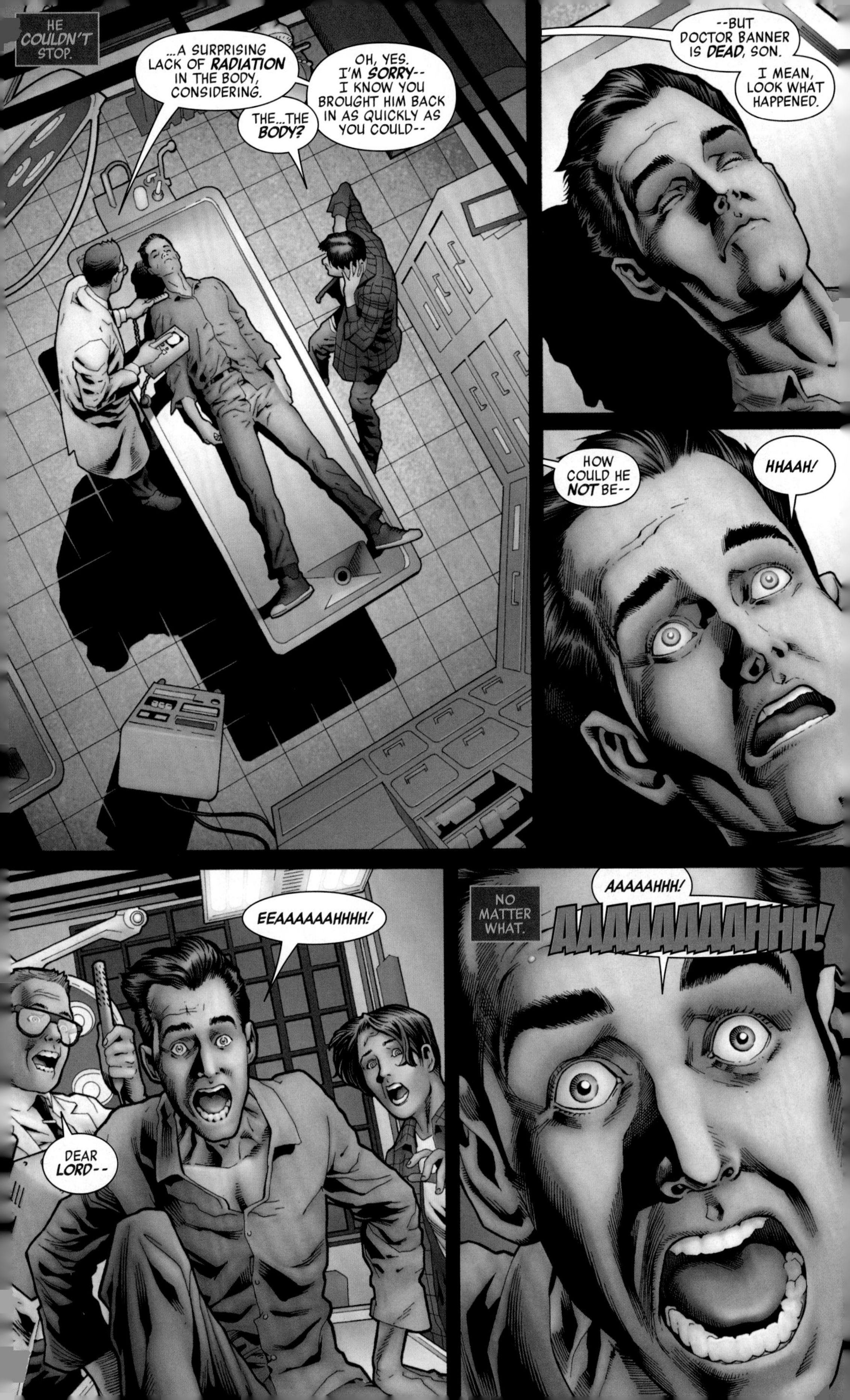
HE COULDN'T STOP.
...A SURPRISING LACK OF RADIATION IN THE BODY, CONSIDERING.
THE...THE BODY?
OH, YES. I'M SORRY-- I KNOW YOU BROUGHT HIM BACK IN AS QUICKLY AS YOU COULD--
--BUT DOCTOR BANNER IS DEAD, SON.
I MEAN, LOOK WHAT HAPPENED.
HOW COULD HE NOT BE--
HHAAH!
EEAAAAAAAHHHH!
DEAR LORD--
NO MATTER WHAT.
AAAAAHHH!
AAAAAAAAAHHHH!

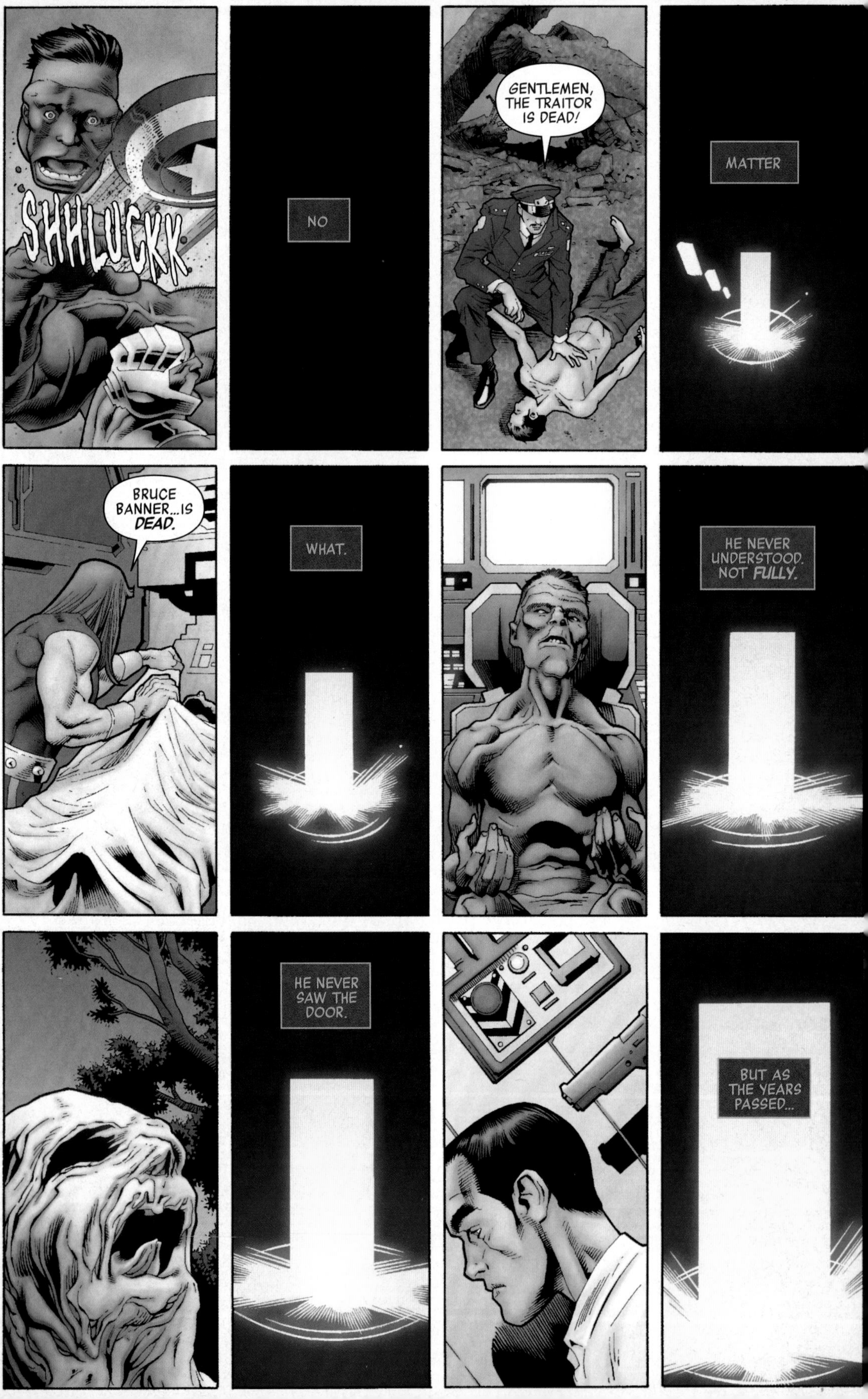
SHHLUCKK
NO
GENTLEMEN, THE TRAITOR IS DEAD!
MATTER
BRUCE BANNER...IS DEAD.
WHAT.
HE NEVER UNDERSTOOD. NOT FULLY.
HE NEVER SAW THE DOOR.
BUT AS THE YEARS PASSED...

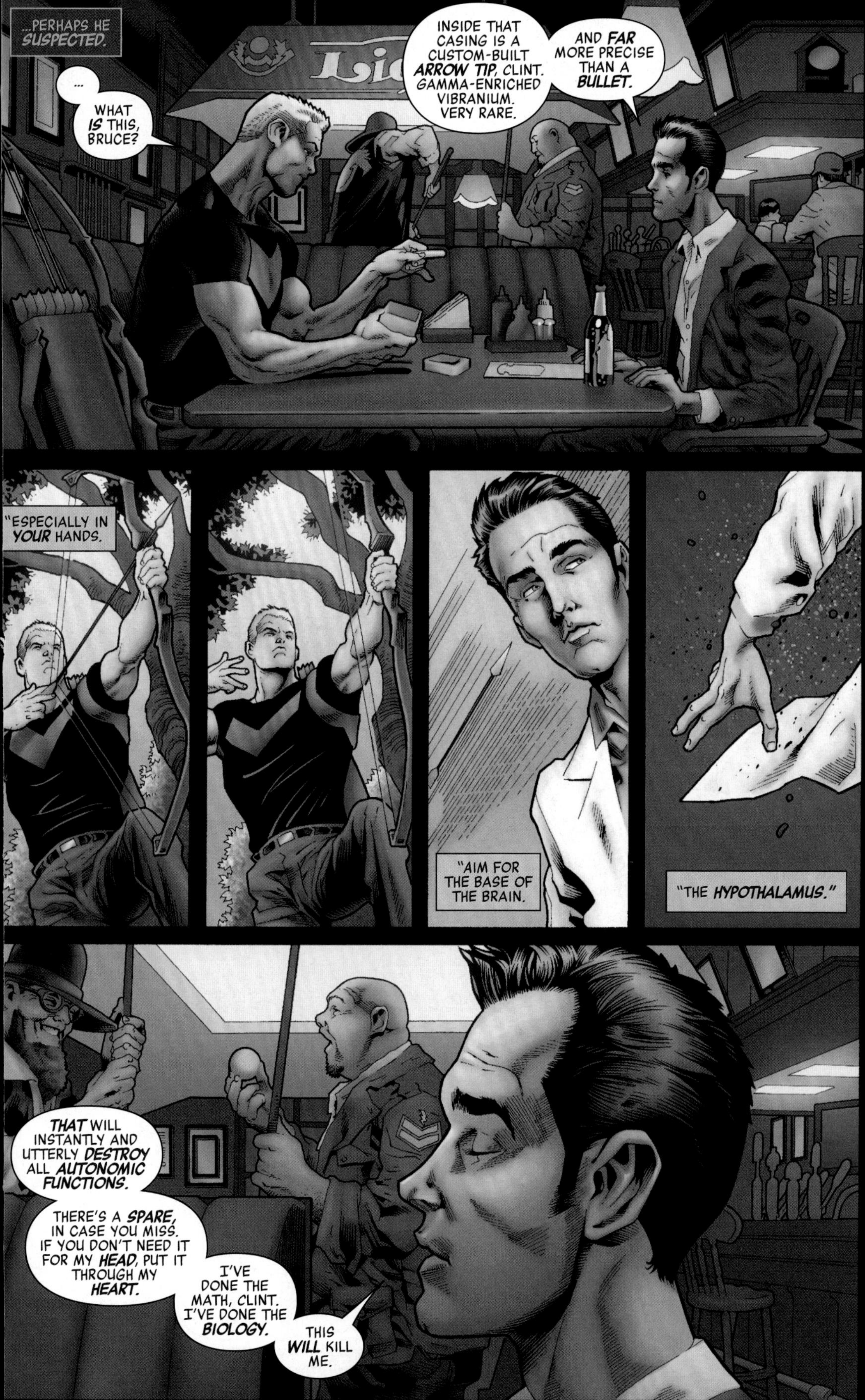
...PERHAPS HE SUSPECTED.
... WHAT IS THIS, BRUCE?
INSIDE THAT CASING IS A CUSTOM-BUILT ARROW TIP, CLINT. GAMMA-ENRICHED VIBRANIUM. VERY RARE.
AND FAR MORE PRECISE THAN A BULLET.
"ESPECIALLY IN YOUR HANDS.
"AIM FOR THE BASE OF THE BRAIN.
"THE HYPOTHALAMUS."
THAT WILL INSTANTLY AND UTTERLY DESTROY ALL AUTONOMIC FUNCTIONS.
THERE'S A SPARE, IN CASE YOU MISS. IF YOU DON'T NEED IT FOR MY HEAD, PUT IT THROUGH MY HEART.
I'VE DONE THE MATH, CLINT. I'VE DONE THE BIOLOGY.
THIS WILL KILL ME.

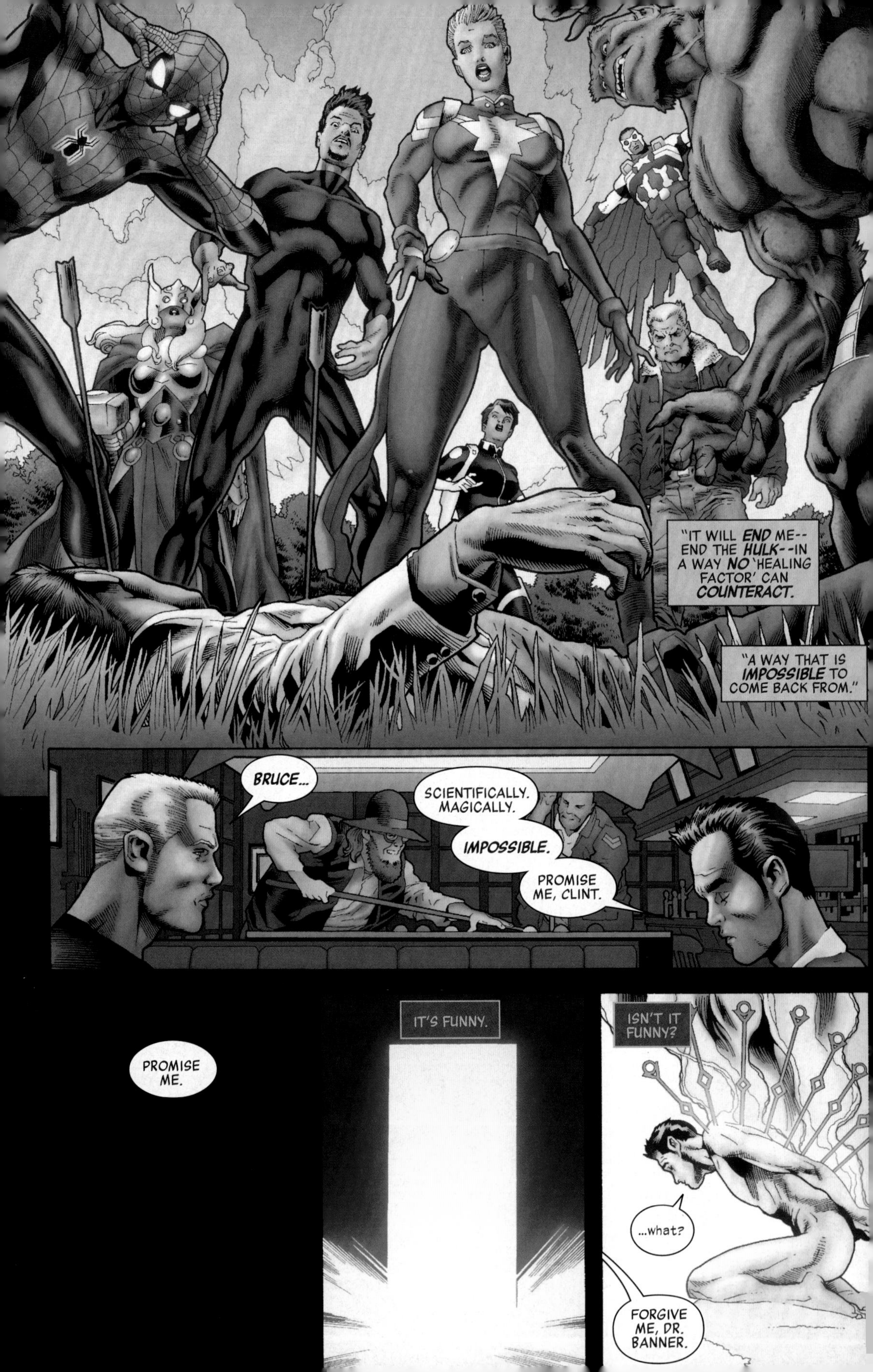
"IT WILL END ME--END THE HULK--IN A WAY NO 'HEALING FACTOR' CAN COUNTERACT.
"A WAY THAT IS IMPOSSIBLE TO COME BACK FROM."
BRUCE...
SCIENTIFICALLY. MAGICALLY.
IMPOSSIBLE.
PROMISE ME, CLINT.
PROMISE ME.
IT'S FUNNY.
ISN'T IT FUNNY?
...what?
FORGIVE ME, DR. BANNER.

# THE ASSEMBLY

He cannot be killed. He cannot be contained. He is THE IMMORTAL HULK, and he'll NEVER stop.
But where did he begin? Here's your roadmap to follow the story events, old and new, that are referenced
in our Hulk prologue:

**Pages 2-3:**
**INCREDIBLE HULK #1**

**Page 4, Panel 1:**
**AVENGERS: ULTRON FOREVER #1**

**Page 4, Panel 3:**
**TALES TO ASTONISH #69**

**Page 4, Panel 5:**
**INCREDIBLE HULK #225**

**Page 4, Panel 7:**
**INCREDIBLE HULK #367**

**Page 4, Panel 9:**
**INCREDIBLE HULK #446**

**Page 4, Panel 11:**
**INDESTRUCTIBLE HULK #20**

**Pages 5-6:**
**CIVIL WAR II #3**

**Pages 6-7:**
**UNCANNNY AVENGERS #17**

**Page 8:**
**SECRET EMPIRE #5**

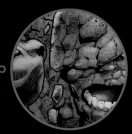

**Page 9:**
**SECRET EMPIRE #6**

## "WHAT DO YOU THINK?"

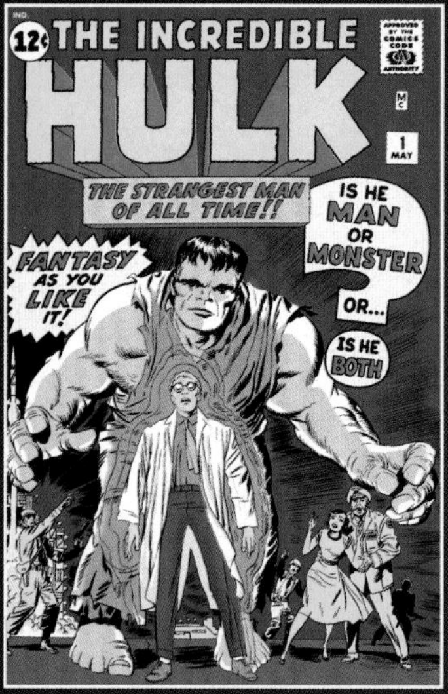
12¢
THE INCREDIBLE
HULK
1
MAY
THE STRANGEST MAN OF ALL TIME!!
IS HE MAN OR MONSTER
OR...
IS HE BOTH
FANTASY AS YOU LIKE IT!

When I was small - 7, maybe 8 - my school library had, squirreled away on a bookshelf like a hidden secret, a pocket-sized reprint of the first six issues of *Incredible Hulk*. A comic about my favorite super hero that I could read during actual reading period! As if it were a real book! Truly, this was buried treasure!

And it was. Those first six issues are the primal meat, a bubbling primordial soup of Stan Lee, Jack Kirby and Steve Ditko, all trying to work out exactly what kind of monster they've made. It was a horror book, to begin with - Bruce Banner, sitting and waiting for the night to come. Waiting to change into his terrifying opposite, the Jungian shadow-side - everything he hid from the world and tried to pretend wasn't inside him. "How do I know I won't keep changing," he breathes, with a thousand-year stare that's a strange mix of fear and desire, "into that brutal, bestial mockery of a human — that creature which fears nothing - which despises reason and worships power!"

Who was this nighttime Lord of Misrule, this shambling monstrosity pretending to be the gentle giant from my TV cartoons? What had he done with the Hulk I knew?

Even the cover of issue #1 - faithfully reproduced - seemed strange and sinister. "The Strangest Man of All Time!!" howled the strapline, a promise of something weirder and more eldritch than the jolly green goliath I knew. But what really grabbed the eye was a stylish question-mark caption, asking "is he MAN or MONSTER or..." - a break in the caption, a pregnant pause - "is he BOTH". No punctuation - the caption itself was the question mark at the end of the sentence - and that made it seem even more ominous and significant to my child eyes. It felt like a key.

These are the things that echo in your head for 30 years and change.

And 30-years-and-change later, through luck and synchronicity — and, yes, the hard graft of pitching and competing and turning down other work to make room for it — I got the job of writing the Hulk. A Hulk who was ping-ponging back and forth from death like a yo-yo. A Hulk who was technically dead...but whom no writer seemed to be able to leave that way. How could they? The Hulk was too powerful. Too vivid. The Hulk just couldn't be dead.

The Hulk couldn't die.

Imagine a Hulk like that. A massive breathing engine of muscle and power, that we only saw in mirrors, or in the darkest corner of the night. As immense and potent as a childhood symbol. The strongest there is. The strangest man of all time.

When that Hulk looks back at us - can it see what we are? See our souls as clearly as our bodies? Smell our lies as we tell them? Does it know everything we've done, everything we are? And when it speaks - in that terrible voice, like granite crumbling, like the tomb breaking open - what judgment will it pass upon us?

Are we man or monster or...are we both?

What do you think?

- AL EWING

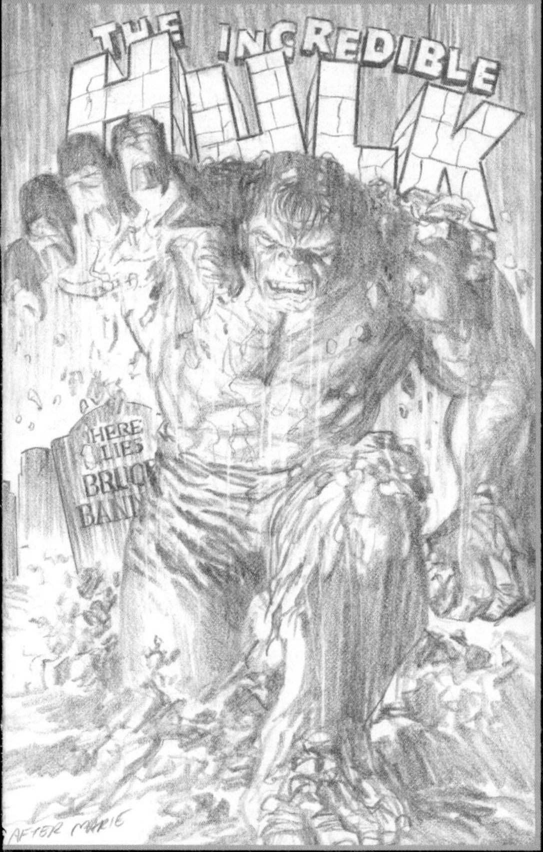
THE INCREDIBLE
HERE LIES BRUC BAN
AFTER MARIE

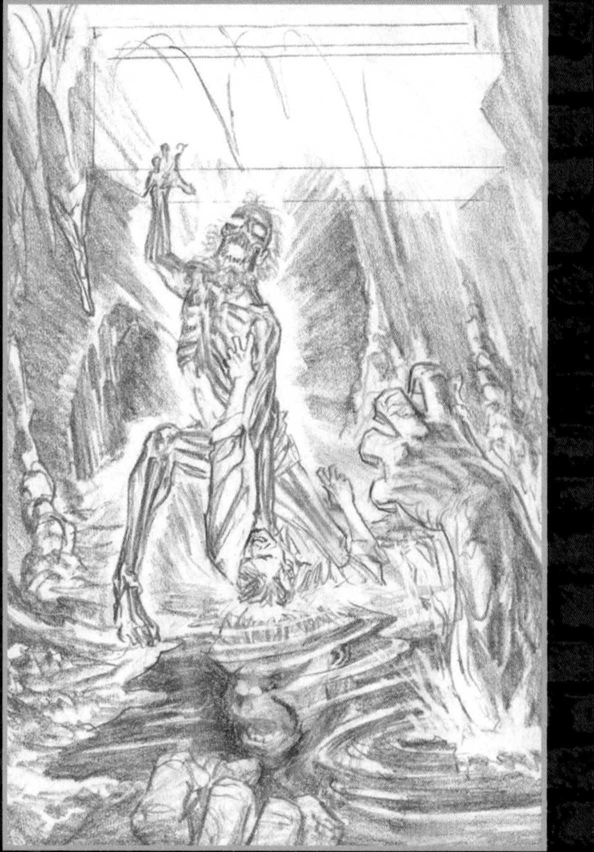

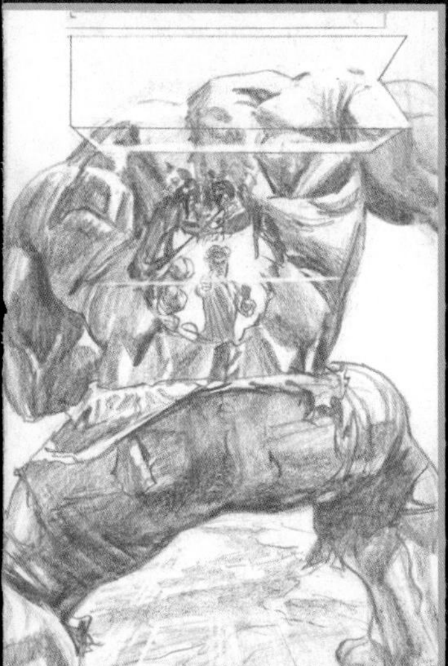

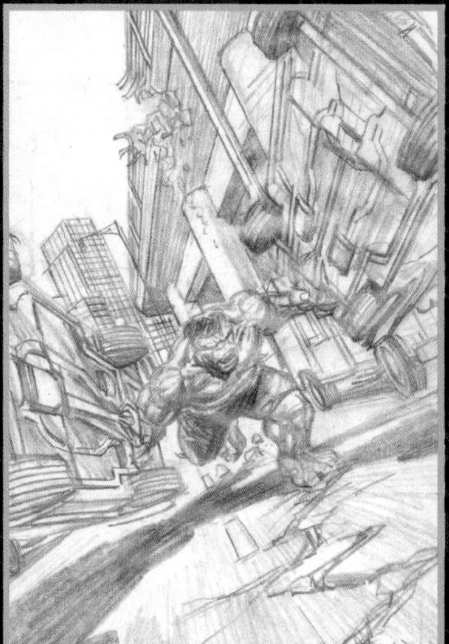

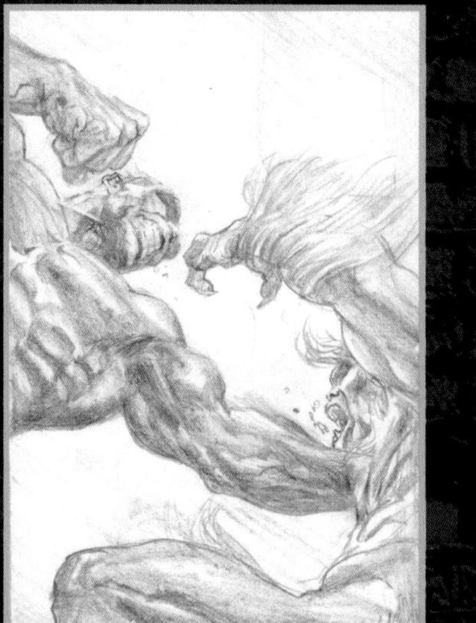

THE IMMORTAL HULK

**ALEX ROSS**
COVER SKETCHES & LOGO DESIGN

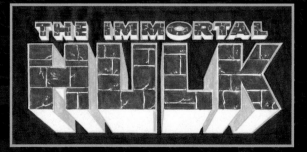

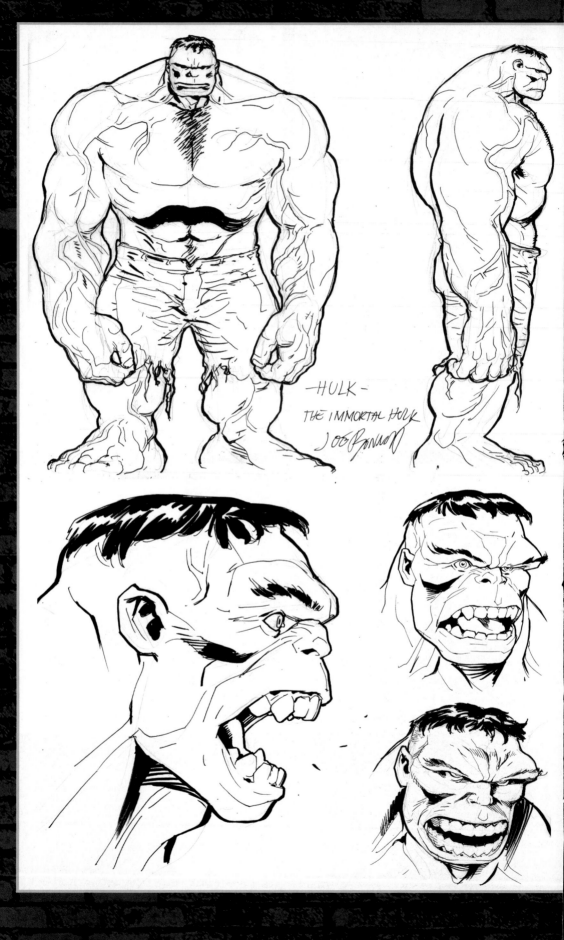

- HULK -

THE IMMORTAL HULK

Joe Bennett

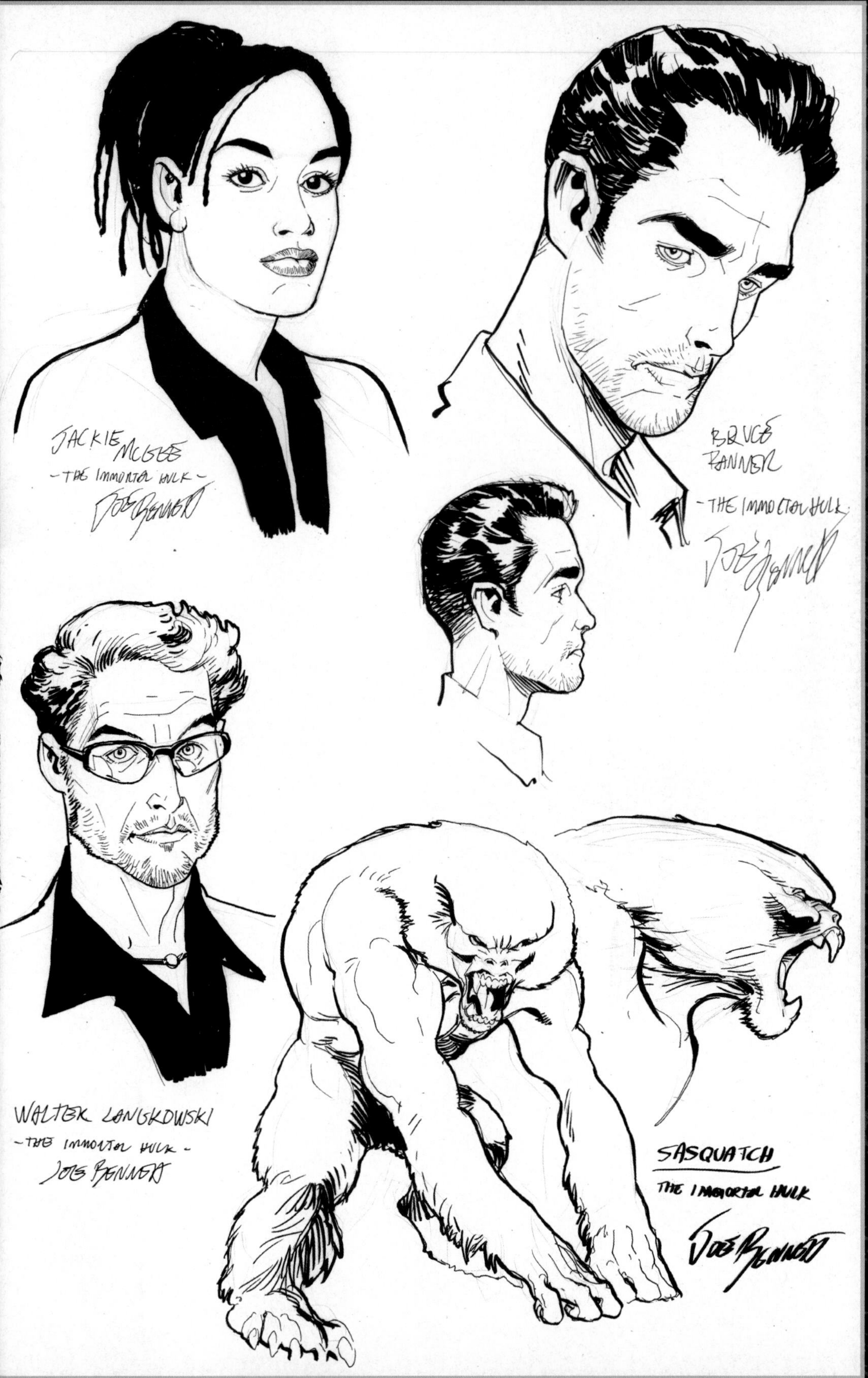
JACKIE MCGEE
-THE IMMORTAL HULK-
JOE BENNETT
BRUCE BANNER
-THE IMMORTAL HULK
JOE BENNETT
WALTER LANGKOWSKI
-THE IMMORTAL HULK-
JOE BENNETT
SASQUATCH
THE IMMORTAL HULK
JOE BENNETT

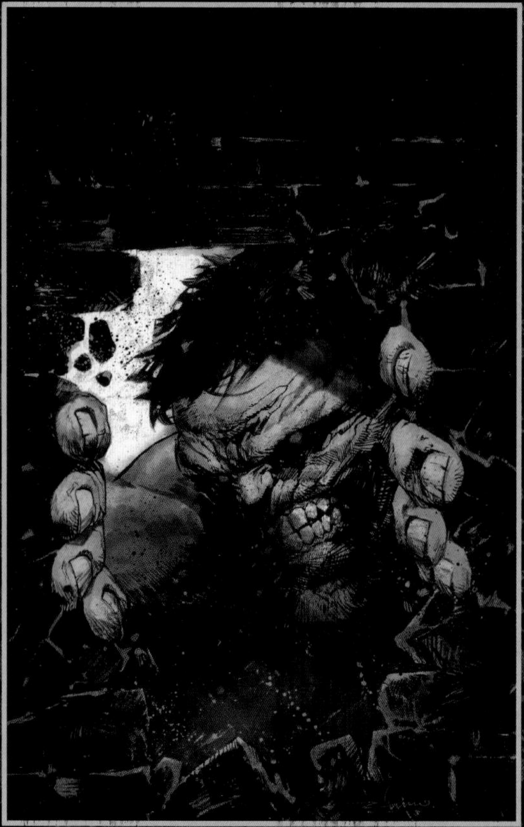

**GERARDO ZAFFINO**
#2 VARIANT

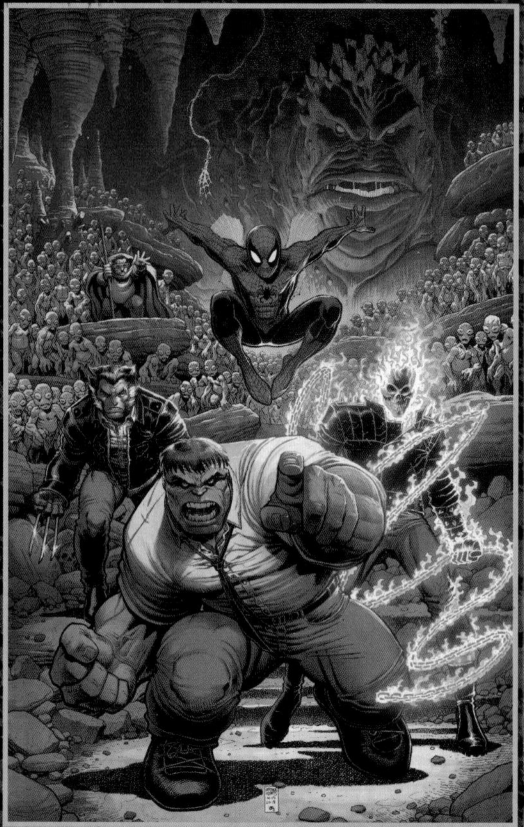

**ARTHUR ADAMS & FRANK MARTIN**
#4 FANTASTIC FOUR VARIANT

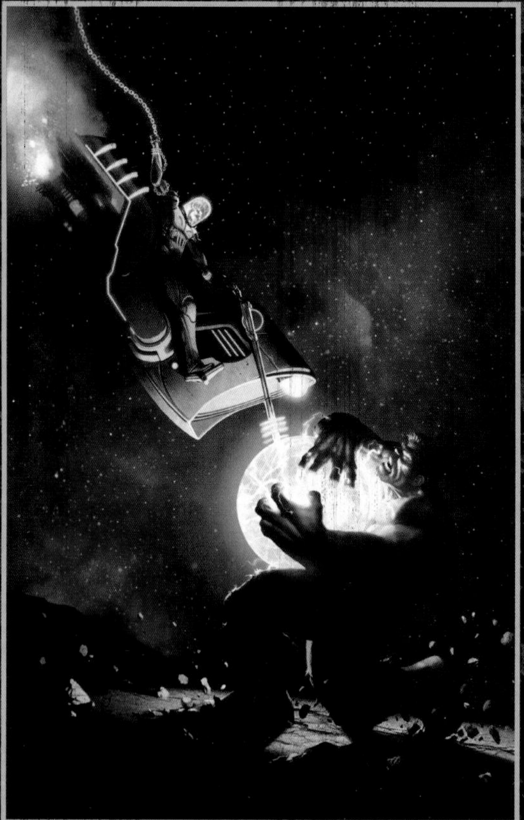

**RAHZZAH**
#5 COSMIC GHOST RIDER VS. VARIANT

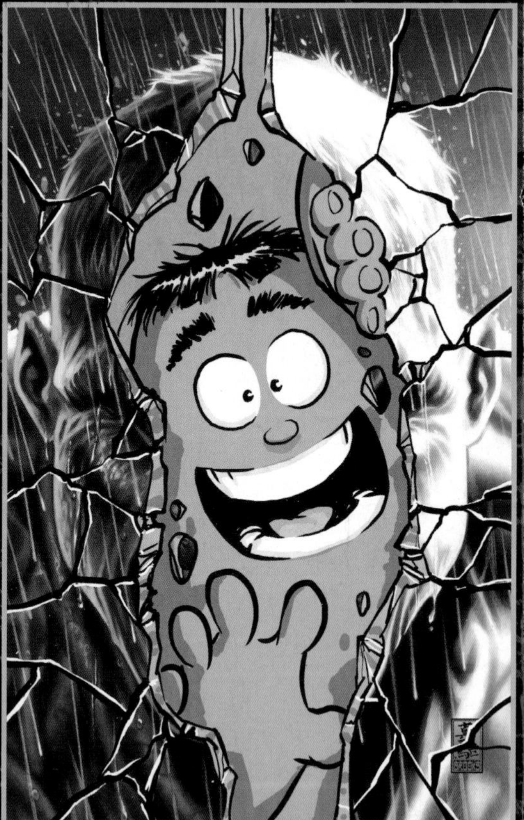

**SKOTTIE YOUNG**
AVENGERS #684 VARIANT